Islamic Law
and Society

Islamic Law
and
Society

An Introduction

Jamila Hussain

BA, LLB, Dip Ed, Dip Shariah Law & Practice,
MCL (International Islamic University, Kuala Lumpur)
Lecturer in Law, University of Technology, Sydney

The Federation Press
1999

Published in Sydney by

The Federation Press
71 John St, Leichhardt, NSW, 2040
PO Box 45, Annandale, NSW, 2038
Ph: (02) 9552 2200 Fax: (02) 9552 1681
E-mail: info@fedpress.aust.com
Website: http://www.fedpress.aust.com

National Library of Australia Cataloguing-in-Publication data:
    Hussain, Jamila
    Islamic law and society: an introduction

    Bibliography.
    Includes index.
    ISBN 1 86287 327 5

    1. Islamic law. I. Title.

340.59

Typeset by The Federation Press, Leichhardt, NSW.
    Printed by Southwood Press, Marrickville, NSW

PREFACE

This book has been written principally to meet the needs of Australian professionals, teachers, students and members of the public who wish to acquire an introductory knowledge of Islamic law and culture to assist them in their work or studies or in their dealings with Muslim people in Australian society.

Islam is professed as a religion by more than a quarter of the world's population, in countries ranging from Africa, through the Middle East, to the Indo-Pakistani sub-continent, and from there through South East Asia, western China and the republics of the former Soviet Union. As well, there are large Muslim minorities in several European countries as well as in North America. The Australian Muslim population is estimated at more than 300,000 and is growing.

There are wide variations in culture and custom among these people, and several different schools of religious thought.

Islamic law encompasses a vast field of knowledge. Just as it would be impossible to describe and explain all the details and variations of the common law in one short book, so it is impossible to explain all the intricacies of Islamic law. Aspects of the law differ somewhat from place to place and from culture to culture. There is also a range of opinions on many issues, from the ultra-conservative to the radical. This book therefore contains merely an overview of Islamic law and culture. The reader who is seeking a greater depth of knowledge will be able to move on from here to the many excellent works which are now being published in English, which deal with different aspects of law and culture more fully.

I would like to acknowledge my gratitude to Tan Sri Datuk Ahmad Ibrahim, the Dean of the Kulliyyah of Laws at the International Islamic University, Kuala Lumpur, who invited me to work and study at the University and taught me Islamic Family law; to the other professors and lecturers of IIU who also taught me; to Jenny Blokland, former Dean of the Faculty of Law at Northern Territory

v

University, who encouraged me to write this book; to Professor Nabil Baydoun, Dean of the Faculty of Business at NTU; and to my friends, Aziza Abdel Halim, Saleha Kasif and Katy Nebhan for their helpful comments and for reading the draft of the text.

Jamila Hussain
January 1999

CONTENTS

المقدمة ❊

INTRODUCTION TO ISLAMIC LAW

There is no doubt that Islam has a bad press. Since the end of the Cold War and the collapse of the former Soviet Union, Islam and Muslims have replaced Communism and Russians as the major threat to civilisation in the eyes of the Western media. Islam is equated with terrorism, oppression of women, backwardness and religious fundamentalism. The ordinary Australian, knowing this, could be excused for believing that it is best to give all things Islamic a wide berth, and that knowledge of Islamic law and culture is not relevant to people in this country.

Muslim populations and Islamic revival

However, there are more than 200 million followers of Islam living in countries close to Australia. The population of Indonesia exceeds 200 million, and of these 85 per cent are Muslims. Malaysia has a Muslim majority population and there are substantial Muslim minorities in the Southern Philippines and Southern Thailand to our immediate north, and also in other parts of Asia and Africa including India, the former Soviet republics of Central Asia and China. There are also many Muslim majority countries with which we trade, including Pakistan, Saudi Arabia, the Gulf states and Iran.

In the post-colonial era immediately following World War II, it was widely believed that the emerging nations of Asia and Africa would rush to imitate the ways of their former colonial masters and would complete the work of westernising their societies in the shortest

1

possible time. For a while many did. The elites lived, dressed, ate and followed the same lifestyles as near as possible to Europeans; Western-owned corporations continued to dominate the business and commercial life; laws continued to be based on Western models adopted wholly or in part during the colonial era. In many Muslim countries Islam was seen as performing a ceremonial function to which the majority paid lip service only.

However, this situation has changed. Since the 1970s the Muslim world has experienced an Islamic revival which has slowed and even reversed the rush towards uncritical westernisation. The reasons for this revival are complex and are beyond the scope of this work, but its results have been that many Muslim countries have embarked upon a program of part or complete "Islamisation" of their societies, economies and legal systems.

The most dramatic example of this process was the revolution in Iran in 1979, which swept away the Western supported regime of the Shah and declared the country an Islamic state. In Pakistan under General Zia ul-Haq in the late 1970s, a start was made on bringing the country's legal and economic systems into line with Islamic *Shariah*; in Malaysia, a more gradual process of Islamisation has proceeded under Dr Mahathir Mohamed as Prime Minister; in Indonesia, a country often considered only superficially Islamic, there are indications of growing religious belief and involvement among Muslims, and even in secular Turkey, the Islamist parties have gained huge popular support. So, what is likely to be the impact of these developments on Western countries?

Islam in trade and commerce

In spite of occasional setbacks caused by regional financial crises and so on, the countries of South-East Asia, which are substantially populated by Muslims, remain potential markets and trading partners, and are also of importance from a defence and foreign relations perspective. In our own interests, we who live in the "West", should understand their culture and way of life, which is at least partly determined by Islamic religious laws which today are being taken very seriously by governments and populations in these countries.

For example, Islamic law determines what foods and drinks are *halal* (legal or permitted) and may be consumed by Muslims. It also determines the way they dress, what entertainments they may see and how they should behave. These things may be relevant to the success or otherwise of international relationships, trade and commerce with these countries. For example, pork and non-*halal* meats are forbidden to Muslims as food, and drinking alcohol is prohibited also. Therefore it would not make sense, commercially, to spend a lot of money on promoting the sale of these commodities in Muslim countries. Even in the case of acceptable trade commodities – the *halal* meat industry is worth millions of export dollars to Australia by itself – it may be wise to take Islamic law into account before embarking upon expensive promotions.

In one lunch hour in Kuala Lumpur, I passed an Australian meat industry promotion. A real Aussie barbeque had been set up in the forecourt of a hotel and "real Aussie" chefs were busy barbequing lamb and offering samples to passers by. They were probably puzzled as to why there were few takers for their generosity. Obviously, no one had told them that it was the month of *Ramadan* when Muslims are forbidden to eat or drink from sunrise to sunset!

Islamic law also prohibits gambling, the giving or taking of interest in financial transactions and some types of personal relationships, such as de facto relationships, which are acceptable in Western countries. The extent to which these rules are enforced does vary from country to country – casinos, for example, exist in some Muslim countries, though in many they are off limits to the locals. The majority of commerce even in the strict "Islamic" countries is still interest based, although Islamic banks and financial institutions are growing in strength and popularity. Western tourists are welcomed in most places, although some still manage through ignorance or lack of sensitivity to give offence to the locals.

Muslims as migrants

On the domestic front, the dropping of the "White Australia" policy and increased migration from the Middle East and Asia since the 1970s has lead to an increase in the number of Muslims who now call Australia home. Although there are still some in politics and elsewhere who believe that every new migrant should hasten to assimilate completely into Australian society, the majority can see that the policy of multiculturalism has eased the transition for migrants and enriched Australian society at the same time.

In the early days, Muslim migrants to Australia had a very rough time. Not only did they have no established community to welcome them, but they found it almost impossible to obtain *halal* food, to build mosques and Islamic schools or to bury their dead according to Islam. Many of these difficulties appeared to arise out of a lack of understanding on the part of both the mainstream and Muslim communities. Some of these difficulties have been overcome, but some remain.

Islamic law and personal relationships

In the area of personal relationships, many more people are marrying spouses of other nationalities and faiths, and inter-cultural disputes arise more frequently in family law than they did in the past. People who have been brought up in cultures where Islamic family law prevails can find themselves with widely differing expectations of marriage and family life from those of a spouse brought up in a Western society. The law and the judicial system may fail to understand these differences when a family law matter comes before the court.

A prominent and sad example of this kind of problem was the Raja Bahrin/Gillespie dispute over the custody of two children of a failed marriage between a Malaysian aristocrat and an Australian citizen between 1985 and 1993.[1]

Following breakdown in the marriage, the wife had brought the children to live in Australia and had obtained an *ex parte* order for custody in her favour from the Australian Family Court. The husband applied for and was granted custody in the Chief Kadi's court in the Malaysian State of Trengganu. The husband applied to the Australian Family Court for a discharge of the orders made in the wife's favour and consequently the Family Court had to decide whether the dispute should be resolved in Australia according to Australian family law or in Malaysia according to the law there.

Although the Family Court heard evidence from two Malaysian legal practitioners, it appears that there was some misunderstanding of the law and legal system in Malaysia on the part of the court, in

---

[1]   See Frank Bates, "The Story of B: Australian Family Law and Policy in an Asian Context", *Asia Pacific Law Review,* Vol 3 No 2, 1994, pp 33-46 and also Abdul Majid, "An Aspect of Islamic Law in the Judgement of the Family Court of Australia in *In the Marriage of B and B* [Kidnapping]", *Asia Pacific Law Review*, Vol 4 No 1, 1995, pp 91-99.

failing to appreciate that the High Court in Malaysia does not have jurisdiction to hear family law proceedings relating to Muslims, and also the effect of an order that the wife resume cohabitation made by the Chief Kadi's Court in Trengganu.[2] The Family Court ultimately ordered that the wife have custody. The husband removed the children from Australia and took them back to Malaysia in contravention of the Family Court order.

A great deal of emotion was generated in the press in both Malaysia and Australia. The Malaysian press and public strongly supported the father's case and blamed the mother and the Australian Family Court for the problem; in Australia the reverse position was taken. There was a great deal of misunderstanding on both sides, and the case did nothing to improve the relationship between Malaysia and Australia, which then was not at its best.

This case received more publicity than most, but there have been, and will be, many other cases where similar problems arise. An understanding on each side of the beliefs and value systems of the other and how the legal system supports those beliefs and value systems should make it easier to understand the other point of view and so reduce potential for conflict and international misunderstanding over these issues.

Approaches to Islam and its law

We are all products of our own environment and upbringing. It is natural to consider the way things are done in our own culture as the norm, and to view other people's ways as strange and aberrant. We are comfortable with what we are used to and are suspicious of foreign influences. The law is traditionally a conservative profession and has never demonstrated much willingness to inquire whether aspects of other people's legal systems, whether European or Asian, might be worthy of consideration here.

Moreover, we are influenced by what other people tell us. We are particularly influenced by the media which is all pervasive and which still presents an unrealistic white, Anglo-Saxon, and secular-Christian view of the world. If we rely on the media for information, we can easily come to the conclusion that we have a real reason to fear Islamic law and that we should oppose Islamic movements

---

2   Frank Bates, op cit p 34; Abdul Majid, op cit p 94.

whenever we come across them. However, let us consider whether that fear is based on fact.

Seeing ourselves as others see us

It would come as a surprise to Western people that in some sectors of some Asian societies, it is widely believed that Western women are immoral. The natural reaction is to be shocked and angry that these people have the temerity to make the assumption that American/ Australian/English women are immoral. How could these people have got this ridiculous idea? Most likely their answer would be: that they have seen many films and television programs produced in the West; European magazines with naked women on the covers; and films and television programs showing unmarried couples jumping into bed with each other and engaging in many acts which are regarded as immoral in other societies. Therefore the picture the media gives is accepted as true and the assumption is made that these are examples of the way most people live in Western societies.

The dangers of cultural and religious stereotyping

Think about whether we make the same assumptions about other cultures from the reporting of sensational events in our media and judging other people's ways by our own standards. Consider the following passage from *Asiaweek* magazine on 16 June 1993:[3]

> In the eyes of the Christian world, the Muslim is easy to identify. The Western press, by subtle and unconscious prejudice more often than outright bigotry, has made sure of that. The Muslim is the one in the white robe, with swarthy features and wild eyes. He has a bomb factory in the basement. His children can break down and reassemble an AK-47 in minutes. His four wives are secluded at home, happy in their ignorance, and only venture out in sacks and veils. Seeing this man on the sidewalk, a good citizen hastens to alert the CIA ... the Islamic world is a dangerous hotbed of terror, a monolithic threat whose ultimate aim is a holy war against Western governments, religion and life. The archetypal Muslim is George Habash, the leader of the Popular Front for the Liberation of Palestine ... Habash, unfortunately, is a Christian — as are some 10% of Palestinians most of whom are fervent Arab nationalists.

The article goes on to point out that religious fanaticism is not exclusive to Muslims, or indeed, to any one religious group, but that

---

3   Page 24.

terrorism when committed by the Irish Republican Army is not attributed to Roman Catholics generally, nor to Christians generally when Christian Serbs raped, mutilated and murdered Muslims in Bosnia.

However, the media has the habit of automatically attributing terrorism to Muslims as it did in the case of the Oklahoma bombing, where it turned out later, that the perpetrators were right wing Americans. Nowhere were these terrorists described as "Christians", nor were their actions attributed to Christianity. When Pakistan exploded a nuclear bomb in 1998, it was immediately labelled the "Islamic" bomb by some sections of the press. Curiously, the nuclear bomb exploded by India a few days before was not called the "Hindu" bomb. The arsenal of nuclear weapons possessed by the United States, Israel and China are not referred to as the "Christian", "Jewish" or "Atheist" bombs.

Even when Muslims do engage in terrorism, their motives are not likely to be religious. The root of much "Islamic" terrorism has been the Palestinian struggle to regain lost national territory and to establish an independent nation in Palestine. A quote which comes to mind is that "one person's terrorist is another person's freedom fighter". This conflict has affected Palestinian Christians as well as Muslims, as noted above. An unbiased study of the whole political and economic situation in the Middle East might reveal a situation which is much less "black and white" than is commonly described in the media.

The resurgence of Islam and the re-emergence of Islamic law in the legal system of Muslim countries are not necessarily things which should be feared and denounced in the West. In fact uncritical support by Western countries of heavy handed dictators who suppress even moderate Islamic opposition can be counter-productive as it convinces Muslims everywhere that the West is against them.

Islamic law as a different system of law

Islamic law is a very different system of law from the common law that we are used to in Australia. It developed in a very different context, and its solutions are sometimes very different from those of Anglo-Australian law. This does not mean automatically that those solutions are wrong, especially in the context of the societies to which they relate. We should try to approach Islamic law with an open mind. It is dangerous to rely on the media, or even books, since unfortunately, there are few books by Western writers which do not reflect the authors' own prejudices and many contain substantial errors.

The major difference between Islamic law and other legal systems is that Islamic law is based on religion, while the common law and civil law systems are secular in origin. In the past, there have been other religion based legal systems in the world – the Hindu legal system and the Jewish legal system, for example. Nowadays, the Hindu system has been all but supplanted in India by a secular system based on the common law, and Jewish religious law is not enforced, even in Israel, although there are moves by religious parties there to ban driving on some roads during the Sabbath and to ban pork in accordance with Jewish religious law.

In common law countries, speakers sometimes refer to the "Judeo-Christian ethic" as being the basis of our legal system. What does this mean? Generally, it means that our legal system is supposed to be based on Christian principles. It certainly does not mean that our laws have been adopted from the Bible, or from a legal system established by the church – consider how many of the Ten Commandments are still enforceable by law. True, there have been church or ecclesiastical courts in England, but their jurisdiction was limited to divorce and probate and church affairs. There was almost no divorce until the passing of the secular *Divorce Act* in 1857 and the probate jurisdiction of the ecclesiastical courts also came to an end in the 19th century. Today, even such survivals of church influence on our law as the *Sunday Observance Act* have been abolished, and the common law system is secular and insists upon separation of church and state.

On the other hand, Islamic law is entirely religious. In theory, there is no separation between church and state. Indeed, there is no church in the sense of a religious hierarchy separate from the ruler. In classical Islamic thought, the ruler is the *Imam*, the religious leader of the people as well as the person who carries out the normal functions of government. This is still the theory in many Muslim countries today, in the same way that the Queen is in theory the head of the Church of England, but mostly the functions of government are carried on by people who are not religious officials. One exception is Iran. In the media, Iran is sometimes called a "theocracy" which means rule by priests, but this is not strictly correct, as Islam has no priests.

The theory and the reality – Islam and Muslims

One mistake which is easy to make is to judge Islam through the behaviour of individual Muslims or even Muslim societies as a whole. Muslim societies contain their share of good and bad people some of

8

whom claim to be good Muslims. The actions of Muslim rulers and governments have often not been in accordance with Islam, just as those in Europe have often fallen far short of the ideals of Christianity. Looking around the world today, you could not find one true Islamic society parallel to that of the Prophet in Medina, just as you will not find any society which can truly call itself Christian.

The influence of culture

Muslim societies stretch throughout the world from Africa to Southeast Asia. They include people of many different races, from the dark skinned people of Nigeria to the Arab peoples of the Middle East, Indians, Chinese, Malays and Indonesians to people of European stock in Bosnia and Albania. Not surprisingly, despite their common religious allegiance, these people have different cultural backgrounds and speak different languages. Although Muslims are often equated with Arabs, in fact only about one sixth of the world Muslim population are Arabs, and, except for these, only the educated may have more than a slight understanding of the Arabic language.

In some regions, culture has most certainly influenced the practice of Islam as it is interpreted in that area. For example, Mandelbaum[4] has identified a "purdah zone" stretching from Pakistan through the Indian State of Uttar Pradesh, Afghanistan and Bangladesh, where seclusion of women is practised in a very similar way by both Muslims and Hindus. The necessity for female seclusion is strongly insisted upon by these Muslims as a requirement of Islam. However, in southern India and even more so in Southeast Asia, purdah is not seen as a necessary requirement of Islam and women participate in society to a much greater extent.

On another level, a recent television series entitled "Women of Islam"[5] interviewed a number of Muslim women in Mali about the practice of "female circumcision". Three of the four women were sure that this was an Islamic practice and a girl could not be a "proper Muslim" unless she had undergone it. Only one woman correctly stated that it was a very ancient cultural practice – she thought derived from ancient Egypt – and it had nothing to do with Islam. In fact, clitoridectomy is practised in African countries (and elsewhere) by some Muslim, Christian, Jewish[6] and pagan communities, and

---

4   David G Mandelbaum, *Women's Seclusion and Men's Honour*, 1988, pp 2-3.
5   Shown on SBS television, August 1996.
6   In Ethiopia.

9

according to Nawal El-Saadawi,[7] there is a *hadith* in which the Prophet spoke against the practice and tried to limit it.

Most Muslim countries are still very much in the "developing" or "third world" bracket. Many of their inhabitants suffer from grinding poverty and truly shocking rates of illiteracy among both men and women. Even the relatively well educated among those brought up as Muslims may have very little idea of Islamic religious laws and principles. In such countries, where educational opportunities of any kind are few and poorly resourced, even the *mullahs* and the *qadis* who preside over the lower courts are not necessarily well educated in Islamic law, and may make decisions in accordance with custom and tradition rather than what is truly Islamic.

The Bangladeshi writer, Taslima Nasreen, received widespread publicity, even acclaim, in the West when she criticised Islamic laws and was quoted as calling for the thorough revision of the *Quran*. Anti-Taslima demonstrations and threats made against her caused the Western press to represent her as a female Salman Rushdie, denied freedom of speech and conscience in her own country.

The Australian writer, Hanifa Deen[8] took time to research the Taslima story during a recent visit to Bangladesh. She was puzzled that Taslima had received little support from Bangladeshi feminist groups. She found that some of Taslima's activities were totally outrageous in the context of Bangladeshi society. For example, she appeared on TV smoking a cigarette while she criticised the *Quran*. Incidents like this not only infuriated the conservatives, but led progressive women to believe that Taslima's outspoken and ill-founded statements set their cause back years. As Hanifa Deen puts it: "her religious learning was superficial. It rested on a literal acceptance of the Qur'an and misogynist aHadith interpretations that many Muslims do not themselves accept as authentic. Even liberal Muslims were dismayed by what they saw as a lethal combination: a lack of knowledge and a loud mouth".[9] In such societies, the best advice may be to hasten slowly.

---

7   *The Hidden Face of Eve*, 1980 p 39.
8   Hanifa Deen's account of the lives of women in Bangladesh and Pakistan is published in *Broken Bangles,* 1998.
9   Ibid p 43.

2

A BRIEF SURVEY OF ISLAMIC HISTORY

Islam in outline

Islam is one of the world's three major monotheistic religions, the other two being Judaism and Christianity. They have much in common, and, of course, significant differences, but all developed from a common root. All revere the Old Testament prophets, Abraham (Ibrahim in Arabic), Moses (Musa), Jacob (Yacub), Joseph (Yusuf), David (Dawud), Solomon (Sulaiman) and so on. Muslims also recognise Jesus (Isa) as a prophet, but reject the idea that he was "literally" the son of God.

Judaism and Islam are more like each other than Christianity. Both have a well defined system of religious law. Both forbid the eating of pork and other meat which has not been ritually killed (*kosher* to the Jews, and *halal* to Muslims). Both forbid the making of statues and religious images. In ritual and practice there are many similarities. Both insist on the unity of God and reject the Christian idea of the Trinity. Muslims reject the Christian concept of original sin and the idea that there can be any intercessor between a person and God, since in Islam, each person is responsible for his or her own salvation which can be achieved by faith and good deeds, and by striving to keep God's law which is laid down in the *Quran*.

The five pillars of Islam

The "five pillars" represent the basic principles of Islam. They are:

1. Belief in God, and belief that Muhammad is the Messenger of God. Muslims are also required to believe in the angels, the prophets and God's revelations in the *Quran*, which represent a complete guidance to mankind.

2. Prayer – Muslims are required to pray five times a day – at dawn. midday, mid-way through the afternoon, after sunset, and at night. The prescribed prayers are recited in Arabic, but believers may make their personal prayers in their own language, if it is not Arabic.

3. Fasting – fasting is prescribed in the month of *Ramadan* which is the ninth month of the Islamic calendar (a lunar calendar). At this time, adult Muslims, who are in good health, may neither eat nor drink during daylight hours. They should also make a special effort to lead a pure life during this time.

4. Giving *zakat* – each year a Muslim should give a defined proportion of his or her accumulated wealth to the poor and needy by way of this compulsory payment.

5. The pilgrimage to Mecca (*Hajj*) – this should be undertaken by every Muslim who can afford it once in a lifetime. The *hajj* proper can only be made at one time of the year, at the time of Eid ul-Adha, and at this time every year up to two and a half million Muslims of all nationalities are present in Mecca. A pilgrimage to Mecca at other times of the year is called *umra*.

The *Quran*

The *Quran* is the holy book of Islam. It consists of the revelations received by the Prophet Muhammad from God. It was revealed in the Arabic language and has been preserved, unaltered, in Arabic since its revelation. Great importance is placed on the recital of the *Quran*. Children are encouraged to complete their *khatme Quran* (complete reading of the *Quran*) while young.

The *Quran* is treated with reverence by Muslims. It is usually carefully wrapped and kept on a high shelf. It is never placed on the floor. A person reading the *Quran* should have *wudu*, that is be ritually clean, as for prayer.

Muslims are encouraged to read the *Quran* and understand it since it is a guidance for life. Unfortunately, the majority of Muslims do not have Arabic as their first language, and so for them, reading and understanding the *Quran* in its original language remains an impossible ideal. The *Quran* has been translated into numerous languages and translations made be used for study, but translations convey neither the beauty of the original language nor are they considered the authentic source of knowledge.

The mosque

The mosque (*mesjid* in Arabic) is not only the centre of religious worship, but also a place of learning, a community centre, and sometimes even a courtroom. A mosque is a simple structure, consisting basically of a prayer hall, with facilities outside for washing, since it is a requirement of Islam that believers be physically and mentally clean before prayer.

Many Westerners are surprised by the austerity of the interior of the mosque. The prayer hall is simply a large empty room, with an alcove (*mihrab*) in one wall which serves the purpose of indicating the direction of Mecca, which Muslims face as they pray. There is no altar, no chairs for the congregation, no pictures and no statues. There may be decorations of Arabic script containing quotations from the *Quran*, and bookshelves containing religious books around the walls. There will be a raised pulpit (*mimbar*) for the Imam (prayer leader) to use to give a sermon during Friday prayers.

Men and women pray in separate areas. Usually the men's space is larger than the women's since it is compulsory for men to attend the Friday congregational prayer, but optional for women.

Objections have sometimes been raised to the building of mosques by local communities on the grounds of noise. This is a mistaken idea. The traditional architecture of a mosque provides for at least one minaret, from which in the past, the *muezzin* called the faithful to prayer. In Muslim countries today, the call to prayer, or *azan*, is quite likely to be amplified through loudspeakers. In non-Muslim countries, *azan* will simply be recited within the mosque.

Day time prayers are silent, even in congregation, and early morning and night prayers recited only by the Imam. There are no bells, musical instruments or community singing. In terms of noise, the mosque is much quieter than the average church during the times of service.

The Imam

The Imam is the person, invariably male, who leads the congregational prayer. An Imam is not a priest, since there are no intermediaries between God and man in Islam. There is no ordination and no sacraments or rites which only a religiously sanctified person can perform. In theory, any respectable man with sufficient religious knowledge can act as Imam, and in cases where for some reason, a particular mosque is left without a formally appointed Imam, a member of the congregation will fulfil the function as and when necessary. However, full-time Imams are usually people who have undertaken religious studies, often at Al-Azhar university in Egypt, or in Saudi Arabia.

In some Muslim countries Imams and other mosque officials are appointed, paid and supervised by the government and may be expected to support the government in its policies. In other countries they are appointed by the local mosque committee which also pays their salary. Imams are normally married and have families the same as any other Muslim. In Western countries where Muslims are in a minority, the Imam frequently finds himself called upon to act as community counsellor, Islamic judge/arbitrator and welfare officer as well as prayer leader.

Festivals and feast days

The two major festivals are *Eid ul-Fitr* called *Hari Raya Aid-il-Fitri* or *Hari Raya Puasa* in South-East Asia, and *Eid ul-Adha* (*Hari Raya Korban*). *Eid ul-Fitr* falls at the end of the fasting month of *Ramadan*. Since the Islamic calendar is lunar, this means that it moves forward approximately eleven days each year. *Eid ul-Adha* commemorates Prophet Ibrahim's (Abraham's) willingness to sacrifice his son at God's command and falls in the month of *Dzul-hijjah*, at the time of the *hajj*.

In Muslim countries, *Ramadan* itself is a very special time. Families get up before dawn to eat their *suhur* (early morning meal) and pray *fajr* before perhaps going back to sleep until the sun rises. After the endurance of fasting during daylight hours comes *iftar* the long awaited breaking of the fast immediately after sunset. Often friends are invited to join the *iftar* meal. During *Ramadan* working hours may be shorter and on the way home, purchases of tasty foods to eat at *iftar* may be made from stalls set up along the roadside for the occasion.

The celebration of Eid itself varies according to the custom of various countries, but normally involves attendance at Eid prayers at the mosque, and much visiting of friends and relatives afterwards. At *Eid ul-Adha* a goat, sheep or other animal should be sacrificed and the meat distributed to friends, neighbours and the poor. In Western countries, this obligation is usually discharged by payment of money to a charitable organisation which will arrange for meat to be distributed to poor Muslims in a third world country.

The concept of *jihad*

Jihad in Arabic means "struggle". It is usually thought of in the context of a "Holy war" often represented as a war to force unbelievers to convert to Islam. The latter understanding is quite incorrect since history shows that for the most part, the spread of Islam was peaceful, and Christian and Jewish minorities lived side by side with their Muslim neighbours throughout Islamic history. For example, Jewish culture flourished in Islamic Spain, only coming to an end when Christian forces under Ferdinand and Isabella defeated the Muslims and gave non-Christians in their domain three choices — exile, conversion to Christianity or death. Jews fled to other parts of the Muslim empires and lived there up to about the time when the state of Israel was founded. Substantial Christian populations still exist today in the heartland of Islam, the Middle East.

On the other hand, Islam differs from Christianity in not advising believers to "turn the other cheek" if they are attacked. Permission for *jihad* was given to the Prophet only after persuasion and migration from Mecca to Medina had failed to stop attacks on the Muslims by their enemies in Arabia.[1] But the Muslims should not start the fighting and if their enemies seek peace, they should make peace with them.[2]

The other meaning of *jihad* is simply to struggle against evil, whether it be against wrongdoing by those in authority, in which case it may be by speech or writing or even legal action, and also in a personal sense, to struggle to overcome unworthy desires in one's self.

---

1   'Abdur Rahman i Doi, *Shari'ah: The Islamic Law,* 1984, pp 438-439.
2   *Quran,* 8:61.

The *Ummah*

The word *ummah* means the worldwide community of believers, or the body of Muslims everywhere. Like Christianity, Islam is a universal religion, making no distinction between its followers on the basis of race, colour, ethnicity, language or social class. This principle is no-where made more clear than at the time of the *Hajj* in Mecca, when all male pilgrims, whether prince, prime minister or pauper, must dress alike in two lengths of unsewn white cloth and perform exactly the same rites in exactly the same way (there is no prescribed dress for women).

Islam transcends national boundaries. In theory, all Muslims are brothers and sisters in religion and should treat each other equally well. In practice the ideal of the *ummah*, remains just that, an ideal. National and ethnic rivalries are just as noticeable in the Muslim world as outside it. Muslims divide themselves on the basis of being Arabs or Turks, Pakistanis or Bangladeshis, Malays or Indonesians. Even in countries such as Australia, where Muslims are a minority, in any city where there is a substantial Muslim population, mosques will be established and supported by particular ethnic groups. There are few mosques which are truly multicultural, although none will deliberately exclude people of other ethnic groups.

A very short history of Islamic civilisation

History, as most people in the West have learnt it at school, is Eurocentric. Students learn about the civilisations of ancient Greece and Rome. Some attention is given to Ancient Egypt, there may be a cursory mention of the Hittites, Sumer and Babylon, then the story moves on to Medieval times – a period when art and literature and learning did not flourish in Europe and ignorance prevailed. Then, the student moves on to the Renaissance, the Voyages of Discovery and the Industrial Revolution when the countries of Europe and North America became the leaders of the world.

To read most history books, nothing of importance ever happened in China or Japan, India or Africa, and the history of the Muslim world is totally ignored. To fill in a little bit of the missing picture, let us now take a very brief look at some of the major historical developments in the Muslim world from the time of the Prophet to the present day.

The origins of Islam

According to Muslims, Islam is the original religion of the first prophets, such as Adam and Abraham, which has been altered by the Jews and Christians over the years, so that their holy books, the Torah and the Christian Bible, no longer reflect the true word of God. Hence, God sent a final prophet, Muhammad, and a final revelation, the *Quran*, as a last guidance to all mankind to follow the correct path.

Muhammad's early life

Muhammad[3] was born in Mecca in what is now Saudi Arabia, in AD 570 into a tribe known as the Quraysh who were prominent in the area. His father, Abdullah, died before he was born and his mother, Amina, died when he was about five years old. He was therefore brought up first by his grandfather, Abd al-Muttalib, and after his grandfather's death, by his uncle, Abu Talib. The first years of his life passed relatively uneventfully. As a boy, he made a journey to Syria with his uncle who was a merchant. As a young man, he was renowned for his honesty and received the nick-name *al-amin* – the trustworthy. At the age of 26 he married a widow, Khadijah, who had employed him to look after her trading business. Although Khadijah was much older than he was, the marriage was happy and lasted until Khadijah's death when Muhammad was nearly 50 years old.

The first revelation

Tradition tells us that Muhammad rejected the idol worship which was practised by most of the Arabs, and that from time to time, he repaired to a lonely cave on Mount Hira for solitude and contemplation. On one such occasion, in the month of *Ramadan*, he was shocked suddenly to find himself in the presence of an angel, Gabriel, who ordered him to recite the words embroidered on a length of green brocade. Despite Muhammad's protests that he could not recite, the angel held him in a fierce embrace until he was able to recite the words, which thereafter became engraved upon his heart:

---

3   There are various transliterations of the name "Muhammad". "Mohammed" is also common, while "Mahomet" is an older Turkish/French spelling which is not much used today.

Recite in the name of thy Lord who created –
Created man from a clot (germ cell).
Recite, and thy Lord is most bountiful,
He who taught by the pen,
Taught man what he knew not.[4]

Fearing that he had become possessed, Muhammad fled from the cave, hearing as he left, the angel's words "O Muhammad, you are the Messenger of God, and I am Gabriel". Fearful and disturbed, Muhammad reported the experience to his wife, Khadijah, who shortly afterwards went to see her cousin, Waraqah, a wise Christian man, who assured him that the vision was genuine and that God had appointed Muhammad to be a prophet to his people.

For some months there was no revelation, and then Gabriel began to appear to the Prophet again, bringing revelations which Muhammad had to recite aloud. At first only his wife, Khadijah, and his immediate family believed in his mission, but gradually he began to gather around him a small band of followers. The Quraysh did not take kindly to this new preacher who urged people to abandon the worship of idols and worship only the one God, and they persecuted Muhammad and all who followed him.

The *Hijrah*

Finally, the persecution became so severe, that Muhammad and his followers left Mecca and migrated to Medina where they were welcomed by the inhabitants. The year of migration (*hijrah*) marks the first year of the Muslim calendar which is represented by the letters "AH" (after *hijrah*). The year was AD 622.

In the following years, Muhammad became established at Medina, but he and his ever increasing band of followers had to fight many battles before they were able to overcome the opposition of the Quraysh and return to Mecca where the idols in the *Ka'bah* were destroyed and Islam was victorious. By the time of the Prophet's death, Islam had spread throughout the whole of Arabia.

Muhammad at Medina

Muhammad proved himself to be not only a prophet and capable military leader, but also an able administrator and judge and the paramount example of the kind of person every good Muslim should

---

4   *Quran*, 96: 1-5.

aspire to be. The Islamic society of Medina at the time of the Prophet and in the years immediately following his death, is accepted as the ideal Islamic society which should be emulated by Muslims everywhere. The American author, Michael J Hart, gave Muhammad first place in his ranking of the one hundred most influential persons in history, since "he was the only man in history who was supremely successful on both the religious and secular levels".[5] The Prophet died, following a short illness, in AD 632.

The spread of Islam

After the Prophet's death, the leadership of the Muslims passed to his great friend and companion, Abu Bakr, the first of the four "rightly-guided" Caliphs. At the time, there was a state of war between the Muslims and Byzantium and a hostile relationship with Iran. During Abu Bakr's caliphate, and that of his successor, Omar, victory was gained over both of these powers, and the Islamic empire reached from (modern day) Libya to Afghanistan, and north to Armenia. Under the next Caliph, Othman, the Empire spread south through Nubia, across the straits of Gibraltar, taking in part of Spain (Al-Andalus), and occupied the islands of Crete, Cyprus and Rhodes in the Mediterranean. The Byzantine Empire was confined to a small area around Constantinople, which did not fall to the Muslims until it was conquered by the Ottoman Turks in 1453.

Contemporary documents suggest that the origin of these wars was political, rather than a desire to spread Islam by the sword, which in fact is prohibited by the *Quran*. Generally the Muslims were more lenient and just rulers than those they replaced and they were often welcomed by the populations of the territories they occupied.[6] In time, most of these populations became Muslims.

The Umayyid dynasty

After the death of Othman, the succession of the fourth Caliph, Ali, was disputed and wars of succession broke out. The government was ultimately stabilised under Abd al-Malik (AD 685-705), and the Empire expanded further to include Morocco and Spain, and the

---

5   *The 100: A Ranking of the Most Influential Persons in History*, 1987, p 33.
6   M Hamidullah, in his *Introduction to Islam*, 1974, pp 197-198, refers to contemporary documents indicating that the Muslims were lenient and popular rulers, and respected and protected Christian churches and priests.

northern part of the Indian sub-continent. Even some cities in France, such as Bordeaux and Toulouse passed temporarily into the hands of the Muslims, until they were turned back at the battle of Tours in 732.

The capital of the Empire was moved from Medina to Damascus. With this change came a decline in religious piety and the adoption of foreign habits of luxury and squandering of wealth. However, intellectual activity was also encouraged and the city became the centre of studies of medicine and the sciences, many treatises being translated from the Greek into Arabic.[7]

One of the caliphs, 'Umar ibn 'Abd el-Aziz who ruled from 717 to 720 was renowned for his piety and impartial administration of justice. He encouraged learning and Muslim scholars made significant advances in the field of science and religious studies.

However, rebellions arose in various parts of the Empire. These lead to the overthrow of the Umayyid rulers and the beginning of the Abbasid dynasty.

The Abbasid Caliphate

The Abbasids came to power in AD 750 and their rule ended in AD 1256 when the Mongols sacked Baghdad which had become the capital of the Abbasids in place of Damascus. About the same time, a rival caliphate was set up at Cordova in Spain, and thereafter the Islamic Empire was divided. Later, independent states appeared in other areas. The most famous of the Abbasid caliphs is probably Harun al-Rashid who reigned from AD 786 to 809.

The golden age of the Abbasids extended from AD 750 to about 847. Intellectual and religious thought flourished. The art of paper making was introduced from China through Samarkand, and paper mills set up. Books became widely available and great libraries held vast collections. The Abbasid rulers encouraged the sciences and invited renowned scientists and intellectuals to their courts. Schools and colleges were established everywhere. The Greek philosophers such as Plato and Aristotle were studied and their works translated into Arabic. In this way, the ideas of the great thinkers of classical Greece were preserved. Some renowned Muslim philosophers of the time were al-Kindi (d AD 873), al-Farabi (d AD 950), Ibn Sina (d AD 1036), known as Avicenna in the West, and al-Ghazali (d AD 1111).

---

7   Ibid p 199.

The founders of the four great schools of Islamic law, Abu Hanifa (d AD 767), Malik ibn Anas (d AD 795), Muhammad ibn Idris as-Shafii (d AD 820) and Ahmad ibn Hanbal (d AD 855), all lived during Abbasid times. So did the great compilers of *hadith*, al-Bukhari (d AD 870), Muslim (d AD 875), Tirmidhi (d AD 892) and Abu Dawud (d 888).

The Abbasids maintained a sophisticated system of administration, with a bureau of taxes, a police force and even a postal service. The administration of justice was considered a religious duty and was entrusted to trained judges known as *qadis*.

The Moors in Spain

Islam first came to Spain in AD 711 when King Roderic was defeated by Tariq, the leader of the invasion of the Moors from North Africa. Roderic's territories known as al-Andalus were added to the Muslim Empire. In AD 758 the Umayyid prince Abd al-Rahman became the ruler of an independent state. Later, the Muslim empire in Spain split up into a number of independent kingdoms, which in time, were conquered, one by one by the Christian states which remained in the northern part of the country. Muslim rule in Granada held out until 1492 when the Moorish rulers were defeated by Ferdinand and Isabella.

While the rest of Europe languished in the Dark Ages, civilisation flourished in Spain. It became a centre of learning, its universities attracting non-Muslim students from all over Europe. Magnificent buildings were constructed, agriculture was encouraged, trade promoted. Great advances were made in the study of science and medicine. Some of the many famous Muslim scientists and philosophers who lived in Spain were Abul Qasim whose surgical works were used in Europe until 1497, Ibn Rushd (d 1198), the rationalist philosopher, known in Europe as Averroes, and Ibn Khaldun (d AD 1406) "a master of the science of human behaviour and a forerunner of modern anthropology".[8] Many new ideas, inventions and discoveries were passed through the Muslims in Spain to Europe, where their origin was not always acknowledged due to the religious prejudices of the time.

---

8   Pervez Hoodbhoy, *Islam and Science*, 1992, p 115.

The Mughals in India

Muslims arrived in India in three separate waves – the Arabs in the 8th century who conquered Sind, the Turkic Muslims from the kingdom of Ghazni in the 12th century who gained control of almost all of India north of the Deccan, and Turkic Muslims from Afghanistan under Babur in the 16th century. Babur's grandson, Akbar expanded the new Mughal empire from the Bay of Bengal in the east to Kabul in the north, into the Deccan in the south. A later successor, Aurangzeb increased Mughal territory to include almost all of India except the tip of the sub-continent. However, this vast territory could not be held for long and by the beginning of the 18th century the Mughal empire had begun to decline. Eventually it broke up into a number of Sultanates which came directly or indirectly under British rule.

In the 13th century during the Mongol invasions which devastated most of the Islamic territories of the Middle East, northern India became a sanctuary for refugees from the invasions, and quickly became a centre of artistic and intellectual civilisation. Later rulers such as Akbar encouraged the arts, literature and music. A descendant of Akbar, the ruler Shah Jahan, constructed the gem of Mughal architecture, the Taj Mahal as a mausoleum to his dead wife, Mumtaz Mahal.

The Ottoman Empire

The Seljuk Turks became established in Baghdad in the 11th century. During the 12th and 13th centuries, the Turks established their rule over Anatolia at the expense of the Byzantine Empire, which was then still administered from Constantinople. In the 14th century, under the leadership of the Ottoman ruler, Osman, Turkish territory was expanded into Thrace and Macedonia. Between that time and the 16th century, Murad I created an empire stretching from the river Danube to the Euphrates. In 1389 at the battle of Kosovo, a combined Serbian, Bosnian and Bulgarian army was defeated, and in 1453, the capital of the Byzantine Empire, Constantinople itself, was captured by the Turks. By the middle of the 16th century, the Turkish armies had defeated the Mameluke dynasty in Egypt and added that country, plus Syria, Palestine and Arabia to the Empire. The height of Turkish power and prestige was reached in the reign of Suleiman the Magnificent, who laid siege to Vienna unsuccessfully in 1529. The

Turks were finally driven back after a final unsuccessful siege in 1683.

After that the Ottoman Empire began to decline, and although the decline was temporarily arrested at times by attempts at reform, it gradually lost territory as it suffered defeat in wars with neighbouring states such as Russia and the Holy Roman Empire. Moreover, the Turkish rulers failed to recognise the power of the newly industrialised European states of the 18th and 19th century, and to deal with them effectively, so that European countries were able to gain economic advantages within the Turkish Empire. As a final blow, the Ottomans found themselves on the losing side in World War I and were only with difficulty, able to avoid coming under the control of occupying Greek, French, British and Italian forces. In 1923 the Turkish republic was proclaimed by Kemal Ataturk, and the sultanate ceased to exist.

Islam in the 20th century

For much of the 20th century, the Muslim world has been ruled directly or indirectly by European colonial powers – the British in India and Malaya, the Dutch in Indonesia, the French and Italians in North Africa, with much of the Middle East being at least indirectly under European control. Islamic laws were supplanted by laws derived from European systems, the influence of Islam was widely believed to be dying under the pressures of westernisation. Everywhere, Muslim peoples were economically downtrodden and disregarded. Islamic civilisation had all but disappeared.

The end of the second World War saw the beginning of changing fortunes, with independence movements in many Muslim countries striving against their former colonial overlords, and finally managing to achieve independence. In most cases the leaders of the new nationalist movements were the Western educated elite, most of whom paid only lip service to Islam while they stressed modernisation for their countries. However, Islamic movements developed influenced by the writings of prominent Muslim thinkers such as Muhammad Abduh and Rashid Rida in the Middle East and Maududi in India. In 1979 the Iranian revolution galvanised the Muslim world with its promise to establish an Islamic state. Islamic movements gained new impetus all over the world, and several countries have now moved towards the "re-Islamisation" of their cultures and legal systems.

The revival of Islamic law

Most Muslim countries have, at some time in the recent past, been colonised by European powers, and Islamic law has been largely supplanted by Western systems except in the areas of family law and inheritance. It was widely expected that in the course of time, Western-based laws would be adopted in most Muslim countries and Islamic law would die out. However, in the past 20 or 30 years particularly, the predicted demise of Islamic law has not happened and there has been a resurgence of Islamic feeling, with many countries beginning to "Islamise" their legal systems again.

Before 1979, the only country in the world with a completely Islamic legal system was Saudi Arabia. Since then, Iran has replaced its Western style laws with an Islamic legal system and the same thing has happened in Sudan, and to a less complete extent, in Libya and Pakistan. There has been a revived interest in Islamic law in Malaysia with a strengthening of the *Shariah* court system, the introduction of Islamic banking in parallel with the secular banking system, and the proposal by the Kelantan State Government – opposed by the Federal Government and now apparently abandoned – to introduce Islamic criminal law in the State of Kelantan.

Most of these changes are not changes which affect trade or commerce or even the tourist industry, and so have not had a serious effect on international relationships. Even in Kelantan, where the PAS party government has attempted to introduce a strict Islamic regime, tourists are not affected by the law which requires strict Islamic dress for Muslim women, and limits the serving of alcohol and various types of entertainments.

However, poverty and desperation breed extremist political movements and in many countries revolutionary movements have appropriated Islam as their slogan and have promised to impose their generally narrow and conservative version of Islamic law on their own countries when they come to power.

An example of this is the recent ascendancy of the Taliban in Afghanistan. This country had been torn apart by constant warfare for the past 17 years, first in the struggle to expel the Russians and then by continual fighting between rival groups of *muhajideen* reflecting tribal rivalries and the ambitions of various warlords and their external backers. Inspired by religious fervour of the particularly narrow variety which is common in the northern regions of the Indian sub-continent, the Taliban succeeded in overthrowing the warlords and establishing a uniform, strict Islamic code on most of the country. While this has serious negative implications for women, it is unrealistic to expect revolutionary regimes to embrace instant democracy in third world countries which have never had a democratic tradition.

Unfortunately, similar situations exist in other parts of the Muslim world. In other countries the poor and desperate have turned to Islamic movements in desperation as the alternatives have failed them. The world is likely to see more, rather than less, of these versions of Islamic law in the future.

❊ القضاء

3

ISLAMIC JURISPRUDENCE

The concept of law in Islam

The concept of "law" in Islam is much wider than the concept of law in Europe or in the common law countries. Islamic law encompasses aspects of belief and religious practice which would not be considered "law" elsewhere. These include rules relating to belief, prayer, fasting, the making of *hajj*, giving *zakat* and also aspects of everyday life such as behaviour towards other people, dietary rules, dress, manners and morals. It also includes laws relating to crime and evidence, international relations, marriage, divorce and inheritance, commercial transactions and many other subjects which would be included under the Western definition of law. This book deals only with the second aspect of Islamic law, that which roughly corresponds with the categories of law we are used to.

Islamic law is known as the *Shariah*.[1] The Arabic word means literally "a way to a watering place", and thus, a path to be followed. According to Muslim belief, it is the path ordained by God for the guidance of mankind,[2] and must be followed by all Muslims. The origins of *Shariah* are the *Quran* and *Sunnah* (the primary sources) and the interpretations and opinions of the learned jurists (the secondary sources).

---

1   There are various spellings in common usage, including *Shari'ah* and in SE Asia, *Syariah*.

2   Abdur Rahman i Doi, *Shari'ah: The Islamic Law*, 1989, p 2.

Primary sources

1. *Quran*

According to Muslim belief, the *Quran* was revealed to the Prophet Muhammad through the agency of the Angel Gabriel (*Jibra'il*) during the last 22 years of the Prophet's life. The verses of the *Quran* were preserved by the companions of the Prophet, who committed them to memory and/or wrote them down on whatever material came to hand as they were revealed. All these different records were brought together after the Prophet's death, by order of the Caliph Abu Bakr, who commissioned Zayd ibn Thabit, the Prophet's chief scribe, to compile one standard and complete copy in the order of chapters (*suras*) used by the Prophet. This version was checked and approved as correct by the Companions who had heard the original from the Prophet's own mouth. During the time of Caliph Othman, this standard copy was distributed to the far-flung regions of the Arab Empire with instructions that it was to be read according to the pronunciation of the Quraysh, the people of Mecca, from whom the Prophet had come. This version of the *Quran* has been in use, unchanged, ever since.

The authoritative text of the *Quran* is the Arabic text. Translations may be used for personal study, but where there is any question of meaning, the Arabic text must be consulted.

The *Quran* is not a legal text. It does however contain approximately 500 injunctions of a legal nature, which 'Abdur Rahman i Doi has classified under four headings:[3]

  (i) The concise injunctions – these are precise commandments but the *Quran* does not give detailed rules about how they are to be carried out. Examples of these are prayer, fasting, payment of *zakat* (the religious charity/tax paid usually in *Ramadan*).

 (ii) The concise and detailed injunctions – these are commandments about which some details are given in the *Quran*, but further details may be discovered from the *hadith* and other recognised sources. Examples of these are the rules about relations with non-Muslims.

(iii) The detailed injunctions – the *Quran* gives complete details about these commandments and nothing further is required or may be sought eg the *Hadd*[4] punishments.

---

3   Ibid, pp 38-39.
4   *Hadd* literally means "limit". These are particular crimes mentioned in the *Quran*. See Chapter 10 – Criminal Law – for further explanation.

(iv) Fundamental principles of guidance – these principles do not have clear cut definitions and the way to put them into effect must be determined through *ijtihad*,[5] eg principles such as freedom, equality, public interest, consultation and justice.

It is generally agreed that the injunctions contained in the *Quran* must not be changed, though there is one precedent for permitting change where circumstances changed. That is in the fact that Caliph Omar did not distribute *zakat* to one of the categories of people specified as recipients of *zakat* in the *Quran* – those whose hearts may be reconciled to Islam. This was on the basis that, by his time, Islam was strong enough not to need to give such encouragement to converts. In spite of this example, the rule stands that the *Quran* must not be altered. It can be interpreted but only by those who are qualified to do so. In modern times it is very difficult to get agreement on who, if anyone, is sufficiently qualified to interpret the *Quran*.

2. *Hadith* and *Sunnah*

The word *Sunnah* means a beaten track, and thus an accepted course of conduct. Among the Arabs before Islam, it meant the traditional practices of the community. Gradually, in Islamic thought, it came to mean all the acts and sayings of the Prophet as well as everything he approved. The word *Hadith* (plural *Ahadith*) means a narrative or communication and is used for a narration of the conduct of the Prophet, whereas *Sunnah* is the example or law which is deduced from the *hadith*.[6] Only *Sunnah* of a legal nature is held to form part of the *Shariah*. Personal practices of the Prophet, such as the way he dressed and ate, and sayings relating to such matters as agriculture and strategy of the wars fought at the time, are not considered to form part of the law.[7] The *Quran* takes priority over the *Sunnah* as a source of law, and jurists should resort to the *Sunnah* for legal guidance, only when no clear guidance can be obtained from the *Quran*.

The *Sunnah* is used by Muslim jurists for the following purposes in ascertaining the law:

- To confirm the law which has already been mentioned in the *Quran*
- To give an adequate explanation to matters which have been mentioned in the *Quran* in general terms only

---

5   Use of personal reasoning.
6   Mohammad Hashim Kamali, *Principles of Islamic Jurisprudence*, 1989, p 59.
7   Ibid pp 64-65.

- To clarify verses in the *Quran* where there may be some ambiguity
- To introduce a new rule which is not mentioned in the *Quran*, for example, the prohibition on marrying an aunt and niece at the same time.

The *hadith* were assembled from the recollections of the Companions of the Prophet, and were recorded in writing only some considerable time after his death.[8] In the course of time, many thousands of *hadith* appeared, and many were clearly forged to suit political or other purposes. Therefore, a science of *hadith* was developed to sort out the doubtful and the forgeries from the authentic *hadith* and to classify them according to reliability. Many *hadith* were rejected. The others were assembled into collections in the 9th century. The most esteemed collections are those of:

Al-Bukhari (d AD 870)

Muslim (d AD 875)

Abu Dawud (d AD 888)

Al-Tirmidhi (d AD 892)

Hadith are classified according to the reliability of their transmitters and the strength of their *isnad* (chain of narrators), as:

(i) *Muwatir* – a *hadith* reported by a large number of trustworthy people in such a way that its authenticity can virtually be guaranteed.

(ii) *Mashhur* – this is a *hadith* which has originally been reported from one or more Companions of the Prophet, but has become well-known and has been transmitted by a large number of people. It must have been disseminated during the first or second generation following the Prophet's death.

(iii) *Ahad* – (or solitary) – this is a *hadith* which is reported by only one person and does not meet the requirements of the first two classes of *hadith*. The jurists disagree on the value of this type of *hadith*, but the majority agree that it can be accepted provided that the transmitter is a competent and trustworthy

---

8   There are differences of scholarly opinion concerning how early the *hadith* commenced to be recorded. The earliest systematic collection which has survived was the *Muwatta* of Imam Malik (d 179 AH), see Daniel Brown, *Rethinking tradition in modern Islamic thought*, 1996, p 94.

adult Muslim, who is known to have possessed a retentive memory and that he has heard the *hadith* directly from his immediate source. Also the contents of the *hadith* must not be contrary to the *Quran* and other principles of *Shariah*. Imam Abu Hanifa imposed additional requirements, and Imam Malik required that it not be contrary to the practice of the people of Medina.

Additionally, certain principles of criticism of *hadith* were established:[9]

- The *hadith* should not be contrary to the *Quran*.
- It should not be contrary to reason, the laws of nature or common experience.
- It should not be contrary to the accepted traditions.
- It should not praise any particular tribe, person or place.
- It should not contain dates or details of future events.
- A *hadith* which purports to contain remarks of the Prophet which are not in accordance with his accepted position or Islamic belief in the Prophethood should be rejected.

Al Bukhari is said to have examined 600,000 *hadith*, but to have accepted only 7397. Even so, the authenticity of *hadith* generally has been criticised both by Orientalists such as Goldziher and some Muslims who have questioned the characters and memories of some of the Companions of the Prophet and the methods by which the authenticity of *hadith* were established.[10] Even some *hadith* which have been accepted by the two most authoritative of the compilers, Al Bukhari and Muslim are considered by some to be open to doubt. An example of a *hadith* which has been rejected is the one which says that anyone who names his son Muhammad is guaranteed entry to Paradise for both himself and his son. This alleged *hadith* is contrary to the *Quran* which insists that reward in the Hereafter is earned solely by faith and good deeds, and so it has been rejected.

---

9   Abdur Rahman i Doi, *Shari'ah: The Islamic Law*, 1989, p 55.
10   Fatima Mernissi points out that Abu Huraira, for example, may have had his own reasons for recounting some of the *hadith* he passed on.

The secondary sources: the major schools of law (*madhab*)[11]

The secondary sources of Islamic Law are the opinions and writings of the jurists which were formulated after the Prophet's death. There have been numerous learned Islamic scholars over the ages, many of whom gathered their own supporters, and founded their own schools of law. Some of these schools endured; others faded away in the course of time. At present there are five major schools of law in the Islamic world:

1. The Shia, which comprises about 10 per cent of Muslims, and resulted from the early political differences in the Muslim world over whether the leader of the Muslims should always be of the family of 'Ali, the Prophet's nephew and husband of his daughter Fatima. This school, which has various sub-sects is predominant in Iran, and has significant numbers of followers in Iraq, India and the Gulf states. There are considerable differences between the Shia and the four Sunni schools of Islam mentioned below.

2. The *Hanafis* who follow the school of thought established by Imam Abu Hanifa (80 – 150 AH) and his famous pupils Abu Yusuf and Muhammad. They emphasised the use of reason rather than blind reliance on the Traditions. This is the prevailing school in India and the Middle East.

3. The Malikis follow the school of Imam Malik (b 95 AH) who laid emphasis on the practices of the people of Medina, as being the most authentic examples of Islamic practice. The Moors who ruled Spain were followers of the Maliki school which, today, is found mostly in Africa.

4. The Hanbali school was founded by Imam Ahmad Ibn Hanbal (b AH 164) who had a high reputation as a traditionalist and theologian, and adopted a strict view of the law. The Hanbali school today is predominant in Saudi Arabia.

5. The Shafii school was founded by Imam As-Shafii, who was a pupil of Imam Malik, and is thought by some to be the most distinguished of all the jurists. He was famed for his moderation and balanced judgment, and although he respected the traditions, he examined them more critically than did Imam Malik. Followers of the Shafii school today, are found predominantly in South-East Asia.

---

11   Plural *madhabib*.

The Hanafi, Maliki, Hanbali and Shafii schools are the surviving schools of Sunni Islam, to which approximately 90 per cent of Muslims belong. They do not differ concerning basic religious doctrine, but in their interpretation of points of law. For example, according to the Shafiis, it is essential for every woman to be represented by a *wali* when she is married, but according to the Hanafis, a *wali* is only required when the bride is a minor virgin. Muslims are free to change from one *madhab* (school of law) as they choose, or not to follow any one exclusively at all, if they so wish.

The legal texts

Many of the learned jurists wrote books which have come to be regarded as authoritative legal texts in their particular school. Among these are Imam Malik's *Al Muwatta*, and Imam Shafii's *Al Umm*, An-Nawawi's *Minhaj et Talibin*, the *Hedaya*, a major text of the Hanifi school and the *Fatawa Alamgiri*, compiled by order of the Emperor Aurangzeb in India in the 11th century AH.

Processes for ascertaining the law

The learned jurists developed a number of methods for ascertaining the law to be used only where a clear answer is not to be found in the primary sources – the *Quran* or *Hadith*. These various processes can collectively be described as *ijtihad* – the use of intellectual exertion by a jurist to derive an answer to a question

Ijtihad (personal reasoning)

The authority for *ijtihad* is the well-known *hadith* about Mu'adh ibn Jabal who was sent by the Prophet as a judge to Yemen. In answer to questions from the Prophet, as to how he would judge, he answered that he would rely first on the *Quran*, and if the answer to a problem was not to be discovered there, then on the *Sunnah* of the Prophet. When the Prophet asked him what he would do if he found the answer neither in the *Quran* nor the *Sunnah,* he answered that he would exert himself to form his own judgment. The Prophet approved this answer.

There are many aspects of *ijtihad* about which the jurists disagree. Some major areas of disagreement are discussed below. *Ijtihad* is a continuous process which helps the *Shariah* to adapt to modern conditions and new developments, although it must not be exercised on the following matters:[12]

- the existence of God;
- the truth of the Prophets;
- the authenticity of the *Quran*.

A person who is qualified to exercise *ijtihad* is called a *mujtahid*. To be a *mujtahid*, according to the traditional definition, a person must possess the following qualifications:[13]

- He must be well versed in the study of the *Quran*.
- He must be well versed in the Traditions of the Prophet, and understand the distinction between reliable and doubtful *hadith*.
- He must understand the principles of *Ijma* (consensus of the Jurists).
- He must understand the conditions for *Qiyas*.
- He must be a good and practising Muslim.
- He must be just, reliable and trustworthy.

Some people say that the qualifications for a *mujtahid* have become so strict that it is now almost impossible to find anyone who qualifies. Others disagree and would give permission to exercise *ijtihad* to a much broader range of people. A major disagreement about *ijtihad* is whether it is still possible in modern times.

Some recognised methods of exercising *ijtihad* by the early scholars of Islam were:

Ijma' (consensus of opinion)

Ijma has been defined as "the consensus of opinion of the Companions of the Prophet (*Sahabah*) and the agreement reached on the decisions taken by the learned *Muftis* or the Jurists on various Islamic matters".[14]

Ijma should be based on consultation between jurists and the use of juristic reasoning, taking into account what guidance is given by the *Quran* and *hadith*. *Ijma* cannot cancel out a provision of the

---

12   Abdur Rahman i Doi, *Shariah: The Islamic Law*, 1989, p 78.
13   Ibid p 79.
14   Ibid p 64.

Quran or an accepted *hadith*. The only persons qualified to participate in *ijma* are those designated as *mujtahidun*.

Qiyas (analogical deduction)

Qiyas means a comparison between two things with the view of evaluating one in the light of the other. In *Shariah* it is the extension of a *Shariah* value from an original case to a new case, because the latter has the same effective cause as the former.[15] *Qiyas* may be resorted to discover the law on a certain matter only if no solution can be found in the *Quran* or *hadith*, or in cases covered by *ijma*. An example of a legal ruling developed through *Qiyas* is that on the punishment for drinking alcohol. No punishment for this is specified in the *Quran*. The Companions agreed that the punishment should be the same as that for false accusation on the basis that people who get drunk rave and make false accusations. Another example is that it is deduced that it is *haram* (forbidden) to use drugs on the same basis that alcohol is forbidden – that they alter the state of the mind.

Istihsan (equity)

Istihsan in Islamic law is not identical to Equity in the common law, though there are similarities, for example, they are both inspired by fairness and good conscience and both allow a departure from a rule of positive law when its enforcement will lead to unfair results.[16] The difference between equity and *istihsan*, according to Professor Kamali, is that the former relies on the concept of natural law as an eternally valid standard apart from the positive law, while the latter relies on, and is an integral part of the *Shariah* and recognises no law superior to it.[17] Muslim jurists have differed about the validity of *istihsan*, some rejecting it as a deviation from the principles of *Shariah*.

An example of the use of *istihsan* is in the acceptance of modern forensic evidence as proof in criminal cases. Under classical Islamic law, oral evidence was considered the best and most reliable type of proof and was given precedence over all other types of proof. However, with the development of modern accurate methods of proof through forensic science, *istihsan* allows a departure from the established rule in the interests of discovering the truth by the best method possible.

---

15   Mohd Hashim Kamali, *Principles of Islamic Jurisprudence*, 1989, p 248.
16   Ibid p 309.
17   Ibid p 310.

Maslahah Mursalah (public interest)

Maslahah mursalah is another expression which means virtually the same as *istihsan*. It can be applied in cases where there is no provision in the *Quran* which can be applied to the situation being considered. If it is evident that a particular course of action will result in public benefit it can be followed. This is one of the means by which the *Shariah* can be adapted to meet the need to accommodate social change. One example of the use of *maslahah mursalah* is the principle approved by the Malikis that when the public treasury runs out of funds, the Imam may levy additional taxes on the wealthy to meet the urgent needs of the government and so prevent injustice.

'Urf (custom)

The continuation of a custom of a particular place or community is allowable under Islamic law, and may in fact, be assimilated into the law, as were many of the customs of the Arabs. However, to be permissible a custom must not be contrary to Islamic belief and practices. A custom of toasting the bride and groom in champagne at a wedding, for instance, could not be accepted into Islamic law, since alcohol is forbidden.

An example of a custom which has been assimilated into Islamic law is the Malay custom of *harta sepancharian*, an *adat* practice whereby property obtained by a married couple during their marriage was divided between them in recognised proportions when they divorced. Another is *jual janji*, a security transaction which was developed by the Malays who wanted to borrow money to go on pilgrimage to Mecca without contravening Islamic law by borrowing money with interest from the banks.

Istishab (legal presumption)

Just as there are legal presumptions in our common law system, so there are legal presumptions in Islamic law. One of the most important is the presumption of continuity of a certain state of affairs until the contrary is proved. For example, as in the common law, there is a presumption of innocence until guilt is established. Generally a thing is presumed to be allowable until it is proved to be forbidden.

Disagreement among the jurists

The jurists agree that the primary sources of Islamic law are the *Quran* and *hadith* but there are numerous areas of disagreement amongst them. Some of the matters upon which they disagree are:

- Whether the term *"Shariah"* includes only the *Quran* and *hadith* or whether it also encompasses the works of all the jurists of all the schools of law.

- Whether the *Shariah* is a fixed and immutable body of law or whether it can continue to change with changing circumstances in society.

- Whether any change in circumstances can ever justify a departure from the text of the *Quran* or a clear direction from the Prophet set out in an authentic *hadith*.

- Who, if anyone, is entitled to recommend changes in the *Shariah* and how those changes should be effected.

Closing the gate of *Ijtihad*: The doctrine of *Taqlid*

According to some scholars, at some time between the 10th and 13th centuries AD, there was a consensus of the jurists who lived at that time, that all matters of religious and legal significance had been considered and ruled upon by the great jurists such as Abu Hanifa, Malik, Hanbal and As-Shafii, and there was no further need for *ijtihad*. Henceforth, it was only necessary to follow the doctrine of *taqlid*, which means strict adherence to established doctrine. People were no longer to develop new principles from studying the *Quran* and *hadith* and using their own independent reasoning. This is called "Closing the gates of *Ijtihad*".

Western writers such Gibb, Schacht and Coulson have attributed this supposed abandonment of *ijtihad* to the mood of uncertainty in the Muslim community brought about by the Tartar invasions and the sacking by the Mongols of Baghdad in 1258. This, they say, made the Muslim *ulema* more inclined towards conservatism and less willing to accept innovation in religious thought.[18] This view locked the *Shariah* into a fixed and inflexible mould, and prevented it adapting to modern times.

---

18   Chandra Muzaffar, "Reformation of Shari'a", in Norani Othman (ed), *Shari'a Law and the Modern Nation-State*, 1994, p 22.

However, it is clear that the idea persists in some quarters that there must be no variation from the interpretations of *Shariah* laid down before the 11th century, which is the only "correct" version of *Shariah*. There is still considerable resistance to new ideas. The leaders of some conservative Islamic movements appear to want to return their societies to an imagined past "Golden Age" of Islam which approximates their imaginings of what Islamic society was like in the days of the Prophet.

Re-opening the gate of *Ijtihad*

The idea of "closure of the gate of *ijtihad*" was never accepted by the Shia schools, nor was it accepted by many influential Sunni Muslim writers, such as Ibn Taymiyah in the 14th century, Mohammed Iqbal in Pakistan, and Al-Afghani and Muhammad Abduh in Egypt, who maintained that despite the decline in the fortunes of Islamic civilisation, which continued under Western colonialism, *ijtihad* was still possible and still continued to be exercised.[19] They argue that the four great Imams never claimed infallibility or finality for their interpretations of the *Shariah*, and that it is a necessity and a duty for qualified Muslims to exercise *ijtihad* in the present time. Contemporary Muslim writers such as Abdullahi An Na'im also accept this view.

Patrick Bannerman says that there are four main trends in modern Islamic thought.[20] These are the:

- orthodox conservatives who adhere strictly to the doctrine of taqlid;
- quasi-orthodox conservatives, who hold views similar to the above but are forced to deal pragmatically with Western influences in their countries;
- modernising reformers, who seek to interpret the fundamentals of Islam in the light of existing and constantly changing circumstances;
- conservative reformers, who hold that taqlid is wrong but set limits to the exercise of *ijtihad*.

---

19   Shaista P Ali-Karamali and Fiona Dunne, "The Ijtihad Controversy", 1995 *Arab Law Quarterly*, p 249.

20   *Islam in Perspective*, 1988, p 11-12.

The Westernisation of law in Muslim countries

During the period of Western expansion between the 16th and 20th centuries, most Muslim countries came at some time under the commercial and political domination of one of the major European colonising powers. The British dominated India and Malaya and at various time exercised influence in the Middle East; the Dutch controlled the East Indies (Indonesia), and the French ruled North Africa, and also exercised a sphere of influence over countries in the Middle East after the fall of the Ottoman Empire.

In these countries the *Shariah* was replaced with European type legal systems, except for areas of law such as family law and inheritance which were of little significance to the colonial powers. Even in countries which were not directly colonised by European powers, such as the Ottoman Empire, and its successor state, Turkey, there was a tendency to "modernise" by adopting Western legal systems. By the middle of the 20th century most Muslim countries had a "mixed" legal system, with Turkey at one extreme, abandoning the *Shariah* entirely and only Saudi Arabia, at the other extreme, retaining a complete and traditional *Shariah* legal system.

Towards a modernisation of *Shariah*

As various Muslim countries attempted to modernise and "westernise" their legal systems, it was clear that some of the traditional interpretations caused hardship and injustice – for example, the Hanafi rule prevalent in the Ottoman Empire and India, that a woman could not obtain a divorce without her husband's consent – and a solution in *Shariah* had to be found to alleviate this kind of injustice – since in Family Law the *Shariah* tradition remained strong. The Islamic Modernists proposed three complementary methods of alleviating hardship through *Takhayyur* and *Talfiq*, re-interpreting the *Shariah* texts and the doctrine of *Siyasa Shar'iyya*.[21]

The principles of *Takhayyur* and *Talfiq*

Takhayyur means making a choice from the variety of legal opinions offered by the eminent jurists of the past. It means that if a satisfactory

---

21   See Butti Sultan Butti Ali Al-Muhairi, "Islamisation and Modernisation Within the UAE Penal Law: Shari'a in the Modern Era", 1995 *Arab Law Quarterly*, pp 34-49.

solution to a problem cannot be found within the opinions of the school predominant in a certain area, a solution may be adopted from the opinion of another school. Similar to this is the doctrine of *Talfiq* which means combining part of the juristic opinion of one school with part of the opinion of another school or jurist in such a way as to establish a new legal rule.[22]

Reinterpreting the *Shariah* texts

Islamic modernists further demand the right to be free from the doctrine of *taqlid*, and to be allowed to exercise *ijtihad* to formulate new legal rules from a new interpretation of the *Quran* and *Sunnah*. For example, the *Quranic* verses on polygamy have traditionally been interpreted to give a Muslim man the right to have up to four wives at the same time. Some modernists contend that the *Quran* in fact, effectively prohibits polygamy through the requirement to be just and fair to each of them, and if this is not possible, then marry only one.[23] This is followed by a later verse which says: "You will never be able to be fair and just between women even if it is your ardent desire".[24] Since fairness and justice are impossible, a man must therefore restrict himself to one wife.

The doctrine of *Siyasa Shar'iyya*

The traditional *Shariah* is uncodified. The law is sought through interpretation of the *Quran* and *hadith* and the opinions of the jurists and is not made by governments through legislation. However, the right of a Muslim ruler to make administrative regulations in the public interest where the *Shariah* is silent is acknowledged. The modernists argued that it is in the public interest that governments should promulgate comprehensive codes of law so that modern interpretations of law could be put into effect clearly and comprehensively. Such a method is more certain and convenient than searching through juristic treatises for the appropriate opinion in each case.

According to the conservatives, this method conflicts with established *Shariah* principles and has contributed to the secularisation of *Shariah*.[25] The view of those opposing the modernising

---

22   Ibid pp 39-40.
23   *Quran*, 4:3.
24   *Quran* 4:129.
25   Butti Sultan, Butti Ali Al-Muhairi, "Islamisation and Modernisation Within the UAE Penal Law: Shari'a in the Modern Era", 1995 *Arab Law Quarterly*, p 41.

of *Shariah* is put by Dr 'Abdur Rahman i Doi. He says that the reforms are in truth a deviation from the divine law contained in the *Quran* and the *Sunnah*.[26] While the *Shariah* was revealed for all times and all situations and is eternally valid, these reformed laws are only man-made laws which can be changed as men consider it necessary.

However, such methods have been widely adopted in Islamisation programs in most Muslim countries except Saudi Arabia. For example, all Middle East Arab countries, except Saudi Arabia, now have written constitutions which give the power of law making to the state.[27]

Those advocating a reformation of *Shariah*, such as the modern Sudanese scholar, Abdullahi Ahmed An-Na'im, and the American feminist scholar, Amina Wudud-Muhsin,[28] say that it is a false and unhistorical view to assume that the compilations of the great jurists of the past are a fixed and categorical body of law which must be accepted as divine; the decisions of the jurists were the product of human reasoning – and the reasoning of men, in a patriarchal era, and therefore neglect the views and needs of women – and can and must be changed with changing circumstances.

Some modern examples of the Islamisation of laws

1. Pakistan

From the time of its foundation in 1947 as an independent state, there was a tension in Pakistan between the conservative religious parties, the most famous of which is the *Jamaat i-Islami* founded by Maulana Abul ala Maududi, and the Western oriented liberal elite, neither of which were strong enough to impose their will on the country as a whole. The "Islamisation" of Pakistani law was a product, not of the democratic process, but of the military dictatorship of General Zia ul-Haq following a coup in 1977.

The type of Islamisation introduced by General Zia, and continued to some extent under Prime Minister Nawaz Sharif, is of the conservative variety, which looks more to imposing the letter of the law of the traditional *Shariah*, with little consideration of whether or

---

26   p 465.
27   Ibid p 44.
28   See Abdullahi An-Naim, "Towards an Islamic Reformation", and Amina Wudud-Muhsin, "The Qur'an, Shari'a and the Citizenship Rights of Muslim Women in the Umma", in Norani Othman (ed), *Shari'a Law and the Modern Nation-State*, 1994.

not it is suitable to modern times or just to the people who are affected by it.

Islamic criminal law was imposed in the form of the *Hudood* Ordinances in the late 1970s. The *Offence of Zina (Enforcement of Hudood) Ordinance* of 1979, to take a typical example, imposed the penalty of stoning to death (*rajm*) upon a married person who was found guilty of unlawful sexual intercourse (*zina*). The definition of *zina* did not distinguish between adultery and rape. In accordance with the rules of Islamic evidence, the required proof of *zina* liable to *hadd* is the evidence of four upright Muslim men who had all been present at the same time and had witnessed the act of intercourse with their own eyes. Since few rapists compel their victims to have sexual intercourse in the presence of four upright Muslim men, the crime of *zina* is virtually impossible to prove.

However, the results were, in Pakistan, that a woman complaining of rape was liable to find herself on trial for *zina*, since she could not produce the four upright Muslim males as witnesses to substantiate her claim, but at the same time, she had admitted to sexual intercourse outside marriage by the fact of making her complaint. If she said nothing but unfortunately became pregnant as a result of the rape, this was taken as confession also, and the unfortunate victim would be punished for *zina*. This matter came to a head in the infamous *Safia Bibi* case in 1985, but the victim's conviction was here overturned by the Federal Shariat Court, as were many others.

The imposition of Islamic law in this form had harsh effects upon women and the poor, the more so as it was accompanied by the usual cosmetic changes which reactionary regimes introduce so as to make it seem that they are acting Islamically, strict dress codes for women and restrictions on their participation in public life. However, less attention was paid to the spirit of Islamic law, and no substantial changes were made, for example in the economic system, which might have had the effect of alleviating poverty.

2.   Malaysia

Although under the Malaysian Constitution Islam is the religion of the state, Malaysia is a multi-cultural country where the Malays only slightly outnumber the non-Muslims and non-Malays, and this is a factor which makes it unlikely that the Malaysian Government will introduce drastic Islamisation programs in the foreseeable future.

Hussin Mutalib[29] attributes the rise of Islam as a factor to be recognised in Malaysia to four circumstances:

- The 1969 racial riots which led to more emphasis on Malay identity and eventually to the growth of a more educated Malay elite with a greater Islamic orientation.

- The election of Dr Mahathir Mohamed as Prime Minister in 1981, after which the government introduced many Islamic related programs and policy directives.

- The growth of *dakwah* groups such as ABIM which disseminated Islamic knowledge widely through Malay society.

- The election of the conservative PAS party to power in the State of Kelantan with a stated aim of establishing an Islamic state in Malaysia. It has been argued that pressure from PAS for the government to be more Islamic has influenced Dr Mahathir's Government to move further towards Islamisation in an effort to counter PAS's criticism that the government is not Islamic enough.

Malaysia already has a dual legal system in which family law, inheritance and minor infringements of religious law remain in the province of the *Shariah* courts which exercise jurisdiction over Muslims, while all other matters are dealt with by the secular civil courts. This seems likely to remain the case for the foreseeable future.

In all States Islamic Family Law enactments have been passed, codifying the *Shariah* in mainly Shafii terms. Attempts have been made or are being planned to enact modern Islamic evidence statutes and to upgrade and revitalise the *Shariah* court system which had been considerably downgraded during the time of the British.

Other Islamisation measures which have been taken since 1980 include the establishment of an Islamic bank and some Islamic financial institutions, an upgrade in the status of *Shariah* courts and judges to place them on the same level as their civil law counterparts, a requirement that Muslims in government service demonstrate a reasonable knowledge of Islam, and increased taxes on alcohol and cigarettes as a way of implementing the Islamic value system. A recent example of the influence of Islamic values in Malaysia is the decision of the Cabinet to drop Carlsberg brewery sponsorship of the

---

29   "Islamisation in Malaysia: Between Ideals and Realities", in Hussin Mutalib and Taj ul-Islam Hashmi, *Islam, Muslims and the Modern State*, 1994.

1998 Commonwealth Games in Kuala Lumpur on the basis that alcohol is forbidden by Islam.

With the example of federal initiatives, the States, which have jurisdiction over religious matters, began to follow suit, introducing their own Islamisation programs. The enforcement of laws prohibiting Muslims from drinking alcohol gambling and committing *khalwat* (close proximity of a sexual nature) were stepped up, new Islamic centres built and "un-Islamic" entertainments such as dancing at nightclubs prohibited in some places, notably Kelantan.

Unfortunately, some of these "Islamisation" measures have merely legitimated conservative patriarchal forms of control over women, and encouraged unquestioning conformity to traditional views. However, some modernist thinkers such as "Sisters in Islam" continue to question and re-assess the application of Islamic measures in Malaysian society.

النساء ❂

4

WOMEN IN ISLAMIC LAW

Some general observations about the status of women in world religions

Many writers have documented the changes in the status of women in the world's major religions. In Hinduism,[1] Buddhism[2] and in Christianity,[3] at the foundation stage of the religion it appeared that women enjoyed equal, or almost equal rights with men. This was because of egalitarian statements in the religious texts, and/or because of liberating statements and behaviour by the founder of the religion.

Alvin Schmidt points out, for example, that Jesus was a feminist in the best sense of the word.[4] He broke the ancient Jewish taboos with regard to women, speaking to a woman of Samaria, teaching Mary and Martha religion, forgiving the sins of a prostitute and healing a woman with menstrual problems. All of these actions were quite shocking within the context of his time and culture. Yet, within little more than a hundred years of his passing, the Christian church had taken up the patriarchal practices of the Jews, Greeks and Romans, and women were once again excluded from participation in

---

1   KS Susan Oorjitham, "A Hindu Perspective" in Noraini Othman and Cecilia Ng (eds), *Gender, Culture and Religion,* 1995, p 39.

2   Chatsumarn Kabilsingh, "Women in Buddhism" in ibid p 55.

3   AJ Schmidt, *Veiled and Silenced*, 1989; Dulcie Abraham, "A Malaysian Christian Perspective" in Norani Othman and Cecilia Ng (eds), *Gender, Culture and Religion,* 1995, p 17.

4   Ibid p 175.

religious life. A similar decline in women's status also took place within Buddhism and Hinduism.

Schmidt says that modern people fail to appreciate the revolutionary nature of Jesus' contacts with women as revolutionary in the context of the time, because today Western culture has freed women from patriarchal oppression. However, for centuries Jesus' teachings with regard to women were ignored by the church which defined women as intellectually, biologically, socially and spiritually inferior.[5] The church fathers relied on scriptural verses, such as 1 Corinthians 14:34[6] which appeared to require the subordination of women, and forgot about those which were favourable to women, because they interpreted scripture in the context of the patriarchal societies they lived in. Asghar Ali Engineer summarises the problem:

> [S]ocial attitudes are so pervasive that even progressive scriptural norms become affected and thus are interpreted in a way that reflects prevailing mental attitudes. Thus, male-dominated societies often harnessed even just and egalitarian norms laid down for women in divine scriptures to perpetuate their hold.[7]

Thus the church fathers and other men spoke out against women's equality. St Thomas Aquinas said "Women are defective and misbegotten". Martin Luther said "a man is nobler than a woman". Theologians also insisted that it was a woman's duty to be subordinate to their husbands.[8] Until quite recently the common law held, following St Paul, that upon marriage a husband and wife became as one. Naturally the husband was the one. This doctrine was used to deny married women a separate legal entity and among other things, to refuse them the right to own their own property, control their own money, or sue their husband in tort. These principles led to manifest injustices, which have been extensively documented elsewhere.[9]

Unfortunately, the same process can be traced in Islam. In the beginning Islam was a liberating religion which gave women unprecedented rights, many of which were opposed by the men of the time, but in due course these rights were whittled away in practice, so

---

5   Ibid p 165.
6   "The women should keep silent in churches. For they are not permitted to speak, but should be subordinate, even as the law allows".
7   Asghar Ali Engineer, *The Rights of Women in Islam*, 1992, p 1.
8   Schmidt gives many examples of such sexist statements, *Veiled and Silenced*, 1989; Dulcie Abraham, "A Malaysian Christian Perspective" in Norani Othman and Cecilia Ng, (eds), *Gender, Culture and Religion*, 1995, pp 70-76.
9   See, for example, Jocelynn A Scutt, *Women and the Law*, 1990.

that today, women in Muslim countries are among the most oppressed in the world.

The position of women in the *Quran*

Amina Wudud-Muhsin has made a careful study of the position of women in the *Quran*.[10] She notes that in the *Quran*ic story of creation, the human species was created from a single *nafs* (soul) and in the fall from the Garden, Adam and Eve were equally guilty and were equally forgiven by God. The *Quran* does not say that Eve was made from Adam's rib and thus came second and inferior in creation.[11]

There are many verses in the *Quran* which attest to the equality of men and women. Men and women are spoken of in the same terms with regard to spiritual matters and their religious duties:[12]

> For Muslim men and women –
> For believing men and women,
> For devout men and women,
> For true men and women,
> For men and women who are patient and constant,
> For men and women who humble themselves,
> For men and women who give in charity,
> For men and women who fast (and deny themselves),
> For men and women who guard their chastity, and
> For men and women who engage much in Allah's praise, –
> For them has Allah prepared forgiveness and a great reward.

The *Quran* endorses the right of women to own property, and to deal with it and their own earnings as they wish – "to men is allotted what they earn and to women what they earn".[13] Women are not normally obliged to use their own earnings or property to support themselves or their children since "men are the protectors and maintainers of women",[14] and they are entitled to *mahr* on marriage.[15] *Mahr* is a gift of money or property given by the bridegroom to the bride. It remains her own property and cannot be taken away from her by the husband or by her own family. Female infanticide was forbidden and polygamy limited to four wives, which was a considerable reform in a society where tribal chiefs prided themselves on having ten wives or more at

---

10 *The Qur'an and Woman*, 1992.
11 Asghar Ali Engineer, *The Rights of Women in Islam*, 1992, p 43.
12 *Quran*, 33:35.
13 Ibid 4:32.
14 Ibid 4:34.
15 4:4.

a time. For the first time, women were given a share in inheritance, even though that share was generally half that of a man.[16] They also had the right to divorce to escape from an unhappy marriage.[17]

If we compare the legal position of women according to the *Quran* with that of women in Western Europe at the same time that is in the 7th century and indeed, right up to the middle of the 19th century, we can see that in principle Muslim women were a lot better off. Legally, they were separate individuals, not mere appendages of their husbands – Muslim women do not usually even change their names on marriage – and they were entitled to work, keep their own earnings, inherit property, and deal with it as they wished. In England, married women did not gain the right to own their own property or to keep their own earnings until the passing of the *Married Women's Property Act* 1870. Divorce was not generally available until the late 19th century.

The position of women in the *hadith*

There are many indications from the *hadith* literature, that the position of women in the early Islamic society was not secluded and sub-servient. There are many instances of women coming to the Prophet for advice, both in the mosque and outside it. There were women who worked for a living, and women who fought in battle alongside their menfolk. The Prophet's wife, Ayesha, was a renowned recounter of *hadith* and for many years after the Prophet's death she taught both men and women and gave rulings on religious questions.[18] Later she led her troops in battle in the battle of the Camel. Another of his wives, Umm Salama, was often consulted by the Companions on religious issues.

The Prophet himself set a good example in his treatment of women. He exhorted his followers to treat women kindly. He never struck a woman or a slave and even helped his wives with the household chores. He encouraged the Muslims to learn from Ayesha.

In the early days of Islam, there were many examples of women who played a prominent role in society. There are examples of women

---

16   The justification for this difference is that men have the obligation to support family members, while women are not obliged to support any one else financially and can rely on male relatives for their own support.

17   Islamic law allows women the right to divorce by *khula'* – see Chapter 5.

18   Kaukab Siddique, *The Struggle of Muslim Women*, 1987, pp 47-50.

who worked to earn their living, such as Asma, the daughter of Abu Bakr, women who fought alongside their menfolk in battle, and women who participated in business and government office, such as Shifa bint Abdullah who was appointed by Caliph Omar as the inspector of markets at Medina. In the early Abbasid period, many women rose to positions of prominence and influence in public life. The sister of Caliph Harun al-Rashid, for instance, was noted for her genius and culture, and often attended the Caliph's meetings where her opinions were listened to and accepted.[19]

The position of women in Islam according to the traditional view

In the centuries following the Prophet's death, scholars studied, pondered over and interpreted the basic sources of Islam, the *Quran* and *hadith*, and sought to formulate a *Shariah* law which was complete in every respect. Unfortunately, almost all of these scholars were men. Naturally, they approached their task from a male perspective, and frequently overlooked aspects of the revelation and the Prophet's sayings and deeds which were favourable to women.

Moreover, as the Islamic empire expanded throughout the Middle East and around the shores of the Mediterranean, the Muslims came into contact with older, more sophisticated civilisations, such as that of the Persians and Byzantines, and they were influenced by their customs, especially that of the veiling and seclusion of women. Gradually Muslim women found their rights whittled away, and the learned jurists interpreted the *Quran* in such a way as to place women completely under the domination of their male relatives. By the end of the 10th century, women were generally secluded and excluded from participation in society.[20]

Just as Christian theologians had seized upon 1 Corinthians 14:34 and other verses like Ephesians 5:22-24[21] and Peter 3:1[22] to keep women in their place, so the Muslim jurists took delight in verse 34 of Sura an-Nisaa which says:

---

19 Abdullah Muhammad Zin, *The 'Abbasid Caliphate*, 1993, p 22.
20 Ibid.
21 "Wives be subject to your husbands as to the Lord. For the husband is the head of the wife as Christ is the head of the church... As the church is subject to Christ, so let wives be subject in everything to their husbands".
22 "Likewise you wives, be submissive to your husbands".

> Men are *qawwamuna* over women, on the basis that Allah has preferred some of them over others and on the basis of what they spend of their property. So good women are *qanitat* guarding in secret that which Allah has guarded. And as for those from whom you fear *nusyuz,* admonish them, banish them to beds apart and chastise them. Then, if they obey you, seek not a way against them.

This verse was interpreted by the conservatives to mean that:

   (i)   men have authority over women, and

  (ii)   all men are superior to women,

 (iii)   women must obey men,

 (iv)   men can beat their wives.

The meaning of the verse turns on the translation of the Arabic words *qawwamuna, qanitat* and *nusyuz. Qawwamuna* is variously translated as "authority" or "have responsibility". Modernist thinkers interpret it to mean that men have a responsibility for the protection and maintenance of women to relieve them of the burden of supporting themselves while they are pregnant or caring for small children (which in those days, would have been most of the time). To balance this responsibility, men have some advantages, for example they get a double share of inheritance, since they must use their money to support women, while women can keep their share for themselves.

    Qanitat is translated as "obedient". Modernists say this particular word means "obedient to God" not to the husband.[23] Likewise the word *nusyuz* (usually translated as "disobedient) is also used of the relationship of a man towards his wife and is best translated as "disruption of marital harmony", which may be the fault of either, or both parties to a marriage. The word *daraba*, often translated as "beat" or even "scourge" should be translated as "a single strike", and in a time when cruelty and violence against women was rampant, was meant to be a last resort. Moreover, the jurists agreed that such a strike should be merely symbolic, as with a toothbrush or folded handkerchief.[24]

    In spite of their relatively liberal views on the question of beating, most of the views of the jurists who formulated the traditional *Shariah* were not so favourable to women. They all agreed that the *Quran* gave women equality, but relying on the *Quran*'s stress on modesty and prohibition of sexual relationships outside of marriage,

---

23   Sisters in Islam, *Are Muslim Men Allowed to Beat their Wives?*, 1991, p 5.

24   Ibid p 8.

they proceeded to divide the world into two separate spheres: woman was "Queen of the Home" in complete charge of domestic life within the four walls of the home; men's sphere was everything outside it. This kind of sexual apartheid thinking is still prevalent today among many Muslims, educated and uneducated.

Thus many restrictions came to be placed on women. Today, nowhere is there a more marked divergence between traditional Muslim thought and more liberal modern thought than with regard to the question of women's rights and behaviour. Some controversial areas relating to Muslim women are:

Dress

The *Quran* requires modesty in dress for both men and women, and makes reference to the fact that women should "draw their veils (clothes) over their bosoms".[25] A *hadith* recounts that the Prophet told Asma that once a woman reaches puberty, she should cover all of her body except for her hands and face. This was modest dress in the context of that place and time.

Later, religious teachers began to insist that women should also veil their faces and wear gloves in case men should be tempted to sin by the sight of a pretty face or shapely hand. Ultimately, women in some countries, such as the northern regions of the Indian sub-continent, were obliged to cover their whole bodies in a shapeless tent called the *burkha* which even covered the eyes with a rectangle of material which was supposed to be transparent enough for women to see through without allowing men to be led into sin by the beauty of their eyes.

Today, there is a variety of opinion about what women should wear.[26] The conservative view is that women should still cover themselves at least as completely as the Prophet recommended to Asma, and some demand that women should in addition cover their faces with veils when outside the house. To many Muslims, a woman's religious commitment is still judged by the amount of material she is wearing. On the contrary, there is rarely any objection voiced to men dressing in Western dress where ever they may be.

---

25   24:30-31.
26   See "To Veil or not to Veil: Malaysian Muslims Debate How Women Should Dress", *Asiaweek*, 17.8.1994, p 32.

In a letter to the *New Straits Times* in Malaysia,[27] Sisters in Islam, a Muslim women's group, wrote:

> The question of dress for women is always paramount in any Islamisation programme both here and abroad. in fact, it is an obsession for some that dressing in a certain way is reflective of one's faith. One culmination of such obsession is a proliferation of attempts to enforce faith through authoritarian means. . .

> Women have been told that a particular mode of dress would protect them from evil. Yet social realities have shown that dress cannot shield women from sexual violence.

> In fact, for the protection of women's dignity, the *Quran* (in Surah Al-Nur 24:30-31) first orders men, if they be believers, to lower their gaze and guard their own modesty. Some men have disregarded this responsibility, but have forced women to accept forms of veiling and seclusion. Women have been made responsible for limiting men's lustfulness and for any loss of their self-control.

In Malaysia, as recently as August 1996, the leader of the PAS party which governs the State of Kelantan, Nik Aziz, urged Muslim women to abandon wearing lipstick lest it attract men's attention to them, a recommendation which was treated with derision by most of the Muslim women interviewed on the issue by the *New Straits Times* newspaper.[28]

Although almost all religious authorities say that women should cover their hair, this practice has not been universally followed, especially in rural areas. In fact as country women frequently work in the fields, it is not practical for them to wear a voluminous covering. The wearing of the veil and complete covering has always tended to be a prerogative of the wealthier classes which can afford to keep its womenfolk in enforced idleness.[29]

With the Islamic revival in recent years, more women are wearing *hejab* voluntarily, for religious reasons, and because it is also a statement of their Islamic identity, and a message to the men that they are not interested in sexual advances. Women in Saudi Arabia, Iran, Sudan and the Malaysian State of Kelantan are forced to wear their country's version of "Islamic dress" whether they like it or not. In Iran, it is compulsory for girls to wear a scarf from the age of six.[30]

---

27   14 November 1991.
28   "Much ado about a dab of colour", 16.8.1996, "Life and Times" p 1.
29   David G Mandelbaum, *Women's Seclusion and Men's Honour*, 1988, p 35.
30   Golnar Mehran, "The Education of a New Muslim Woman in Postrevolutionary Iran", *Muslim Education Quarterly*, Vol 8 No 3, 1991, p 7.

Women who are guilty of "bad hejab" in the past have risked been beaten by the authorities, but there are some indications that a more liberal view is being taken in Iran today. In Kelantan, women risk only being fined for violation of the dress laws.

On the other hand, in countries like Malaysia (excluding Kelantan), Indonesia and Egypt, there is a great deal of variety in the dress of Muslim women. Malaysian courts have refused to uphold a woman's right to wear the veil if she is employed in the government service.[31] On a recent television program, an Indonesian woman spoke out against the "Arabisation" of Muslim culture in Indonesia, represented by religious people urging women to adopt the veil.

Segregation

As a means of preventing opportunities for sexual misconduct, religious teachers insisted that women should be kept completely away from men who were not their *mehrem*, that is members of their immediate family, although this was not the case in the day of the Prophet since the *hadith* recount many instances of women coming by themselves to seek advice from the Prophet. Women were kept at home, and not allowed to venture out unless covered from head to foot and accompanied by a husband or other male escort from the family. The rationale is that this prevents women being harassed by men, and of course it also prevents them making the acquaintance of male outsiders. This ensures that unmarried daughters do not have the opportunity of meeting and marrying someone not approved by the family and it keeps all women under the control of their male relatives.

This is still the custom in Saudi Arabia and among Muslim communities in India and Pakistan. It prevents women participating fully in education,[32] the workforce, business, social life and public life. Women are also prohibited from driving cars in Saudi Arabia, but this has nothing to do with Islamic law.

Many Muslims still insist that "Islam requires the complete separation of men and women", but there does not seem to be any basis in the *Quran* or *hadith* for this long and firmly held dogma. Modern thinkers say there is no reason that women and men cannot

---

31   See *Halimatussaadiah v Public Services Commission Malaysia* [1992] 1 MLJ 513.
32   Other than single-sex education.

meet together for work or other "proper" purposes, though most add "as long as the women are properly (ie 'Islamically') dressed".

Education

The Prophet Muhammad said that every Muslim should seek knowledge even in China (which of course, in those days, was well beyond the bounds of the Muslim world). In the early days of Islam many women were renowned for their learning and scholarship. Even renowned male jurists were known to have been pupils of such women as Rabi'ah bint Mu'awwad, A'isha bint Sa'd Ibn Abi Waqqas, Sayyida Nafisa and Fatimah bint Qais.[33] There is no question, even today, that women and girls are entitled to an education. Conservatives have tried to limit this to only a basic religious education, and in fact, until recently in many Muslim countries, this was the only education available to the masses whether male or female.

Some Muslim countries have established schools and colleges especially for girls. In Saudi Arabia, one quarter of the students at Riyadh university are women, who are taught by female academic staff or by closed circuit television.[34] It was proposed to set up a Woman's University in Pakistan, an idea which was opposed by women's groups who felt that it would confine Pakistani women to a segregated domestic science based education. However, most Muslim countries are desperately poor, with enormous illiteracy rates among both men and women,[35] and the prospects of setting up separate educational facilities for women must be close to zero. Of course when there is only enough money to provide schools for one sex, and it is decided to provide single sex educational facilities, you can be sure it is the girls who miss out.

In higher education, the renowned Islamic university of Al-Azhar in Egypt opened its doors to women students in 1961, establishing an exclusive faculty of them. At the International Islamic University in Malaysia, provision is made for both men and women to learn side by side. Dress rules are strict, especially for women, and in the library some tables are marked exclusively for men and some

---

33 'Abdur Rahman i Doi, *Women in Shari'ah*, 1990, pp 142-144.
34 Khawla Fadhil Mohammed Al-Zubaidy, "The experience of Muslim women: considerations of education and employment opportunities", *Muslim Education Quarterly*, Vol 8 No 3, 1991, p 48 at 50.
35 For example, the illiteracy rate among women in Afghanistan is 98 per cent.

exclusively for women. In classes, the men normally sit on one side of the classroom and women on the other, and the women who make up at least 50 per cent of the student body in faculties such as Law, are encouraged to participate on the same basis as the men, and do equally well in their studies. Both sexes participate voluntarily in student activities such as mooting and in (segregated) sport, although the sight of young women rowing or engaging in martial arts in full *hejab* and tracksuits in the hot, humid Malaysian climate, is a startling one to the Western observer.

Employment

Even conservative Muslims grudgingly agree that a woman has the right to work outside the home with her husband's consent. But the traditionalists insist that they must not work in any occupation which brings them into contact with men – a woman must work in a factory or office which does not employ men, or if in business, she must not deal with male customers or suppliers. The conservative view is expressed by 'Abdur Rahman i Doi in his book *Women in Shari'ah*. He says:

> Islam does not require women to participate in trade, the vocations or professions unless it is very necessary. . . A Muslim woman can work in a factory if it is run by women. . . Trading by a woman is not forbidden in the Shari'ah. . . A woman's trade or business must not take her to the marketplace where she will have to mingle with her male counterparts. . . But if women engage in trading in their own house where the buyers are small boys and girls from the neighbourhood there is absolutely no harm. . . Women can learn and establish small scale cottage industries in their homes or may engage in dress designing or sewing. . . A Muslim woman can teach small children, whether male or female, in primary schools where the other teachers happen to be women. In the case of secondary schools and colleges and universities, they should be engaged to teach in girls' institutions only . . . Muslim ladies should be encouraged to join the medical profession and take up nursing as their career, but they should seek employment in female wards and hospitals.[36]

Professor 'Abdur Rahman i Doi places so many restrictions on the employment that a Muslim woman may legitimately undertake, that very few women would be able to work at all. Few would disagree that Muslim women need to be trained in the medical profession, since Muslim women have suffered diseases in silence and even died

---

36   'Abdur Rahman i Doi, *Women in Shari'ah,* 1990, pp 147-149.

for being unable to consult a female doctor, but he does not face the issue of how Muslim women are going to get such training if they are never to be allowed to come into contact with an unrelated man.

For millions of poor women throughout Asia and Africa, the issue is academic. They must work in the fields and gather firewood and fetch water and work at whatever jobs they can find to keep themselves and their families alive. Yet, the idea that it is shameful for women to work, or to speak to men or even to be seen by unrelated men helps keep their needs unrecognised and their work unvalued.

The current trend in Muslim countries, as in the West, is for women to become more involved in the workforce, through economic necessity or otherwise. Some governments (for example in Malaysia) encourage the entry of women into the workforce, regarding this as essential for national development, and have passed laws giving women entitlement to maternity leave, vocational training and other benefits. For some Muslim women, participation in the workforce is actually easier than for their sisters in the West, since traditional extended families, and/or the availability of cheap domestic help removes much of the burden of trying to do two jobs at once and the feelings of guilt at leaving children to go out to work.

Women in the legal system

There are differences of opinion concerning the extent to which women may legitimately participate in the legal system, other than as litigants. There are three views – that women are precluded from being judges, that they may be judges except in *hudud* cases (on account of their tender nature), and thirdly, that there are no restrictions on the appointment of women to judicial office.

Professor 'Abdur Rahman i Doi, representing the conservative view, would allow women to do welfare work in the juvenile courts. In Iran, according to the Shia opinion, women can become lawyers, but not judges, and immediately after the Iranian revolution in 1979 all women judges were dismissed. However; since 1993 women have been able to be appointed as jurisconsults to advise judges in the courts. In Malaysia, women are lawyers and judges in the secular courts but not yet judges in the *Syariah* courts, although no one has forbidden it; in Indonesia women do sit as judges in the *Syariah* courts.

There is much controversy over the evidence of women as witnesses. One *ayat* only in the *Quran*[37] refers to the need to have two male witnesses or one man and two women if two men are not available. This verse refers to commercial transactions involving future obligations, a field in which women were not experienced in the days of the Prophet. On the basis of this one verse, the traditional jurists have made it a general rule that the evidence of two women is required where the evidence of one man would otherwise be satisfactory. There are exceptions to this rule in relation to situations where men would not traditionally be expected to have knowledge, such as childbirth, and in some circumstances the evidence of one woman alone can be accepted.

Participation in religious life

Although the Prophet told his followers not to forbid women going to mosques, in Saudi Arabia women are not allowed to attend mosques and in many other countries they are strongly discouraged. The reason advanced for this is that it is not compulsory for women to attend congregational prayer on Fridays, or at any other time, while it is compulsory for men. What appears to be a concession for women, recognising their need to care for children, and their more limited mobility, has been turned almost into a prohibition in countries such as Pakistan and Turkey, although not in South-East Asia.

If women do attend the mosque, traditionally they pray separately from the men. In most mosques, they are separated by being secluded in a separate room, or if allowed into the prayer hall itself, they will be divided from the men by a curtain, which is meant to protect the women's modesty, but equally restricts them from invading men's space both during prayers and on other occasions.

Sometimes this has ludicrous results. At a Sydney mosque which is largely attended by Muslims from Pakistan and India, a "Sunday school" prize giving was arranged. The small children from the *madrasah* (religious school) attached to the mosque were to give recitals from the *Quran* and answer religious questions and were to be given prizes for their efforts. Their proud parents were invited along to applaud. The mothers were told to take their place in the back of the mosque behind a thick brown curtain which excluded all sight of

---

37   *Quran*, 2:282.

the activities, and also muffled the sound so that the women could neither see nor hear their little ones perform. Naturally the women became bored and began to talk among themselves. The men blamed them for their inattention. However, from the women's point of view there was very little point in being there, since they could neither see nor hear the activities for which they were invited.

On the other hand, there are some Islamic associations where the participation of women is invited, and women are encouraged to serve on the Committee of the Islamic Society along with men.

Women and leadership

Those who oppose women occupying any positions of leadership in society are fond of quoting a *hadith* to the effect that: "a nation can never prosper which has assigned its leadership to a woman". This *hadith* was quoted extensively by those opposed to Benazir Bhutto's leadership in Pakistan. Some scholars reject this *hadith* on the basis that it is contrary to the *Quran*, which speaks approvingly of a woman as leader of a nation, in the person of Bilqis, Queen of Sheba. Also, Fatima Mernissi says that the *hadith* is unreliable because of the circumstances in which it was recalled by Abu Bakra, a companion of the Prophet.[38] Abu Bakra stated that he remembered this *hadith* which he said was recounted by the Prophet some 25 years before, after the Battle of the Camel, at which the forces of the Prophet's widow, Ayesha were defeated by Ali. At the time, Abu Bakra's personal position was tenuous since he had to justify his non-participation in the battle. It was providential for Abu Bakra to remember such a *hadith* at the time. Fatima Mernissi says:[39]

> let us take a brief look at the attitude of the *fuqaha* (Muslim scholars) of the first centuries towards that misogynistic Hadith that is presented to us today as sacred, unassailable truth. even though it was collected as *sahih* (authentic) by al-Bukhari and others, that Hadith was hotly contested and debated by many. The *fuqaha* did not agree on the weight to give that Hadith on women and politics. Assuredly there were some who used it as an argument for excluding women from decision making. But there were others who found that argument unfounded and unconvincing. Al-Tabari was against it, not finding it a sufficient basis for depriving women of their power of decision making and for justifying their exclusion from politics.

---

38   Fatima Mernissi, *Women and Islam*, 1987, pp 49-58.
39   Ibid p 61.

Other Muslims oppose the idea of a woman as leader on the basis that her position would inevitably bring her into contact with unrelated men, which to those who believe that neither women nor men are able to control their sexual appetites when in the presence of unrelated members of the opposite sex, is something which cannot be countenanced.

Dr Anis Ahmed, the former Dean of the Faculty of Revealed Knowledge at the International Islamic University in Malaysia, told his students at a lecture in 1994 that a woman could not be head of state because national security might require her to meet in private with the head of the armed forces. In support of his views, he quoted a *hadith* which says that Satan is a third presence whenever an unrelated man and woman meet in private. Such a view is quite unrealistic and demeaning to both men and women.

Muslim women's rights and the CEDAW Convention

Western critics of Islam most frequently point to the poor record of treatment of women in Muslim countries as the major fault of the Islamic system. It must be remembered, however, that not all aspects of Western life and society would be enthusiastically embraced by even modernist Muslim thinkers. The prevalence of sexual promiscuity, high divorce rate and breakdown of the family are perceived not to be worthy of emulation by Muslim societies. International conventions such as CEDAW are seen by some as being just another attempt to impose inappropriate Western values and practices upon Muslims in their own countries.

Norani Othman argues that much of the criticism of CEDAW in Muslim countries is based upon a desire to maintain the regressive authoritarian view of the traditional *fiqh* towards women, and that Muslim women must evaluate the *Shariah* to press the point to their own societies that the *Quran* itself stresses gender equality and promotes rational, egalitarian and justice-oriented ideals.[40] As such there is not so great a division between the true Islamic view of women's rights and that of CEDAW as the upholders of the traditional view would have us believe. Many of those who oppose

---

40   Norani Othman, "Shari'a law and the rights of modern Muslim women: an overview of the implementation of CEDAW in Muslim countries, with special reference to current developments in Malaysia", paper presented at IWRAW Round Table Meeting on Women, Islam and CEDAW, New York, 14.1.1995.

CEDAW are demanding exemptions and protections "not for the core religious and spiritual values of the Qur'anic revelation but for the historically contingent edifice of codified *Shari'a* (and often also the various iniquities and abuses that managed to survive in Islamic history alongside the *Shari'a*, even though they confronted the core religious and social ideals of that revelation)".[41]

That is one view. Unfortunately, from the point of view of women's equality, the majority of Islamic revivalist movements seem much more inclined to try to take their societies back to their version of a revival of the Islamic past, which includes for them, veiling and seclusion of women and their exclusion from public life. Thus the Taliban, on taking Kabul, immediately ordered working women out of their jobs regardless of hardship. In Algeria, women risk being shot by the fundamentalists for not wearing *hejab*, and by government supporters for wearing *hejab*. As a practical matter, the full implementation of CEDAW is presently unlikely in most Muslim countries.

---

41   Ibid p 16.

 الزواج

5

MARRIAGE IN ISLAMIC LAW

Islam discourages celibacy and encourages every Muslim to marry:

> And among His signs is this, That He created for you mates from among yourselves, that you may dwell in tranquillity with them, And He has put love and mercy between your (hearts): Verily in that are signs for those who reflect.[1]

Also, the Prophet said:

> O you young men! Whoever is able to marry should marry, for that will help him to lower his gaze and guard his modesty.[2]

The jurists of all schools of Islamic thought agree that marriage is recommendable or even obligatory for a man who can afford to support a family and for a woman. A man who does not have the means to support a wife, or one who is suffering from a serious illness, or one who possesses no sexual desire at all need not be obliged to marry.[3]

Marriage is a contract, not a sacrament, as it is in Hinduism and Christianity. However, the contract does have religious overtones. Although it is not strictly essential, in most cases there will be some religious ceremonies associated with the marriage. Also many of the rules and principles pertaining to marriage are laid down in the *Quran*, and elaborated on in the *Sunnah* of the Prophet.

---

1   *Quran* 30:21.
2   *Sahih Al-Bukhari.*
3   'Abdur Rahman i Doi, *Women in Shari'ah*, 1992, p 33.

Betrothal

In many societies, marriage is preceded by betrothal or an engagement. This is not essential according to Islamic law, and the Hanafi school, for one, does not recognise betrothal as having any legal consequences, though engagement ceremonies may still take place according to custom in areas where the Hanafi school prevails. However, in parts of Southeast Asia where the Shafii school is predominant, betrothal is a recognised practice with a formal ceremony of betrothal and gifts being exchanged between the parties. Most of the Islamic Family Law enactments of the Malaysian States contain a provision about the return of gifts if the marriage is called off, but do not provide for any other penalties for breach.[4]

The essential requirements or *rukun* for marriage are:

1. Marriage must be between a man and a woman.

2. The bride and the bridegroom must have reached marriageable age.

3. A Muslim man may marry a Muslim or a *kitabiyyah*, but a Muslim woman may marry only a Muslim.

4. The parties must not be within the prohibited degrees of affinity.

5. The parties must both consent to the marriage, and the consent of the bride's *wali* (guardian for marriage) may be required.

6. *Mahr* or *Mas-kahwin* must be paid by the bridegroom to the bride.

7. There must be offer and acceptance so as to form a contract.

8. The parties should be equal in status (*kufw*).

9. The parties must not be in *ihram* for *hajj* or *umrah*.

10. The bride must not be married or in *iddah*, and the bridegroom must not have more than three other wives.

Marriage must be between a man and a woman

Homosexuality is forbidden in Islam and so it is an essential requirement that one party be male and the other female. In Malaysia, the *Islamic Family Law Enactment* 1983 of Kelantan specifies in the Fourth Schedule that marriage requires as an essential condition a prospective husband who is male and a prospective bride who is female.

---

4   See, for example, s 15 of the *Islamic Family Law (Federal Territory) Act* 1984.

The age of marriage

What is considered marriageable age varies. Child marriage was quite common among Muslims in the past, as it was among other communities. In traditional communities marriage was more a matter of alliance between families, and protection of family property than a matter of individual choice. Thus when an opportunity arose to make an advantageous arrangement through marriage, it was taken up, regardless of the age of the intended bride and groom. The practice of child marriage was also fortified by the desire of Muslims to ensure that a girl was protected by marriage as soon as possible from being tempted into any immorality, and by the example of the Prophet, who was reputed to have married his great love, Ayesha, at the age of six and taken her to live with him when she was nine or ten. However, some modern scholars dispute this story saying that the great extent of Ayesha's knowledge indicates that she must have been much older than 18 when the Prophet died.

Thus child marriage was held to be valid, but the parties should have reached puberty before they commence married life together. The attainment of puberty is a matter of fact, but, in the absence of evidence to the contrary, the minimum age was set by the Hanafis at 9 years for girls and 12 for boys. A more modern view is that puberty is deemed to have been attained at the age of 15 years for both sexes.

Child marriage has now been forbidden absolutely in Pakistan and India.[5] Most Muslim countries today have legislated to provide a minimum age of marriage. For example, the minimum age of marriage is 21 for males and 18 for females in India; 18 for males and 16 for females in Pakistan and Malaysia and several of the Arab states, and 15 for males and puberty for females in the Philippines. There a girl is presumed to have attained puberty at the age of 15 years, but there is provision for the marriage of a girl under 15 years but more than 12 years, if a petition is made to the court by the girl's *wali*.[6]

Restriction on marriage with persons of a different religion

The *Quran* prohibits marriage with polytheists,[7] but permits a Muslim man to marry a woman from the "People of the Book" (*Ahl al-Kitab*),

---

5   *Child Marriage Restraint Acts* 1929-78.
6   Code of Muslim Personal Laws of the Philippines, Article 16(2).
7   2:221.

which is usually interpreted as being a woman from the Jewish or Christian communities.[8] Such women are called *kitabiyyah*. All Sunni schools allow marriage with a *kitabiyyah*, though many Muslims consider it undesirable, because such a wife (if a Christian) may eat pork and drink wine and sing hymns and so lead her husband and family astray. Some Shia schools do not permit such a marriage. The definition of who is a *kitabiyyah* also varies, with the Shafii school adopting so restrictive a definition – a woman whose ancestors were Jews before the time of the Prophet Jesus or Christians before the time of the Prophet Muhammad – that few women can qualify, and so marriages with non-Muslims under Islamic law are almost unknown in areas where the Shafii school prevails.[9] A Muslim woman is prohibited from marrying anybody except a Muslim. This is a universal rule.

Where a non-Muslim wants to marry a Muslim outside these rules, that person, if a man, must convert to Islam, since a marriage with a non-Muslim is void, or becomes void if one half of a married couple converts to Islam and the other does not.[10] In multicultural societies like Malaysia, and Sri Lanka, there have been many cases on this point. Problems have arisen where the Muslim husband wishes to exercise his religious right to practise polygamy,[11] where it is necessary to ascertain whether a marriage is in existence to determine entitlement to a pension,[12] or where one party claims an earlier marriage is indissoluble, as in *Pedley v Majlis Ugama Islam Pulau Pinang*, where the husband was a Roman Catholic and the wife converted to Islam, which, according to Islamic law, rendered the marriage invalid.[13] In such cases, there have been conflicts between the provisions of Islamic law and the civil law.

---

8   *Quran* 5:6.

9   The Kelantan *Islamic Family Law Enactment* 1983 in fact provides in s 16(3) and (4) that neither a male nor a female may marry any person who is not a Muslim.

10 In some countries such as India and Indonesia, it is possible for Muslims to marry non-Muslims under civil statutes, but these marriages are outside Islamic law. In other countries, such as Malaysia, it is legally impossible for a Muslim to marry outside Islamic law.

11 *Attorney-General of Ceylon v Reid* [1965] 2 MLJ 34; *PP v White* (1940) 9 MLJ 214.

12 *Eeswari Visualingam v Govt of Malaysia* [1990] 1 MLJ 86.

13 [1990] 2 MLJ 307.

The prohibited degrees of affinity

The prohibited degrees of affinity are laid down in the *Quran*.[14] A person may not marry his or her ascendants, descendants, siblings, nieces and nephews, aunts and uncles, in-laws, step parents and step-children and their descendants. The prohibition also applies to foster relatives, as a family relationship is deemed to come into existence between a woman who breast feeds a child and that child. This was an important provision in the early days of Islam as it was the custom for children of Meccan society to be fostered out to country women during infancy. Marriages between cousins are not prohibited and are quite common in Muslim societies.

In addition there are some temporary bars to marriage, for example a man may not marry two sisters at the same time or a woman during her *iddah* (waiting period after her husband's death or divorce).

Consent

Although arranged marriages have been common in Muslim societies, in theory at least, the free consent of both parties is required. There are several *ahadith* in which the Prophet is reported to have stated that the consent of a girl to her marriage must be sought, although if the girl is shy, her silence may be taken to be her consent. In traditional Muslim societies, there are few, or perhaps no, opportunities for a young person to meet the opposite sex and choose a marriage partner. Most young people accept that their parents will arrange a suitable match for them, and although the prospective bride or groom has the right to refuse a particular match, in practice, it is rare for them to do so. Romantic love is not thought to be an essential ingredient for a marriage to take place. More attention is paid to factors such as good reputation, social and economic position, family relationship, and more recently, educational achievement in choosing a spouse. The chances of incompatibility are thus reduced and there is no evidence that such marriages are less happy as a general rule, than those contracted according to Western criteria.

The *wali* is the bride's marriage guardian, and will usually be her father or paternal grandfather. In the absence of these, another male relative, such as a brother or uncle, may act as *wali*. The consent

---

14   4:22-23.

of the bride may be given through her *wali*, and the Shafii school holds that the *wali's* consent is essential in all circumstances. However, according to the Hanafi school, the *wali*'s consent is essential only for the marriage of a minor virgin, and when a woman reaches the age of majority, whether she is a virgin or not, she can marry without her *wali*'s consent. If the bride has no male relative who is able to act as her *wali*, or if her proper *wali* unreasonably refuses his consent to a marriage, the Shafii school allows the appointment of the Sultan as *wali raja* to consent to the marriage.

Imam Shafii also held that it is permissible for a father or paternal grandfather to arrange the marriage of a virgin girl without obtaining her consent, interpreting the Prophet's words as meaning that it is commendable, but not essential, to obtain the bride's agreement to the marriage. This ruling appears to have been based on the idea that a properly brought up virgin girl will not be in a position to judge what is best for her in a marriage partner, and her father would not act against her interests in arranging her marriage. This idea might possibly have had some validity in Imam Shafii's time, if it can be accepted that all fathers will always choose a daughter's husband in her interests and not for some other reason, but is clearly not of universal application today.

This issue came before the court in Malaysia in 1959 in the case of *Syed Abdullah Al-Shatiri v Shariffa Salmah*[15] when a proud Arab father disapproved of his daughter's choice of prospective bridegroom and promptly married her off to a relative without her consent. The Syariah Appeal Board upheld the father's right to do so but allowed a *fasakh* divorce as the young woman was adamantly opposed to the match and had left home to live with her chosen suitor's family anyway. The *Islamic Family Law (Federal Territory) Act* in Malaysia omits this principle and requires the consent of both parties to a marriage, but the traditional position still prevails in Kelantan.[16] The *Code of Muslim Personal Laws* of the Philippines requires consent of both parties.[17]

---

15   [1959] 2 MLJ 137.
16   *Islamic Family Law Enactment* 1983 s 13(2).
17   Article 15(b).

Mahr

Mahr (called *mas-kahwin* in Southeast Asia) is a compulsory payment which must be made by the bridegroom to the bride (not to her relatives) at the time of the marriage. It becomes her own property and cannot be taken from her by her relatives or taken back by the husband. However, the wife may agree to remit all or some of it of her own free will. Unpaid *mahr* may be recovered as a debt from the husband on divorce or on his death, and in those circumstances, the wife has a right to retain the husband's property until the *mahr* is paid.

By religious tradition, the maximum amount of *mahr* cannot be limited. The traditions relate that Caliph Omar attempted to place a maximum limit on the amount of *mahr* which could be paid, as extravagant amounts were being given by the people of his time. He was forced to change his opinion when a woman challenged his decision in the mosque, reciting from the *Quran* the verse which refers to the giving of a "whole treasure for dower", and questioning his right to specify less. The minimum amount has been fixed by the Hanafis at 10 *dirhams* (a *dirham* was an Arab form of currency), and by the Malikis at 3 *dirhams*, but according to a tradition of the Prophet, it may be as little as an iron ring or the teaching of verses from the *Quran* where the husband has no other means. If no *mahr* is agreed at the time of the marriage, then the wife is entitled to a proper amount according to local custom and her station in life.

Payment of *mahr* may be prompt (paid at the time of marriage) or deferred. In Southeast Asia the amount of *mas-kahwin* is usually quite small – less than A$100 – and is paid at the time of marriage. In the Indian sub-continent, perhaps for reasons of show, quite huge amounts are sometimes agreed as *mahr*, but are rarely paid in full. According to Mandelbaum,[18] in the northern parts of India and Pakistan, specification of a large *mahr* is a matter of family honour, but wives usually receive only a token payment and then are induced by local custom to formally release the husband from payment of the remainder. In theory the purpose of *mahr* is to provide the woman with some means of her own in case of divorce or the husband's death, but in practice, in neither of the above situations does it usually provide any real financial security for the woman.

Mahr may be in the form of money, or possessions such as furniture or land, or as we have seen above in other forms as approved

---

18   *Women's Seclusion and Men's Honour*, 1988, p 44.

by the Prophet. Some examples of *mahr* included in marriage contracts by modern Muslim women were recently listed in *Sisters*, a magazine for American Muslim women.[19] Some of them were:

- a new car and $20,000;
- a promise to teach her *Juz 'Amma* and *Juz Tabarak* (sections of the *Quran*);
- $1 with a deferred *mahr* of $100,000 in the event of divorce;
- Arabic lessons, a home computer, and a home gym;
- a trip around the world with stopovers in Mecca, Medina and Jerusalem.

The payment of *mahr* should not be confused with the Hindu custom of dowry, where the bride's parents make a large payment to the intended bridegroom and his family. Although this custom of giving dowry has led to many evils and has been prohibited by the *Dowry Prohibition Act* 1961, it still continues in India and has been taken up by some Muslims living in areas where it is practised by Hindus. The giving of dowry in this way is quite un-Islamic and should not be practised by Muslims.

The marriage contract

As marriage is a contract, there must be offer and acceptance (*ijab* and *kabul*). The bride's acceptance may be given through her *wali*. Some jurists have likened the marriage contract to a sale, with the *mahr* being consideration for the husband's purchase of the bride. This is not a correct interpretation. The *Quran* repeatedly emphasises that marriage should be a partnership of mutual love and affection. The pre-Islamic Arabs treated women as property allowing a man's sons to inherit his wives when he died. The *Quran* specifically forbade this practice.

No particular form of marriage ceremony is prescribed and it is not necessary for the marriage to be performed by a religious official. Some modern legislation allows the bride's *wali* to perform the marriage.[20] Often there will be some ceremonies in accordance with the cultural practice of the parties, such as the *bersanding* ceremony

---

19   August/September 1996 p 16.
20   See *Islamic Family Law (FT) Act* 1984 s 7 and *Islamic Family Law Enactment* 1983 (Kelantan) s 9, *Code of Muslim Personal Law* (Philippines) Art 8.

which is usual in Malaysia and Indonesia. This is not an Islamic ceremony, and is not an essential part of the marriage. It is considered *sunnah* to hold a celebration, which need not be elaborate, for the friends and families of the parties. The religious ceremony may be held at an earlier date than the public celebration.

There must be two adult witnesses to the marriage and the fact of marriage must not be kept a secret.

The marriage contract itself should be in writing, and may contain conditions agreed to by the parties. Tanzil ur-Rahman says that "generally speaking Muslim jurists are not favourably inclined to allow absolute freedom in a contract of marriage",[21] but stipulations are commonly made as to:

- the place of residence;

- payment of periodic sums of money to the wife;

- restriction on the husband's right to marry a second wife.

However, agreements that the wife should continue to live in her parents' house have been held to be void.[22] According to the well known text of Hanafi jurisprudence, the *Fatawa Alamgiriyya*, Muslim jurists have approved the following conditions in marriage contracts:[23]

- that the husband cannot absent himself from the matrimonial residence for a specified period of time;

- that the wife cannot be forced to prepare food or wash dishes;

- that the husband shall not keep the wife in the same house as his other wife;

- that the husband shall not stop the wife from going to her parents once a week and to other near relations once a month;

- that the husband shall not indulge in gambling or drink liquor;

- that the husband shall not maltreat the wife or use filthy language to her;

- that the husband shall pay the wife a specified amount of maintenance by or on regular specified dates;

- that the husband shall not leave the place where they are living without the wife's permission.

---

21   *A Code of Muslim Personal Law*, Vol I, 1984, p 298.
22   Ibid p 300.
23   Ibid pp 304-5.

Such conditions can be enforced by the Islamic courts in the same way as normal contractual conditions are enforced. Provisions concerning the enforcement of conditions in a marriage contract were included in the Ottoman Family law of the Turkish Empire, under which non-compliance with such conditions were grounds for divorce at the option of the wife, without any penalty upon her.[24]

Sharifa Alkhateeb says that a Muslim marriage contract will be enforceable in most States of the USA providing it is in writing and signed by the parties and registered at city hall or county office before the marriage takes place. It can include provisions which are contrary to the assumptions normally made by United States law. For example, she suggests that the wife might include a stipulation that she will not be economically legally responsible at any time during the marriage.[25]

In Australia, at common law, pre-marriage contracts were not enforceable. The question of whether such contracts should be recognised by law was considered by the Australian Law Reform Commission in 1992. Its recommendation was that pre-marriage contracts governing the distribution of property in the event of a dissolution of marriage should be enforceable unless a court decided that enforcement would cause substantial injustice. The Commission did not appear to consider stipulations in marriage contracts other than those about distribution of property on divorce. It would appear that such stipulations would come under the heading of "family agreements" which would not usually be considered to be legally binding under contract law.

The rule of equality in status (*kufw*)

In some Muslim societies it has been considered an essential for marriage that the husband should be equal of the wife in social status (*kufw*). Some jurists disagree with this rule on religious grounds, since the *Quran* states unequivocally that all Muslims are equal,[26] and the Prophet said that no person can be better than another except in piety. In the past this rule of equality was considered to be of great importance, and the wife's relatives were entitled to prevent a marriage on this ground. Equality was required by all schools in religion, meaning that both parties must be Muslims, though not

---

24   Sharifa Alkhateeb, "The Marriage Contract", *Sisters*, Aug/Sept 1996 p 15.
25   Ibid p 16.
26   See sura al Hujurat 49:10 "The Believers are but a single Brotherhood".

necessarily following the same *madhab*. Other considerations were lineage, freedom (from slavery), calling or profession, freedom from defects and character.

Nowadays, not so much emphasis is placed on this rule, but it did come before the court in Singapore in *Re Husseinah Banoo*[27] where a 14-year-old Muslim girl eloped with a man her family considered completely unsuitable. Her father applied to the court to have the marriage annulled on the ground that the man was not her equal in status as he was not of good character and did not pray. The court annulled the marriage.

The parties must not be in *Ihram for hajj or umrah*

Marriage should not be celebrated during the pilgrimage to Mecca.

The bride should not be married or in *iddah* at the time of the ceremony and the bridegroom should not have more than three other wives

In Islamic law, polygamy, or polygyny as it should be called, is a right or privilege available only to men. A woman can have only one husband at a time. If she is divorced, or if her husband dies, she must wait out the prescribed period of *iddah*, which is normally three months or three menstrual periods, before she is able to marry again.

Polygamy is permitted in Islamic law, but it is not recommended or encouraged. Although polygamy is now thought of as an Islamic practice, it was an accepted custom in much of the ancient world, and is still practised in many societies today. Polygamy was accepted in ancient Egypt and Persia; the Old Testament did not limit the number of wives a man might marry, and many of the Prophets mentioned in it were certainly polygamists. Jacob had four wives; King Solomon was said to have had seven hundred wives and three hundred concubines; and European Jews were still practising polygamy in the Middle Ages.[28] It is usually believed that polygamy has no place in Christianity, but there are examples in Christian history of polygamy being tolerated, if not approved, by Christian leaders. Martin Luther, for example, approved the bigamous marriages of Phillip of Hesse, and more recently the Anabaptists and the Mormons have openly

---

27   (1963) 5 MLJ 392.
28   Hammudah 'Abd al 'Ati, *The Family Structure in Islam*, 1977, p 114.

supported polygamy, although it is no longer part of official Mormon doctrine. In Africa where established custom supports polygamy, many examples can be shown of Christian men having more than one wife.[29] Hammudah 'Abd al 'Ati says:

> It was not a preconceived social philosophy, but most probably a combination of aversion to sex, suspicion of women, and preoccupation with soul saving that gave Christianity its doctrinal monogamous character.[30]

Polygamy was permitted in Hindu law before the passing of the *Hindu Marriage Act* 1955, and the taking of secondary wives by those who could afford it was an established feature of Chinese society.

The *Quranic* rules on polygamy were originally a limitation on the then current Arab practice which allowed men to marry as many women as they chose, and a provision for women who were left without male support at a time when there was no social security and every woman was expected to be dependent on some man.

The verse permitting polygamy[31] was revealed immediately after the battle of *Uhud*, when many men in the Muslim community were killed and many women widowed. Polygamy was allowed as a means of ensuring that someone would have the obligation of providing for them.

The *Quranic* verse about polygamy follows immediately after a verse dealing with the obligation to act justly towards orphans and is as follows:

> If you feel that you shall not be able to deal justly with the orphans,
> Marry women of your choice, two, or three, or four;
> But if you fear that you shall not be able to deal justly (with them),
> Then only one, or (a captive) that your right hands possess.
> That will be more suitable to prevent you from doing injustice.

In a later verse,[32] the *Quran* also says:

> You are never able to be fair and just as between women,
> Even if it is your ardent desire. . .

Some scholars see a contradiction in these verses. The first calls for justice between wives, the second says justice is not possible. Some modernists have interpreted this as meaning that a man should have only one wife, but the general opinion is that polygamy is permitted

---

29   Ibid and Abdur Rahman i Doi, *Women in Shari'ah,* 1990, p 65.
30   Ibid p 115.
31   *Quran* 4:3.
32   4:129.

subject to certain conditions. It is certainly not meant as unrestricted licence for any man to indulge his sexual appetites, as is commonly depicted in Hollywood movies about Muslim life.

Generally, if a man wants to take a second (or third or fourth) wife, he should:

- have sufficient income and assets to be able to make financial provision for them;
- be capable of treating all of his wives equally and justly;
- have a good reason for wanting to take an additional wife, such as that the first wife is too old or ill to perform household duties or her marital obligations; that she cannot have children, or if she is of unsound mind;
- obtain the consent of his first wife (or wives).

Polygamy is not common in Muslim countries. Some Muslim countries have now prohibited polygamy altogether,[33] while others[34] require the man to seek permission from the court and to meet its requirements.

An example of such a provision is s 23 of the *Islamic Family Law (Federal Territory) Act* 1984 of Malaysia, which states that no man is permitted to contract a polygamous marriage without the permission of the court. An application must be filed with the court with a statutory declaration setting out the grounds upon which the proposed marriage is alleged by the applicant to be just and necessary, the applicant's present income and financial commitments, the number of his dependants and whether he has obtained the consent of his present wife or wives. The court will then summon the existing wife or wives to attend the hearing *in camera* and may grant permission for the marriage if satisfied as to five conditions:

1. That there is a just and necessary reason for the proposed marriage because of circumstances such as sterility, physical infirmity, physical unfitness for conjugal relations, wilful avoidance of a decree for restitution of conjugal rights or insanity;

2. That the applicant has sufficient means to be able to support all his existing dependants and intended dependants;

---

33   For example, Syria and Tunisia.
34   Morocco, Iraq, Pakistan.

3. That the applicant would be able to accord equal treatment to all his wives as required by Islamic law;

4. That the proposed marriage would not cause *darar syar'i* to the existing wife or wives. This is defined in the Act as "harm, according to what is normally recognised by Islamic law, affecting a wife in respect of religion, life, body, mind or property;"

5. That the proposed marriage would not directly or indirectly lower the standard of living that the existing wife or wives or dependants have been enjoying and would reasonably expect to continue to enjoy were the marriage not to take place.

It is extremely difficult to satisfy the court as to all the above conditions, and so polygamous marriages are rarely approved in the Federal Territory of Malaysia. However, conditions in some other States are not so stringent, (Family Law is a State matter in Malaysia) and so disappointed suitors need only take themselves to a more sympathetic jurisdiction.

In Singapore, in the case of *Aishah binte Abdul Rauf v Wan Mohd Yusof bin Wan Othman*,[35] the court held that the husband's fear of committing adultery was not a sufficient ground for permission for polygamy, but on the other hand, in *Re Giman bin Abdul Samad*[36] where the first wife supported the husband's application and he could provide evidence of his financial ability to support two families, the court granted permission.

Anecdotal evidence is that polygamy is increasing slightly among the Malays as they become better off, but it must be remembered that the right of polygamy carries a corresponding obligation – the necessity of supporting another family, which few men can afford. Recently, a backward step, in the eyes of Muslim feminists, was taken by the Selangor Government when it ruled that it was not necessary for a man to obtain the permission of his first wife before contracting a second marriage, unless a *Syariah* Court judge disagrees.[37]

Arguments advanced in favour of polygamy among Muslims are:

---

35   [1990] 3 MLJ lx.
36   [1991] 1 MLJ xxxiv.
37   Personal communication from Sisters in Islam, Kuala Lumpur, 31.10.1996.

- It avoids the situation where a woman is kept as a mistress with no rights or legal claim on the man concerned. Extra-marital relationships are forbidden by Islam.
- The first wife is not abandoned when the husband falls in love with a younger woman and he has an ongoing obligation to maintain her and care for her.
- A second wife can help the first when the first wife is disabled by ill health or old age.
- Unless he is allowed to take a second wife, a man may be led into adultery to satisfy his natural biological needs. In this regard, it is pointed out that Islam forbids and severely penalises extra-marital relationships, so the alternative of a mistress "on the side" is not available.

From the Western viewpoint the idea of polygamy is shocking. The idea that a man can have four wives while a woman can only have one husband is contrary to ideals of the equality of the sexes. Few women would want to share a husband. However, as Muslim critics are fond of pointing out, Western society condones extra-marital relationships, and accepts that successful older men may discard their first wives once they have passed their "use-by date", in favour of a younger, more glamorous new model. Thus the Western view is not without hypocrisy.

The *Mut'a* or temporary marriage

This is a contract between a man and a woman to enter into a marriage type relationship for a specified period of time. The man must agree to pay the woman an amount of money for her agreement. There are no witnesses and the woman does not inherit from the man, although children have the normal rights of legitimate children. This form of marriage was practised in the pre-Islamic era in Arabia, where it was considered expedient if a man was going off to war or on a journey, and it was not forbidden in the early days of Islam. Some of the *Shia* schools still consider it to be legal, and claim that it was never forbidden by the Prophet, but by Caliph Omar, whom they do not regard as a legitimate ruler.

The view of the *Sunni* schools is that *Mut'a* marriage is equivalent to fornication in disguise, and it is strictly prohibited. According to the *Sunnis* marriage must always be a permanent arrangement, with mutual rights and duties and provision for the upkeep of children. Thus this kind of marriage does not fulfil the conditions of a proper Islamic marriage and so is not considered legitimate. It is not practised by the vast majority of Muslims.

In summary, therefore, marriage is the essential element of the Muslim family. There can be no family without marriage. Over the centuries, in spite of idealistic statements to the contrary, women have, in practice, been disadvantaged in the marriage relationship. As in other areas of Islamic law, patriarchal practices have intruded to diminish the benefits given to women by the *Quran*. Fortunately, in modern times, in most Muslim countries more consideration is being given to women's rights, within marriage, as well as outside of it.

الحياة الأسرية ❈

6

FAMILY LIFE

Everywhere, the family is the basic element of Muslim society. As we have seen in the previous chapter, a family can be formed only through marriage, and the traditional Muslim family is more likely than not to be an extended family. As might be expected, the principles regarding marital and family relationships are laid down in the *Quran* and *Sunnah*:

> And among His signs is this,
> that He created for you mates from among yourselves,
> that you may dwell in tranquillity with them,
> and He has put love and mercy between your hearts.
> Undoubtedly in these are signs for those who reflect.[1]

The relationship between husband and wife

According to the traditional view, men and women have different functions in life, and as God has given men greater strength and a greater capacity to earn than women, men are "in charge of women"[2] or "the protectors and maintainers of women"[3] and the husband is therefore the head of the house. Some women see this as a shield from the distress and inconvenience of participating in public life and do not object. However, modernists particularly, emphasise that family decisions should be made by *shura* or mutual consultation, often involving the children as well as the parents, but the father ultimately has the casting vote.

---

1   *Quran* 30:21.
2   4:34.
3   Alternative translation.

Duties within marriage

Maintenance

It is the husband's duty to support his wife and children. Only in exceptional circumstances will the wife be expected to contribute to her own maintenance or that of the children. If the husband is miserly, the wife is entitled to take sufficient from his property to support herself and the children. According to *hadith*, the wife of a man named Abu Sufyan told the Prophet that although her husband was rich, he did not give her sufficient money to live on. The Prophet told her that she could take money for living expenses from his funds without his consent.

The wife can expect to be maintained at a reasonable standard, according to the financial position of her husband and the standard of her own family. Thus if the wife has been brought up to expect the assistance of a maid, the husband should provide her with a maid, unless he is too poor to do so. A *hadith* recounts that a man asked the Prophet what rights a wife might demand of her husband. The Prophet replied:

> That you should feed her (with the same standard) as you feed yourself, clothe her as you clothe yourself, that you should never hit her face or put her down, or cut yourself off from her unless it occurs in the house.[4]

However, the traditional jurists consider that if a wife is *nusyuz* (disobedient) she forgoes her right to maintenance. Disobedience may entail going out to work without the husband's permission, denying him his conjugal rights while she is living with him or leaving the house to live elsewhere without his permission and without just cause. The wife will not be held to be *nusyuz* if she leaves home because of the husband's ill-treatment, or if a co-wife or the husband's relative (except his incapacitated poor parents) is brought to live in the same house without her consent, or if a proper house is not provided for her.

The wife is not entitled to maintenance if she is in gaol, or if she is travelling without her husband's permission, with some jurists excepting a wife who is travelling with a *mehrem* on *hajj* for the first time. If the husband travels, he should leave the wife sufficient maintenance to cover the time he is away.

---

4   Quoted in Yusuf al-Qaradawi, *The Lawful and the Prohibited in Islam*, 1989, p 203.

Mutual care and consideration

The *Quran* says: "They are as a garment to you, and you are as a garment to them".[5]

A husband should not ill treat his wife, but should be patient with her even if he dislikes something about her. The *Quran* says: "And consort with them in kindness, for if you dislike them, it may be that you dislike something in which Allah has placed much good".[6]

If the wife is persistently adverse to following her husband's instructions the *Quran* recommends that the husband first try to persuade her to his point of view by reasoning with her or admonition; if this method fails, then he may separate from her in bed; then he may take the step of beating her.[7] The interpretation of this verse has led to much controversy. On the one hand it has been taken by some men as giving permission to beat disobedient wives as they choose. On the other hand, most of the scholars agree that any beating should be symbolic only, as where a tooth-stick or similar light object is used. It should not be interpreted as condoning domestic violence.[8] According to the traditions, the Prophet never struck a woman or a slave and spoke frequently of the need for kindness to women.

However, a dutiful wife should be careful to please her husband as much as she can. She should not allow into the house anyone her husband does not approve of, she should not obey anyone who contradicts his orders (unless his orders are contrary to Islam), and she should not refuse to share his bed. It is also a Muslim husband's duty to please his wife, including looking after his appearance for her sake.

Many of the traditional jurists give the husband the power to confine the wife to the home, but the modernists disagree on this point. In some Muslim countries, the tradition of seclusion of women has made it a point of honour for men to boast that their wives have never left the matrimonial home from the day they came to it as a bride until the day of their death – or perhaps only once, to attend the funeral of the wife's father. In such countries men attend to all outside activities, including shopping for food. In other Muslim countries, this tradition which is cultural in origin, has never existed, and women freely leave the home to shop, work and engage in community activities.

---

5   2:187.

6   4:19.

7   4:34.

8   Amina Wudud-Muhsin, *Qur'an and Woman*, 1992, p 76.

Household duties

Care of the home and children is normally considered to be primarily the wife's responsibility but men should not regard housework as beneath them. The Prophet himself used to mend his own clothes and help his wives in the house. Some authorities say that the wife cannot be compelled to cook and sew or do the housework, but should be provided with cooked food and ready made clothes by the husband.[9]

Sexual relationship

Both husband and wife are entitled to a satisfactory sexual relationship with each other. The jurists agree that a wife is at fault if she refuses to sleep with her husband, except for good reason. Maulana Maudoodi says that it is also a form of cruelty for a man to deprive his wife of sexual relations.[10] There is a verse in the *Quran* which indicates that the maximum period for which a man should keep away from his wife is four months.[11] After that, he should resume the sexual relationship, or divorce her.

Care of children

Under Islamic law, children have a right to know their parents and to be cared for and maintained during infancy and to inherit from parents after their death. Only the natural mother and father of a child can be acknowledged as his or her parents, since adoption is not recognised. The status of legitimate children is different from that of illegitimate children who have no claim upon their natural father. As illegitimacy has severe consequences in the Islamic world, some latitude has been allowed by the jurists in calculating the term of pregnancy. The minimum term of pregnancy, according to most of the scholars, is six months and the maximum term allowed by them has varied from nine lunar months according to some of the Shias to five years according to others. Some count the term of the pregnancy from the time of the marriage contract rather than the date of consummation of the marriage.[12]

It is the parents' duty to care for children and to bring them up to be responsible and God-fearing. It is the father's responsibility to

---

9   Tanzil ur-Rahman, *A Code of Muslim Personal Law,* 1984, p 258, Asghar Ali Engineer, *The Rights of Women in Islam*, 1992, pp 116-117.

10   Maulana Abul A'ala Maudoodi, *The Laws of Marriage and Divorce in Islam,* 1987, p 17.

11   2:227.

12   Jamal J Nasir, *The Islamic Law of Personal Status,* 1986 pp 140-142.

provide for their maintenance until they are grown up or, in the case of a girl, until she is married. If the father cannot do this, it becomes the paternal grandfather's responsibility, and only if there are no male relatives to provide does it become the responsibility of the mother. Children's physical needs – food, clothing and shelter – must be provided for, but they should also be educated to the best of the parents' ability and nurtured with love and kindness.

According to the scholars,[13] it is the mother's religious duty to suckle her baby in accordance with the *Quran*ic rule that "the mothers shall suckle their offspring for two whole years…".[14] The Hanafis and Malikis agree that a woman can be compelled to feed her baby, unless of course, she is physically unable to do so, and the Shia also agree with this position with the exception that a woman may hire a wet nurse as a substitute if she wishes. The Hanbalis say that it is the duty of the father alone to provide for feeding the baby. In all cases the father is obliged to provide maintenance or payment for the mother or wet nurse who suckles the baby. If the mother has been irrevocably divorced by the father, she herself is entitled to payment for suckling the child for a period of up to two years.

Children should be treated equally by their parents. According to *hadith*, a man of the Ansar proposed to accede to his wife's request to give a garden or a slave to one of his sons and asked the Prophet to be a witness to the transfer. The Prophet inquired whether such gifts were being made to the other sons, and on being informed that they were not, refused to be a witness saying that he would not be a witness to injustice.[15] However, according to Imam Ahmad bin Hanbal, it is permissible to give special treatment to a child who suffers from a handicap, or in some other unusual circumstances.

There is a *hadith* to the effect that children should not be struck with a cane before they have reached the age of 10, but reason and guidance are preferable means of discipline.

Children, even when adult, are expected to respect and obey their parents. Soraya Altorki[16] mentions that in Saudi Arabia where the *Shariah* is strictly adhered to in social custom as well as by law, it is unthinkable for a child not to obey his or her parents, whether in

---

13   Ibid pp 153-154.
14   2:233.
15   *Hadith* quoted in Yusuf al-Qaradawi, *The Lawful and Prohibited in Islam*, 1989, pp 230-231.
16   *Women in Saudi Arabia*, 1986, p 72.

selection of a marriage partner or a college major. Disobedience to parents is a sin as well as socially unacceptable.

Custody on divorce

There is a presumption in Islamic law that it is for the benefit of a small child to remain with its mother. This is called *hadhanah*. The age at which *hadhanah* ceases varies between the schools, and also with the sex of the child but the very minimum age is two years, and according to the Maliki school the right of *hadhanah* in relation to a daughter lasts until she is married. Once a child has reached the age of discretion, he or she may choose which parent he or she wishes to live with.

A woman may lose the right to *hadhanah* for various reasons including abjuration of Islam, ill treatment of the child, by going away and residing at a distance from the father's residence without his permission so that he loses contact with the child, or marrying someone who is not related to the child. This last reason appears to have been based on fears that a step-father might abuse the child, but the approach of the courts, in Malaysia at least, is to decide whether the welfare of the child is best served by leaving him or her with the mother regardless of her remarriage.

The father retains guardianship over a child regardless of whether the mother has custody. The guardian has power to control the minor's property and to incur debts and enter into contracts on his or her behalf.

Adoption

Adoption is not recognised in Islamic law. Apparently, adoption was common in pre-Islamic Arabia, and Muhammad himself, before the time of his prophethood, had adopted a child named Zaid, who had been captured in a tribal raid and presented to him as a slave. Muhammad freed him and adopted him and he was known as Zaid ibn Muhammad. Later he married the Prophet's cousin Zainab, but when that marriage failed, the Prophet married her after the divorce in accordance with the now revealed Islamic rule that adoption created no family relationship.

The practice of adoption was forbidden in the *Quran* as follows:

> . . . nor has He made your adopted sons your sons:
> That is simply a saying of your mouths. . .
> Call them by (the names) of their fathers:
> That is more just in the sight of Allah,

But if you do not know their fathers,
They are your brothers in faith and your wards. . .[17]

The prohibition of adoption does not mean that there is any objection to a person bringing up someone else's child and caring for it if the child is an orphan or other circumstances exist which justify this happening. However, such a child does not inherit as an heir, although the foster-parent can make provision for him or her through gifts made during life or by a bequest in a will, provided that such bequest does not exceed one third of the testator's estate.

Care of the elderly

The Muslim family is traditionally an extended family comprising of three or more generations, sometimes, but not always, living under the same roof. As we have seen, parents are to be respected and obeyed throughout their lives.

Again, the basic principles are set out in the *Quran*:

> Your Lord decrees that you worship none but Him
> And be kind to your parents,
> If either or both of them attain old age in your lifetime,
> Say not to them a word of contempt, nor repel them,
> But address them in terms of honour.
> And, out of kindness,
> Lower to them the wing of humility, and say:
> "My Lord! Bestow on them
> Your mercy even as they
> Cherished me in childhood".[18]

According to the *Sunnah*, the Prophet emphasised the necessity of respecting, obeying and caring for elderly parents, and gave preference to the rights of the mother, saying that Paradise lay at the mother's feet. The Prophet also spoke of obligations owed to grandparents, other elderly relatives and aged and infirm neighbours.

Children, both sons and daughters, are under an obligation to contribute to the maintenance of their parents, the father, when he is unable to maintain himself, and the mother regardless of her ability to earn money for herself. If the children cannot maintain both parents, then the mother has priority according to some scholars, but others say that available maintenance should be divided between mother and father. If the children cannot maintain the parents in a separate household, then they should make room for them in their own. The

---

17   33:4-5.
18   17: 23-24.

obligation to provide maintenance should be shared among the children according to their means.

The same principles apply to needy grandparents and other more distant relatives, provided that there is not some other family member who has primary responsibility for their maintenance, and that the family member has sufficient means to support himself and his own family. These rules also apply in respect of relations who are not Muslims. No elderly person should be left to fend for himself or herself without the support of some family. If a person has no family at all, then the state must assist through the resources of the *bait ul-mal* (state treasury) or *waqfs* (charitable endowments). However, in most Muslim countries there is no system of social security with pension entitlements such as exists in the West.

In most modern Muslim countries the law gives effect to the *Shariah* principles.[19]

Ownership of family property

Under Islamic law, women are entitled to own property in their own right, and dispose of it as they choose without interference from male relatives. Only the Malikis limit this right by giving the father as guardian the right to control a daughter's property during her minority and for some time after she is married. Women could obtain property through the marriage gift (*mahr*), through gifts or inheritance from family members, or from their own efforts in working or conducting a business. Property brought into a marriage by the husband or the wife remained their separate property and could be taken out of the marriage by them.

There appears to be little discussion of matrimonial property in the classical law texts. It is not clear why this is so, but quite likely it is because custom supervened in most Muslim societies to ensure that in practice, women were unable to exercise control over property which was rightfully theirs. In the literature there are indications that in some Muslim societies, for example Al-Andalus,[20] women did hold and deal with their own property at least some of the time. On the

---

19   See Tahir Mahmood, "Law and the Elderly in the Islamic Tradition-Classical precepts and modern legislation", *Islamic and Comparative Law Quarterly*, Vol IX:1 March 1989, p 33 at 40-44.

20   See Maya Shatzmiller, "Women and Property Rights in Al-Andalus and the Maghrib: Social Patterns and Legal Discourse", *Islamic Law and Society*, Vol 2 No 3, 1995.

other hand, in countries like India, the large amounts of money and property given to a bride as *mahr* – to uphold the family honour – were largely illusory, as she would normally receive a token payment and then be induced to release the balance. Also considerations of keeping family land within the family led to women being persuaded to forgo their share of inheritance in favour of their brothers. In practice a wife's own property was likely to be limited to her jewellery and personal effects.[21]

In Saudi Arabia, Soraya Altorki writes the situation is changing a little in modern times.[22] When once women were not expected even to inquire about the amount of their dower and leave its management entirely to their male relatives, nowadays some have their own income and use it to buy clothes for themselves or keep their *mahr* in a separate bank account.

However, in Malaysia and Indonesia, women have traditionally been able to earn their own income and hold their own property to a much greater extent in practice, as well as in theory. The division of matrimonial property on divorce has long been governed by Malay *adat* (custom) in the form of *harta sepancharian* which provides that the wife should normally receive either a one third, or a one half share of property acquired during the marriage. As well both husband and wife are entitled to their own separate property. In *Re Ketuna Bibi*,[23] the court held that the English common law position that a wife could not steal her husband's goods did not apply to Muslims, since there was no community of interest under Muslim law. A wife may also be entitled to wages for working on property owned by the husband.

The family home

Ideally, the Muslim family home should be a place of privacy and tranquillity for the family. Architectural styles differ from country to country. In the Middle East and North Africa, the typical home presents a walled front to the street, and family living takes place around a courtyard within. The houses of people of means were always built with separate areas for men – public areas where visitors

---

21   David G Mandelbaum, *Women's Seclusion and Men's Honour: Sex roles in North India*, 1988, pp 67-68.
22   Op cit p 139.
23   (1955) 21 MLJ 166.

could be admitted – and secluded areas for the women of the family where no unrelated male could tread.

Fatima Mernissi says, describing the house in Morocco where she was born: "Our house gate was a definite *hudud*, or frontier, because you needed permission to step in or out".[24] Their house gate was guarded by a door keeper with whom it was necessary to negotiate if children wished to step out; grown women had to remain within. Sometimes several generations of a family occupied one large house, with separate quarters within for married sons and their families.

In South-East Asia, the typical *kampung* house was built of timber on stilts, with wide opening windows to admit cool breezes. Even so, in the past, women were not expected to use the front door, opening on to the "public" sitting room, but had to use the back staircase. Today urban dwellings are of the "link" or bungalow variety are little different in architecture to Western housing. In all Muslim homes, if there is space, a separate room or area may be set aside for prayer.

There is no objection to the home being comfortably and attractively furnished, though excessive luxury should be avoided. Gold and silver dishes and utensils should not be used.[25] Statues and portraits should not be used as decorations since they are forbidden by Islam. Some strict Muslims also object to the display of photographs.

It is a universal rule that people entering a Muslim home should remove their shoes, to prevent dirt being tramped in from outside. Since, traditionally, people sat on the floor, ate food from a cloth placed on the floor, and prayed on the floor, this is a sensible rule. Islam places great emphasis on cleanliness, both of the person and the home itself. In bathrooms, a shower is preferred to a bath, and there should be a bidet or at least a water spray so that people can wash after using the toilet.

Cats are sometimes kept as pets in Muslim homes, but not dogs, since dogs are considered unclean. If a dog is kept as a watchdog or a working dog, it must be kept outside the house. Even so, Islam stresses kindness to animals and popular children's stories include one about a woman who went to Hell because she ill treated her cat and another about a man who was rewarded by God for climbing into a well to fetch water for a thirsty dog.

---

24   Fatima Mernissi, *The Harem Within*, 1994, p 21.
25   Yusuf al-Qaradawi, *The Lawful and Prohibited in Islam*, 1989, p 98.

7

DIVORCE

Unfortunately, not all marriages are made in heaven, as the saying goes. In all societies some marriages are good, and some are bad, and some should never have been entered into in the first place. So far as ending dysfunctional marriages is concerned, Muslims, in theory, have been more fortunate than people in the West in that divorce has always been permitted under Islamic law. When a marriage has irretrievably broken down and there is no hope of reconciliation, it is better, the *Quran* says, for the couple to part with kindness than to continue to live together in intolerable disharmony.[1]

However, although it has always been legal, divorce has traditionally been quite rare in most Muslim countries, since the Prophet said that nothing is more hated in the sight of God than divorce. Where there is marital discord between husband and wife, they should resort to the arbitration (or mediation) of relatives to settle their differences:[2]

> If you fear a breach between them twain,
> Appoint two arbiters, one from his family and the other from hers;
> If they wish for peace, Allah will cause their reconciliation:
> For Allah hath full knowledge and is acquainted with all things.

However, if the arbitration is unsuccessful and the parties cannot reconcile:[3]

---

1   *Quran* 2:229.
2   4:35.
3   4:130.

But if they disagree (and must part), Allah will provide abundance for all from His all-reaching bounty: For Allah is He that careth for all and is wise.

There are many different kinds of divorce in Islamic law. The parties may divorce by mutual agreement. This is called *mubarat*, and under the classical Islamic law, it may be effected without the intervention of the court. The right to divorce by *talaq* is the prerogative of the husband, and other types of divorce, known as *khula'* or *fasakh*. may be used by the wife when she wishes to initiate a divorce. Additionally, there are less usual types of divorce such as *li'an* and *ila*.

Divorce at the instance of the husband – *Talaq*

In countries where Islamic Family Law is uncodified, such as India and Saudi Arabia, there is no need for a husband to obtain permission from a court to divorce his wife. He can effect a divorce simply by pronouncing a *talaq* at the appropriate time and under the proper conditions. The word *talaq* means literally to snap off or to separate, and thus to sever the bond of the marriage relationship.[4] This can be done by the husband at will and without any prior formalities, providing that he observes the conditions laid down in the *Quran*. However, most Muslim countries nowadays insist on some formalities, even if it is only registration of the divorce, as is required in Pakistan.[5] In other jurisdictions, such as the Federal Territory of Malaysia, the law now requires the person seeking divorce, whether husband or wife, to approach the court for permission to divorce in the first place.[6]

The husband may pronounce *talaq* either orally or in writing. It may also be pronounced by his authorised representative. Some scholars say that neither witnesses nor the presence of the wife is necessary, but others insist that two witnesses should be present. *Talaq* should be pronounced at a time when the wife is free from her

---

4   Tanzil ur Rahman, *A Code of Muslim Personal Law*, Vol I, 1984, p 309.

5   The law in Pakistan provides that a divorce does not become absolute until 90 days after notice is given to the Chairman of the Arbitration Council. However, there are difficulties in that if the husband does not register the divorce and so legally terminate the marriage, he is free to marry again polygamously, but the wife may be charged with bigamy if she unwittingly enters into another marriage.

6   *Islamic Family Law (Federal Territory) Act* 1984 s 47. However, it appears that if the husband fails to do this, the divorce may nevertheless be effective, but the husband may convicted of an offence.

menstrual periods, so that her unavailability to him during this time should not influence the husband's decision. Some scholars hold that *talaq* pronounced while the husband is intoxicated is ineffective; others believe that it is effective nevertheless if the man has voluntarily drunk intoxicating liquor. Divorce pronounced by a mentally deranged person is ineffective.

Divorce by *talaq* may be revocable, or irrevocable. An irrevocable divorce requires three pronouncements of *talaq*, and after this the couple are unable to marry again, unless the wife first marries another man, and is divorced by him. Otherwise, after the pronouncement of one *talaq*, the husband may revoke the divorce at any time during the wife's *iddah* (waiting period after divorce), and the marriage will continue. Revocation may be by words, or by actions. Having sexual intercourse is considered to effect revocation by the Hanafis, but Imam Shafii's view was that it was first necessary for the husband to make a formal declaration of revocation in the presence of two witnesses. Some modern legislation requires the revocation to be registered.[7]

The authorities differ as to whether the wife can refuse to accept the revocation and insist on divorce. The Hanafi view is that revocation is the right of the husband and the wife has no say in it. In Malaysia, the *Islamic Family Law (Federal Territory) Act* 1984 s 51(9) provides that if a wife has not consented to the revocation, for reasons allowed by the *Shariah*, she shall not be ordered by the court to resume conjugal relations, but the court will send the matter for arbitration.

However, a divorce can only be revoked twice.[8] After the third *talaq* it becomes irrevocable. Asghar Ali Engineer says this rule was introduced to end a custom of the Arabs, in pre-Islamic times, of divorcing their wives, and taking them back time after time, so that the wife had a constant threat of divorce hanging over her.[9]

Types of *talaq*

There are three types of *talaq* – *talaq ahsan*, *talaq hasan* and *talaq bida'a*. The first two are approved types of divorce and require a period of at least three months (strictly speaking, three menstrual

---

7   For example, see *Islamic Family Law (Federal Territory) Act* (Malaysia) s 51.
8   *Quran* 2:229.
9   *The Rights of Women in Islam*, 1992, p 123.

periods) to elapse before the divorce can become final. This time allows the parties to reconsider and reconcile if possible, and it also allows time to ascertain whether the wife is pregnant, in which case the *iddah* continues until the child is born.

The *bida'a* divorce is a disapproved form and takes place where the husband pronounces three *talaqs* at the one time. This kind of divorce provides no scope for reconciliation and revocation, and becomes irrevocable as soon as it is pronounced. This disapproved or *bida'a* form is the one most often depicted in Hollywood movies where the husband simply states "I divorce you" three times on the one occasion, and the wife is irrevocably divorced. Hanafi jurists, however, consider that this triple *talaq* takes effect only as a single divorce, but the Shafiis hold that it is legal and effective, although reprehensible. The danger of this form of divorce, which is certainly against the spirit of the *Quran*, is that divorce may be pronounced in the heat of an argument, and the husband may later regret it and yet be unable to revoke it.

In the Malaysian case of *Re Mohd Hussin bin Abdul Ghani,*[10] such an event occurred. In a fit of pique the husband pronounced a triple divorce against his wife and later reconsidered and wished to revoke it. The wife was pregnant and did not wish to be divorced. Most Malays belong to the Shafii school of Islamic thought which considers the triple divorce to be legal, though reprehensible. The husband's request to the *Syariah* court to enable him to revoke the divorce was refused at first instance. On appeal, it was found that the husband followed the Hanafi school, which considers a triple divorce to count only as one *talaq*. On this ground, the husband was able to revoke the divorce and reconcile with his wife.

Arbitration

In *sura An-Nisaa*, verse 35, quoted above, the *Quran* recommends arbitration of marital disputes. Such arbitration may be informal, and undertaken, as recommended, by family members. However, if one or both of the parties approaches the court, or an official, a formal appointment of *hakam* (arbitrators) can be made. The scholars disagree concerning whether such *hakam* have the power to dissolve the marriage, and various verses of the *Quran* and *ahadith* are quoted to support one or the other view.

---

10   [1990] 2 MLJ lxxv.

However, modern legislation in several Muslim countries[11] has made formal provision for arbitration. For example, s 47 of the Malaysian Federal Territory legislation referred to above, provides that when an application for divorce is made, if the other party does not consent to the divorce, a conciliatory committee shall be appointed by the court, consisting of a religious officer and two other persons, one representing the husband and the other the wife. Preference should be given in appointing representative to close relatives who have knowledge of the case. The committee should endeavour to effect reconciliation for a period of up to six months, but if it is unable to effect reconciliation, it should issue a certificate to that effect, and the court may refer the case to *hakam* (arbitrators) under s 48.

Under s 48 *hakam* may be appointed whenever there are constant quarrels between the parties to a marriage. These *hakam* should also, where possible, be close relatives of the parties. The court may give directions to the *hakam* as to the conduct of the arbitration, and if they are unable to agree, the court may remove them and appoint other *hakam*. Ultimately, if the *hakam* believe that the couple should divorce, but are unable to persuade the husband to authorise a divorce, the court may give the *hakam* the authority to effect the divorce. Under these procedures, divorce cannot be hasty, and must be seen as a last resort.

Divorce through conversion

As we have seen, when considering the Islamic law relating to marriage, a Muslim man is prohibited from marrying any woman who is not a Muslim or a *kitabiyyah*, and a Muslim woman is not allowed to marry any man who is not a Muslim. Therefore, if one party in an existing non-Muslim marriage converts to Islam, the conversion may have the effect of dissolving the marriage. If the husband in a Christian or Jewish marriage converts to Islam and the wife does not, the marriage is not dissolved since he may legally be married to a Jewish or Christian woman. However, if his wife is a Hindu or a Buddhist, the marriage is dissolved. If the wife converts, as happened in the Malaysian case of *Pedley v Majlis Ugama Pulau Pinang*,[12] the marriage is automatically dissolved after three months according to

---

11   For example: Iraq, Egypt, Tunisia, Morocco, Jordan and Syria.
12   [1990] 2 MLJ 307.

Islamic law. The three month period is allowed to give the non-converting spouse the opportunity to consider conversion also.

A particular problem exists in Malaysia, in that the *Law Reform (Marriage and Divorce) Act* 1976,[13] which governs the family law of non-Muslims, lists conversion to Islam as a ground which entitles the non-converting spouse to petition for divorce, but does not give any such right to the party who converts. At the same time the convert cannot divorce his or her spouse in the *Shariah* court, since the *Shariah* court has no jurisdiction over non-Muslims. The *Islamic Family Law (Federal Territory) Act* s 46(2) specifically states that dissolution of marriage by conversion is not effective until confirmed by the court. However, in Pakistan it has been decided that the right of a Muslim husband to divorce his wife by *talaq* has not been taken away by statute and could validly dissolve a marriage solemnised in England under the *Marriage Act* 1949.[14]

Divorce at the instance of the wife

Asghar Ali Engineer says:

> It is very unfortunate that Islam intended to give a woman equal status not only in marital contracts but also in matters of divorce; but the jurists, either enamoured by speculative reason, or dictated by old traditions, or influenced by male domination or swayed by temporary considerations, undermined the woman's position, enforcing arbitrary rules of divorce which went against her interests. She came to depend on the mercy of her husband in matters of divorce.[15]

Most of the traditional jurists placed insuperable obstacles in the way of a wife who wished to initiate divorce. The view of the jurists was that divorce was the prerogative of the husband, and they interpreted references in the *Quran* and *hadith* to the wife's right to divorce very narrowly. As a result, under the Hanafi rules in the Ottoman Empire and in India up to 1939 when the *Dissolution of Muslim Marriages Act* was passed, a Muslim woman was virtually unable to obtain a divorce, and the same situation prevailed over almost the whole Muslim world.

---

13   Section 51.
14   *Marina Jatoi v Nuruddin K Jatoi* PLD 1967 Sc 580 discussed in Ahmad Ibrahim, "The need to amend s 51 of the Law Reform (Marriage and Divorce) Act 1976", [1990] 2 *MLJ* lviii.
15   Asghar Ali Engineer, *The Rights of Women in Islam*, 1992, p 126.

Today, most Muslim countries have enacted legislation allowing divorce initiated by the wife. However, a wife must obtain a divorce through the court in all circumstances. The *Quran* does not say why husbands were traditionally allowed the right of extra-judicial divorce and wives were not. 'Abdur Rahman i Doi has an interesting theory:[16]

> A woman's psychological and physiological make-up is such that every month for a period of five to seven days she is in a state of pathological change. . . There is greater impressionability, greater suggestibility, and, to a variable extent, diminished self-control. . . It is also during this period that, to those women who are pre-disposed to them, certain caprices, fits of ill-temper, moods of depression, impulses of jealousy, and outbursts of self-confession, are more likely to occur. Also during this period when a woman is exceptionally sensitive and irritable, she may be upset by trivial matters which at other times would provoke no discernible response.

Thus, Professor Doi concludes that "[i]f women were given the power of unilateral divorce, it is probable that millions of them would divorce their husbands and it is probable that millions of divorces would have ensued and there would be chaos in society". A study of the reasons for divorce in a jurisdiction which allows equality to men and women in initiating divorce proceedings might be illuminating!

Khula'

Khula' is divorce by redemption. It is founded on the *hadith* about Jamila, the wife of Sabit b Qais who came to the Prophet and said that although she could not find any fault in her husband, she could simply not stand the sight of him, and she wanted a divorce. The Prophet told Sabit to divorce her on the condition that she returned to Sabit the garden he had given her as her marriage gift. Thus, according to the modern interpretation of this *hadith*, a wife who wants a divorce on the grounds of incompatibility can request the court to grant a divorce on condition that she returns her *mahr*.

In another *hadith* reported by Al-Bukhari, a woman named Burairah asked for *khula'*. The Prophet asked her to take her husband back. She turned down the Prophet's request and insisted on her right to divorce.

However, some of the jurists, for example, Imam Shafii, interpreted these *hadith* to mean that the wife could only obtain *khula'* if the husband consented to it, and so closed off this way for women

---

16   *Women in the Shari'ah*, 1992, pp 94-95.

to escape from loveless or violent marriages. This became the traditional interpretation of the law for many centuries. Even the Indian jurist, Maulana Abul A'ala Maududi, who is certainly not known as a champion of women's rights, criticised this interpretation. Writing about the state of affairs in India in 1941, he said that it created great injustice and was contrary to the intention of Islam in that it left a woman at the mercy of her husband. If the court could not grant a divorce to the wife:

> the helpless women who are refused Khula, must either resign themselves to life-long misery, or commit suicide. The other alternatives before them are to satisfy their natural passions through sin or get rid of the marriage bond through apostasy.[17]

Fortunately, two decisions of the courts in Pakistan in 1959[18] and 1967[19] reversed the traditional view and allowed the wife divorce by *khula'* without the husband's consent. The court said that a wife should not apply for *khula'* on some flimsy pretext, but she does not have to prove any ill-treatment to obtain it. It is sufficient if the court can be convinced that the parties are unable to observe "the limits of Allah" in their marriage.

The basis of a divorce by *khula'* is that the wife must "buy her freedom" by returning something of value to the husband. Normally, this is whatever she has received by way of *mahr*, though some jurists hold that the husband can demand more than this. Most agree that where the wife seeks divorce because of ill-treatment by the husband, she should not have to pay him anything.

A divorce by *khula'* is irrevocable. This kind of divorce is called *cerai tebus talak* in Malaysia.

Where the husband and wife mutually agree to a divorce, it is called *mubarat*. It is otherwise similar to *khula'*.

Talaq-i-Tafwid or Ta'liq

This is a delegated divorce. It commonly exists where the wife has included in her marriage contract a condition that the husband delegates his right of divorce to the wife so that she can exercise it herself when any of the conditions of the marriage contact are

---

17 Maulana Abul A'ala Maudoodi, *The Laws of Marriage and Divorce in Islam*, 1987 edn, p 45.
18 *Balquis Fatima v Najmul Ikram* PLD (1959) Lah 566.
19 *Kurshid Bibi v Muhammad Amin* PLD (1967) SC 97.

violated. Thus the wife may reserve the right to divorce herself in this way if the husband takes a second wife, or fails to pay her maintenance of a specified amount or for a stated period. This right can be delegated to the wife at the time of marriage, or afterwards, and may be conditional or unconditional. According to the Hanifis and Malikis, such a divorce is irrevocable. Imam Shafii believed that whether the divorce was revocable or not depended on the intention of the husband at the time the right was delegated to the wife.[20]

In Malaysia delegated divorce is called *ta'liq* and it has been put into statutory form in the Islamic Family law enactments of the various States. The common practice is that when the parties are married, the husband signs a *ta'liq* certificate immediately after the solemnisation of the marriage in the presence of the *kadi* and witnesses, and the certificate is entered into the official marriage register. The certificate usually provides that if the husband leaves the wife or fails to pay her maintenance for a specified period (usually four months), she may approach the court to seek confirmation of the *ta'liq*. If the court finds the wife's complaint is true, and the wife pays $1.00 to the court, the couple are divorced. If the husband denies the allegation, the court will hold a hearing of the matter.

Fasakh

Fasakh is a divorce, more in the nature of an annulment, which can be obtained by the wife (or by the husband according to some scholars) through the court where there is fault on the other side. It is not common for applications for *fasakh* to be made by husbands, since they have the easier alternative of *talaq*. There are differences between the schools as to the grounds upon which *fasakh* can be obtained.

Grounds for *fasakh* – apostasy

Apostasy is a common ground. If the husband converts to another religion, the marriage is at an end, since a Muslim woman cannot legally be married to anyone other than a Muslim. If the wife converts to Judaism or Christianity, the marriage continues, since a Muslim man can legally marry a *kitabiyyah*. If she converts to some other religion, the marriage is at an end.

---

20   Tanzil ur Rahman, *A Code of Muslim Personal Law*, Vol I, 1984, p 351.

Impotency, insanity or certain diseases

Other grounds are impotency. leprosy and insanity, though some of the traditional jurists refused relief for these reasons, however serious the handicap. In the case of impotency of the husband, which was unknown to the wife at the time of marriage, some jurists require that a period of one year be allowed for treatment of the husband's condition, before the marriage can be dissolved. They hold that the same period of time should be allowed when the husband is insane. Maulana Maududi has noted that these conditions have no support from the *Quran* or the *Sunnah*.[21]

Absence on the part of the husband

Differences exist between the jurists concerning the situation where the husband has gone missing without explanation. According to some of the traditional Hanafi jurists, a woman must wait until she receives certain knowledge of her husband's death, or at least until persons of his age would normally have passed away, before she can consider the marriage at an end. This may require her to wait until he would have attained the age of 90 years, though there are different opinions on the length of a normal life span.

Others allow the *qadi* to dissolve the marriage after a reasonable time has elapsed on presumption of death. The Maliki view is that four years is the appropriate time in cases of unknown whereabouts, while different considerations apply if the husband is known to have been taken prisoner in war time or to have disappeared in battle. The Hanafis, Shafiis and Zahiris would not, traditionally, admit a wife's right to dissolution on the ground of her husband's imprisonment; the Malikis and Hanbalis and some Shia *ulema* would permit the wife to ask for separation on this ground.

Cruelty

The traditional jurists did not include cruelty as a ground for *fasakh*. At best, their view was that a complaint of cruelty on the wife's part should lead to the appointment of arbitrators, relying on the *Quran*ic verse which says:[22]

---

21   Maulana Abul A'Ala Maududi, *The Laws of Marriage and Divorce in Islam*, 1983, p 87.
22   4:128.

If a wife fears cruelty or desertion on her husband's part,
There is no blame on them if they arrange an amicable settlement
between themselves; and such settlement is best;

Whether a divorce could be obtained, then depended on whether the prevailing view in that place was that the *hakam* had power to order a divorce. If not, the wife was left without a remedy, though some jurists would allow her to obtain a *khula'*. This, of course, required that she buy her freedom by returning her *mahr*, and perhaps more than that. Until relatively recently, it was all but impossible for a wife to obtain a divorce on the ground of cruelty.

Modern legislation has altered this situation. In India and Pakistan, the *Dissolution of Muslim Marriages Act* 1939 provided for cruelty to be a ground for divorce. In the Middle East, legislation in Iraq, Egypt, Tunisia, Morocco, Jordan and Syria provide for judicial divorce where cruelty is proven. In Southeast Asia, cruelty is a ground for *fasakh* under the *Islamic Family Law (Federal Territory) Act* in Malaysia,[23] and under the Philippines *Code of Muslim Personal Laws*,[24] but not under the Kelantan enactment, since Kelantan tends to follow more closely the traditional view of the Shafii school which did not allow *fasakh* on this ground.

Failure to pay maintenance

Where the wife seeks dissolution on the ground that the husband has failed to pay her maintenance, as is his obligation under Islamic law, the traditional jurists of the Hanafi school would not allow her a divorce. The Maliki school would allow *fasakh* on this ground after the husband, if able to be contacted, was given a reasonable time to pay. The Shafii allow dissolution where the husband is completely insolvent, but not where he has means and refuses to pay, as the wife has a legal right to enforce payment. A minority view of the Shafii school is that the wife can obtain dissolution after she has not been able to receive maintenance for three days.[25]

---

23   Section 52(h).
24   Articles 52(f), 53.
25   Ahmad Ibrahim, "Fasakh for Failure to Maintain", [1970] *Journal of Malaysian and Comparative Law* 329 at 332-3.

Modern legislation

Fortunately for Muslim wives, modern jurists are much more kindly disposed towards a wife's application for *fasakh*, and have allowed relatively broad grounds. Dissolution is allowed on the ground of the husband's imprisonment in Egypt, Iraq, Jordan, Syria, Pakistan, Malaysia and the Philippines, though the term of imprisonment required varies from one year (Federal Territory, Malaysia and the Philippines) to seven years (Pakistan and Kelantan). Dissolution by *fasakh* is also now allowed by legislation on the ground of cruelty, as mentioned above.

The *Islamic Family Law (Federal Territory) Act* 1984[26] of Malaysia lists twelve separate grounds for *fasakh*, including impotence, imprisonment for a period of three years or more, that the whereabouts of the husband have not been known for one year, failure of the husband to provide maintenance for three months, refusal to consummate the marriage and lack of consent.

Other Types of Divorce: *Li'an* and *'Ila*

A divorce by *li'an* takes place where the husband accuses his wife of adultery by a process of making four oaths that she has committed adultery, followed by a fifth oath calling down the wrath of God upon himself if he is lying. The wife, in turn, denies that she has been adulterous under oath in the same manner. *Li'an* can be invoked where there is no positive evidence of adultery to put before the court, or insufficient evidence. *Li'an* is an exception to the rule in Islamic law that failure to prove adultery results in the person making the accusation being punished by 80 lashes for the crime of *qazf*. This form of divorce is not common and the jurists disagree about whether it is revocable.

A divorce by *'Ila* takes place where the husband takes an oath to abstain from sexual intercourse with his wife for a period of four months or more. According to the Hanafis, a divorce takes place automatically at the end of this time. According to the other schools, the *qadi* should ask the man to resume his married relationship with his wife, and if he refuses, the *qadi* dissolves the marriage. The divorce is irrevocable.

---

26   Section 52.

According to Tanzil ur-Rahman, divorce by *'ila* is rare in India and Pakistan but it is still enforceable.[27]

The Option of Puberty (*Khiyar al-Butugh*)

Another possible way of ending a marriage, in Hanafi law, is through the option of puberty. This only applies to the marriage of a minor arranged by a guardian other than the father or paternal grandfather of the minor, or by the father or paternal grandfather if they have acted negligently or fraudulently. According to the Malikis and Shafiis, a marriage contracted by any other guardian is invalid, and so the question does not arise.

The minor has the right to repudiate the marriage immediately upon attaining puberty providing that the marriage has not been consummated, or that it was consummated without her consent. However the marriage does not come to an end until the court issues a decree.

In India, where child marriages have been common, this rule of Islamic law has been put into statutory form, as regards the rights of females, in the *Dissolution of Muslim Marriages Act* 1939, and there has been considerable litigation in respect of it. According to the act, the age of puberty is to be taken to be 16 years.

Void (*batil*) marriages

It is also possible that a marriage may be found to have been void from the start, as if it had never existed in the first place. This is possible under Islamic law as it is under the common law. A void marriage is one which is performed even though some perpetual impediment exists, for example, when the parties may be within the prohibited degrees of relationship with each other. No legal relationship is formed by such a marriage, and children, if any, are illegitimate.

The consequences of divorce: *Iddah* and *Muta'ah*
Iddah

Iddah is the period of waiting which a Muslim woman must go through before she can remarry after divorce, or the death of her

---

27   *A Code of Muslim Personal Law,* Vol I, 1984, pp 498-501.

husband. After divorce, it is usually three months, but if she is pregnant, it lasts until the child is born. If the woman is widowed the period of *iddah* is four months and ten days. There is no *iddah* if the wife is divorced before the marriage is consummated.

The purpose of *iddah* is to ensure that the wife is not pregnant at the time of the divorce. The husband must maintain the divorced wife during the period of *iddah*, and she is entitled to live in his house. There is a difference of opinion as to whether a widow is obliged to live in the deceased husband's house during *iddah*, or whether she can please herself where she resides. Both widows and divorced women are free to remarry once the period of *iddah* is completed.[28]

The *Quran* says that a man who has divorced his wife must continue to maintain her at the same standard as he enjoys during *iddah*:[29]

> Let women in *iddah* live in the same style as you live, according to your means: Annoy them not so as to restrict them. And if they carry (life within their wombs), then spend (your substance) on them until they deliver their burden: and if they suckle your (offspring), give them their recompense. . .

The question of whether a divorced woman is entitled to maintenance after the expiry of *iddah* is controversial. The *Quran* says:[30]

> For divorced women maintenance should be provided on a reasonable (scale). This is a duty on the righteous.

The majority of jurists have held that this duty comes to an end when the *iddah* is completed. After that the divorced woman should rely on her own resources, or if she has none, on her parents or other male relatives to provide for her. As a last resort, if she is destitute, the state should provide for her support through the *bait ul-mal* or public treasury. In theory, the woman is entitled to receive the balance of her unpaid *mahr*, if any, on divorce, but, as we have seen, in practice this may be an illusory right if the amount she has received is nominal, or if she has been prevailed upon to remit it to the husband as is the custom in some countries. She is, of course, entitled to call on the former husband for full maintenance of any children.

A huge controversy erupted over this matter in India in 1985, in the wake of the *Shah Bano* case,[31] when the Indian Supreme Court

---

28   *Quran* 2:234.
29   65:6.
30   2:241.
31   *Md Ahmed Khan v Shah Bano Begum* AIR (1985) SC 945.

awarded an elderly divorced woman a small amount of maintenance beyond the period of *iddah*. Riots broke out as Indian Muslims saw the decision as unwarranted interference by the court in their personal law. Eventually under pressure, the government enacted a law to overturn the decision. The opposition to the award of maintenance in the *Shah Bano* case illustrates the conservative nature of Muslim thought in India, which was prepared to allow injustice to be perpetuated against women on the excuse that the rules formulated by the medieval jurists cannot be changed to take modern realities into account.

Asghar Ali Engineer points out that the *Quran* has not fixed any time limit for maintenance,[32] nor does it place any limit on its amount. It is the interpretation of the Medieval jurists which limits it to the period of *iddah*. This may result in injustice as in Muslim societies women have generally been strongly discouraged from pursuing a career of their own, and, in practice, custom has intervened to ensure that they do not receive anything substantial by way of *mahr*. Thus, a divorce may leave them without means and unemployable, dependent on the charity of relatives or the state.

Where the woman is widowed, the *Quran* says:[33]

> Those of you who die and leave widows should bequeath for their widows a year's maintenance and residence;

According to the Maliki school a widow is not entitled to maintenance, although she is entitled to accommodation in her husband's house during *iddah*. This is said to be because her right of inheritance supervenes.[34] However, the Hanafis allow her maintenance. In view of the fact that the widow's share of the husband's estate is as little as one eighth, if she has children, and only one quarter if she does not, this does not seem overly generous.

Muta'ah

Muta'ah is a consolatory gift which the husband must pay to a wife when he divorces her without fault on her part. Its origin lies in the *Quran*ic verses which says:[35]

---

32   Asghar Ali Engineer, *The Rights of Women in Islam*, 1992, p 130.
33   2:240.
34   'Abdur Rahman i Doi, *Women in Shari'ah*, 1990, p 106.
35   2:236.

> There is no blame on you if you divorce women before consummation
> or the fixation of their dower; But bestow on them (a suitable gift)
> The wealthy according to his means and the poor according to his
> means;
> A gift of a reasonable amount is due from those who wish to do the
> right things.

According to the Hanafi school, *muta'ah* was limited to the situations where the wife was divorced before consummation or fixation of her dower, but in Malaysia where the Shafii school prevails, *muta'ah* is payable in the case of every divorced woman who is divorced by her husband when there is no fault on her part. It is said that *muta'ah* is a consolatory gift which is meant to console the wife for any shame she might feel because of the divorce, to remove any false accusations and to help her in starting up her life again.[36]

In Malaysia, there have been many cases concerning *muta'ah*, and the courts have ordered some quite large amounts to be paid to divorced wives. The parties may agree on the amount to be paid, but if they do not, the court can assess the amount, taking into account the financial position of the husband and the needs of the wife. Malaysian women are generally better off on divorce than women in some other Muslim countries because of the Malay custom of *harta sepencarian*, which intervenes to give a divorced wife either a half or one third share in any property acquired by the spouses during the marriage.

A comparison with Western divorce laws

Professor Ahmad Ibrahim[37] has remarked that in the present day, Western divorce laws have gradually become more like Islamic law in many ways. Until at least the middle of the 19th century, divorce was, to all intents and purposes, legally unobtainable in Western countries, and remained so, until very recently in countries such as Italy and Ireland where the Roman Catholic church is influential. When statutes were first passed permitting divorce in Britain and other common law countries, the "fault" notion was paramount. To obtain a divorce one party had to prove some matrimonial fault such as cruelty, desertion or adultery, and for women adultery was available as a ground only if coupled with another "fault" ground. It was not until 1975 in Australia that the *Family Law Act* allowed irretrievable breakdown as the sole

---

36   Per Hj Harussani b Jaki Zakaria in *Noor Bee v Ahmad Sanusi* [1979] JH(2) 63.
37   Dean of the Faculty of Law at the International University, Malaysia, and a renowned Muslim scholar.

ground for divorce and permitted divorce by agreement between the spouses. Similar developments occurred in Britain and the United States and many other Western countries about the same time. Much emphasis is now placed upon mediation and arbitration in resolving family law disputes in these jurisdictions.

In Islamic law, divorce has always been permitted, although it has been easier for men to divorce their wives than vice versa. A husband could divorce his wife extra-judicially when he considered the marriage had broken down, but the wife has to approach the court with a reason to obtain *fasakh* or prepared to return her marriage gift to be granted a divorce by *khula'*. Indeed, at times, through the interpretations of the Medieval jurists, the right to initiate divorce was taken away from Muslim wives altogether in practice, though in most Muslim countries this is no longer the case. Again this difference between the sexes offends against modern Western ideas of equality. However, the modern trend is to restrict the unfettered right of the husband to divorce and to require all applications for divorce to be dealt with through the courts.

8

INHERITANCE, WILLS AND *WAQF*

The common law allows people almost complete freedom to dispose of their worldly goods by will as they please, subject only to whatever Testators Family Maintenance or Family Provision legislation which may exist in a particular jurisdiction. Such legislation normally only allows a claim to be made against the estate by a near relative who can prove that he or she was dependent on the deceased and had a just expectation of being provided for in his estate. Claims by infant children and by dependent spouses, legal or de facto, who have been left little or nothing in the will, may succeed. Claims by adult children usually do not.

A person may leave his whole estate to charity, or to his favourite barmaid or to a complete stranger, and his adult, non-dependent family have no redress. Alternatively, the testator may favour one family member over others by giving that person a greater share of the estate and the others cannot challenge the will, unless they can bring themselves within the classes of people permitted to apply under the above legislation, or prove that the testator was not of sound mind or subject to duress or undue influence when the will was made.

Only if the deceased person has not made a will, does the law intervene with a statutory distribution to next of kin, beginning with the surviving spouse and children, and in their absence, moving to parents and other more distant relatives, depending on the laws of the particular jurisdiction. If there is no surviving relative entitled to inherit, then the estate passes to the state *bona vacantia*.

The situation is completely different in Islamic law. A testator may dispose of only one third of his or her estate by will. The rest must be divided among the heirs in accordance with the rules of *faraid* (prescribed portions) laid down in the *Quran* and developed and interpreted by the jurists.

The development of the Islamic law of inheritance

In pre-Islamic Arabia, the custom was that only men capable of bearing arms and fighting in defence of the tribe were entitled to inherit. Children and females were incapable of inheriting, and indeed, women were themselves often inherited as property, regardless of their wishes, by the heir of their deceased husband or father. Adoption was a common practice among the Arabs and adopted sons could inherit along with natural sons, provided that they were capable of bearing arms. Men could also make an alliance to inherit from each other.[1]

The coming of Islam resulted in drastic changes to these customary rules. The new laws were revealed in the *Quran* in stages, and in response to certain circumstances. In *Sura Al-Baqarah* 2:180, the believers are instructed, when death approaches, to make a bequest of any goods the might have to parents and next of kin. In *Sura An-Nisaa*, 4:7, 11 and 12, the details of the new scheme are set out:

- Males and females are each entitled to a share of inheritance, regardless of the size of the estate.

- A daughter's share is to be half that of a son's.

- If there are only daughters, two or more are to share two thirds of the estate; if there is only one daughter, she receives one half.

- Parents, both mother and father, are each entitled to one sixth, if there are children, but if there are no children, and the parents are the only heirs, the mother receives one third. If the deceased left brothers and sisters, the mother receives one sixth.

- A husband is entitled to a half share of his wife's estate, if there are no children; if there are children, the husband's share is one quarter.

---

1   Jamal J Nasir, *The Islamic Law of Personal Status*, 1986, p 196.

- A wife is entitled to one quarter share of her husband's estate if there are no children; if there are children, she receives one eighth.

- If the deceased has left neither ascendants or descendants, but has a brother and/or a sister who survive him, each gets one sixth, but if there are more than two, they share in a third of the estate.

- In every case, debts and legacies must be paid before the estate is distributed among the heirs.

In the same *Sura*, verse 19, men are forbidden to inherit women, and in *Sura Ahzab* 33: 4 and 5, the right of the adopted son to inherit is revoked.

The *Quran*ic rules were complemented by the *Sunnah*, and the interpretations of the learned jurists over the ages, so that the following additional principles have been devised:

- Uterine kindred have priority in inheritance over consanguine kindred.

- No Muslim can inherit from a non-Muslim. No non-Muslim may inherit from a Muslim. This is the orthodox Sunni view, but it is permitted by the Shia. However, a legacy under a will may be left to a non-Muslim relative or friend.

- No murderer may inherit from his victim. Accidental homicide does not prevent inheritance.

- A child has a right to inherit as soon as he or she is born alive. If a child is *en ventre sa mere* at the time of the deceased's passing, a share of the estate is to be set aside for the child until he or she is born.

- A grand-mother is to receive one sixth of the estate if there is no mother.

- A maternal uncle may inherit if there is no other heir.

- Illegitimate children cannot inherit, and cannot be inherited from.

- The child of a mother divorced by *li'an* may inherit from the mother and her heirs.

Rules concerning exclusion from inheritance

- Nearer in relationship excludes those who are remoter, for example a father excludes a grandfather.

- A person who is related to the deceased person through another is excluded by the presence of that other, for example a father excludes a brother. However, a mother does not exclude a brother or sister.

- Full blood excludes the half blood, but uterine relations are not excluded on this ground.

Components of the estate

As in the common law, in Islamic law, the deceased person's estate can be made up of property of various kinds. It may include:

- real and movable property;

- debts due to the deceased, including *diyat* (blood money), and revenue from *waqfs* (charitable foundations);

- rights such as water rights and rights of way;

- rights under a contract.

Charges on the estate in order of priority

According to the Hanbalis, Shias and some of the Hanafis, these are, in order:

- funeral costs and burial expenses;

- debts of the deceased;

- valid and effective legacies up to the amount of one third of the estate;

- shares of the heirs.

The Malikis and Shafiis and some other Hanafis place payment of the debts first in priority.

Classes of heirs

The Sunnis categorise heirs into three classes:

(a) Sharers – these are entitled to a fixed share of the estate. The sharers are enumerated as:
- (i) husband;
- (ii) wife;
- (iii) father;
- (iv) mother;

(v)   true grandfather and true grandmother;[2]
(vi)   daughter;
(vii)   son's daughter;
(viii)   full sister;
(ix)   consanguine sister;
(x)   uterine brother and uterine sister.

(b) Residuaries – these are entitled to the residue after the claims of the sharers have been met. They will be entitled to the whole estate if there are no surviving sharers.

Residuaries in their own right are:

(i)   sons and sons' sons – male descendants, with in certain cases, female descendants of equal rank;
(ii)   male ascendants;
(iii)   full and consanguine brothers and sisters;
(iv)   full and consanguine paternal uncles, grand-uncles and their male descendants;

Residuaries through another (all females who need a residuary in his own right to share with):

(i)   daughter with the son;
(ii)   son's daughter with an equal or lower son's son;
(iii)   full sister with a full brother;
(iv)   consanguine sister with a consanguine brother.

(c) Distant relations who do not fall into either of the two above classes. They are entitled to inherit if there are no surviving heirs of the other classes. They are themselves divided into four classes:

(i)   Descendants of the deceased through a female link – daughter's children and grandchildren and son's daughter's children and grandchildren
(ii)   Ascendants of the deceased through a female link – mother's father and mother etc.
(iii)   Descendants of the deceased's parents who are not sharers or residuaries – children of sisters, brother's daughters, sons of uterine brothers and their children
(iv)   Descendants of the deceased's immediate grand-parents ie paternal and maternal aunts and uncles and

---

2   A "true" grandfather and grandmother is an ancestor in the male line, without any female intervening in the line.

their children, paternal grandfather's uncles and aunts and similar relatives.

It can be a very complex matter to determine who is entitled to what proportion of the estate of a deceased person. In some Muslim countries, a declaration as to entitlement is sought from a religious court before distribution of the estate.

The missing person

If a person is entitled to a share in inheritance, but his or her whereabouts cannot be discovered, the estate should be divided on the basis that the person is alive, until it is established definitely whether or not they are alive or dead. If the person is dead, but it is proved that they died after the deceased, the share will go to their heirs of the missing person. If that person predeceases the deceased, there is no entitlement to any share.

Shia rules

These are somewhat different from those of the Sunni school. The Shia do not distinguish between people related to the deceased through agnates and those related by consanguinity. The Shias recognise only two grounds for inheritance, a prescribed share and kinship, in contrast to the three recognised by the Sunnis.

The residue of the estate -*Al- Radd*

If there is any residue left after the sharers have received their share, and there is no one entitled to it, according to some jurists, such as the Hanafi and Hanbali jurists, this residue is to be divided proportionally between the sharers. According to others, for example the Shafii, it will revert to the Public Treasury, the *Bait ul-Mal*, since it would be going against the *Quran* to give any sharer more than the amount allotted in the *Quran*. Some other jurists would divide the residue between only some of the sharers.[3]

---

3   For a detailed explanation of this, see 'Abdur Rahman i Doi, *Shari'ah: The Islamic Law*, 1984, pp 322-324.

Wills and bequests (*Wasiyyah*)

The meaning of the word *wasiyyah* is very similar to the English word "will" in that it refers to a direction by a person as to the disposal of his or her property after death. The difference lies in the fact that the Muslim testator, unlike the testator in common law countries, is permitted to dispose of only one third of the estate by will. The rest of it, as we have seen above, must be divided among the heirs in accordance with Islamic law.

The origin of the rule limiting bequests by will to one third of the estate lies in a *hadith* concerning a wealthy man named Sa'd ibn Abi Waqqas who became gravely ill. He had only a daughter to inherit from him, and he asked the Prophet if he could leave all his estate to charity. The Prophet said no. The Prophet allowed him to leave one third of his wealth to charity, and the rest had to go to his heirs. From this *hadith*, the jurists deduced a general rule and made it applicable to all Muslims.

The form of the will

According to some jurists, the will may be oral, or in writing or even made by an intelligible gesture if the testator is mute and illiterate. However, the Malikis require that a will must be in the form of a written document. An oral will has obvious difficulties of proof, and so most modern Muslim countries require by legislation that a will be in writing or be capable of proof by writing.[4] The will need not be signed or formally attested, provided that the intention of the testator is clear.

A will must not contravene *Shariah* law. Thus, a gift to a mistress will be void.

A will may be made subject to conditions. An invalid condition will not render the whole will void, but will itself be void.

The capacity of the testator

To make a valid will, a person must be adult, of sound mind and making the will of his own volition. Some schools will allow a will to be made by a person under the normal age of majority, or a person

---

4   Jamil Nasir, *The Islamic Law of Personal Status*, 1986, p 239.

under interdiction for prodigality subject to a court order, or in particular circumstances.

According to the Hanafis, if the testator becomes insane and remains so until death, the will shall be void by.

The beneficiary

The beneficiary of a will may be an individual or group of individuals, an organisation or an amount may be designated for some specified purpose, for example the upkeep of an animal, or the maintenance of a mosque. The beneficiary must be:

- identifiable;
- in existence at the time of making the will;
- not a belligerent;
- not the murderer of the testator or accomplice;
- not an heir.

The beneficiary may be identified by name or by an adequate description. Where a will is made in such terms as "to the children of A", the majority of Sunni jurists require that to be included, a child must be in existence at the time of the testator's death. An unborn child must be born within six months of the testator's death to qualify. However, the Malikis and Shias allow a longer time. The Shias require that the embryo must have been in existence at the time of the will being made.

There is much disagreement among the jurists concerning the last requirement, that the beneficiary not be an heir. Some jurists hold that a gift to an heir is absolutely void; others that it is valid provided that it is less than one third of the estate, and others that it is valid only if within the one third of the estate and if the other heirs consent. The last opinion is held by the majority of the schools, other than the Ithna-Asharis, Zahiris and Zaidis.[5]

The bequest made by the will

The property left by will may be real or personal property, money or any other kind of goods or rights which can normally be inherited. These must be in existence at the time of the testator's death, even if

---

5   Ibid p 243.

not in existence at the time the will is made. A gift cannot be made by will of objects forbidden such as wine, pigs, or other things which are considered *haram*. A gift cannot be made by will of things which are public property such as rivers, air and wild creatures.

A bequest may not exceed one third of the estate, after payment of funeral expenses and debts, unless the heirs agree. If some, but not all of the heirs agree, the bequest will be paid from the shares of the heirs who consent to it only.

The mandatory will

This is a provision found in the legislation of most modern Muslim countries in the Middle East for the benefit of grandchildren whose parents predecease the grandparents, who would not otherwise inherit from them. It deems that such grandchildren have been bequeathed the share of the estate which would otherwise have gone to their parents. The authority for it is the *Quran*ic verse 2:180 which reads:

> It is prescribed for you, when one of you approaches death, if he leave
> any goods that he make a bequest to parents and next of kin,
> According to reasonable usage;
> This is due from the God-fearing.

It might be noted that according to many jurists the obligation to make a bequest in favour of parents was abrogated by the later verses of the *Quran* which appointed parents heirs, but it was confirmed for people not entitled to inherit.[6]

Bequests made during death-illness (*mard al-mawt*)

When a person is in his death sickness, Islamic law intervenes to protect the rights of his heirs. A bequest or a gift in such circumstances is considered valid only to the extent of one third of the estate.

Revocation of the will

A will may be revoked by a later will, or by an express declaration revoking the will, or if the testator acts in some way inconsistent with the bequest, for example if he sells or gives away the property bequeathed to another person during his lifetime.

---

6   'Abdur Rahman i Doi, *Women in Shari'ah,* 1990, p 332.

Criticisms of the Islamic law of inheritance

Major criticisms are that:

1. The provision for the surviving widow is inadequate. The widower receives one half of his deceased wife's estate if there are no children, and one quarter if there are children. The widow receives only one quarter in the absence of children and one eighth if there are children. If there is more than one widow, they must share the widow's proportion between them.

2. Females, generally, receive only half the share of a male. Where there are both sons and daughters surviving the deceased, the sons receive twice as much as the daughters.

3. While the law is even-handed and prevents favouritism between relatives, it does not provide for special circumstances which warrant one child, for example, receiving more than the others. This may be quite reasonable in the case of a disabled child.

The answer given by Islamic scholars to these criticisms is as follows:[7]

1. The widow is entitled to receive her deferred dower (*mahr*) on her husband's death. Receipt of this amount should help make financial provision for her. However, in cases where custom or otherwise has intervened to induce the wife to waive the deferred dower, or in South-East Asia where amounts of dower paid are customarily small and paid promptly, this provision is unlikely to assist.

2. The children of the deceased have an obligation to maintain the widow. However, this leaves the widow dependent on the goodwill of her children. In a good Muslim family there should be no reluctance on the part of the children to contribute to the mother's support. However, in practice, some families may fall short of the ideal.

3. A female does not have social and family obligations to maintain other relatives. The obligation to support the women of the family is placed upon males – fathers, sons, brothers and even uncles. In theory a wife, sister or daughter would almost never have to support herself, therefore, the argument goes, she can always of right, call upon a male relative to provide for her. A Muslim

---

7   See, for example, S Khalid Rashid, *Muslim Law*, 1990, pp 231-234.

woman is entitled to keep her own property, whether received as inheritance or otherwise, for herself, and is not obliged to support herself out of it.

4. In traditional Muslim societies, (as in most societies anywhere in the world, ancient or modern) the reality is that the husband will be more likely to have gained more personal wealth than the wife, remembering that there is no community of property between spouses in Islamic law. Therefore the wife is likely to receive arithmetically more from her husband that he will receive from her if she predeceases him, even though her proportion is less.

5. A husband or father can make provision for his wife and daughters after his death by making gifts to them during his lifetime. There is no limitation on his power of gift. Provision can be made for a disabled child in the same way. The opinion of those jurists who hold that it is permissible for a bequest up to one third of the estate to be made in favour of an heir allows for greater flexibility to take account of special family circumstances.

Gifts – *Hibah*

Whilst inheritance is strictly defined and controlled under Islamic law, there are few restrictions on the making of gifts during a person's lifetime. To be valid, a gift must:

• be declared by the donor;

• be accepted by the donee, personally or through an agent;

• be delivered by the donor to the donee.

A gift may be made to any person, although gifts to the poor (*sadaqa*) are especially recommended. If a gift is made to one child, then it is recommended that a similar gift be made to other children, so that they are treated equally by their parents. It is considered reprehensible for a parent to give all his or her property to one child, excluding the others. Husbands and wives can make gifts to each other. Gifts can be made to and received from non-Muslims. Gifts can be made in favour of charity or an institution, and may amount to the whole of a person's property.

If a gift is made by a person on his death bed (*mard al-mawt*), such a gift is treated as a bequest and cannot exceed one third of the estate. It is also subject to the consent of the heirs, since it should not deprive the heirs of their legitimate rights.[8]

Waqf

According to Muslim scholars, *waqf* is the permanent dedication by a Muslim of any property for religious or charitable purposes, or for the benefit of the founder and his descendants, in such a way that the owner's right is extinguished, and the property is considered to belong to God.[9] Establishment of a *waqf* is voluntary.

There are two types of *waqf*:

- *Waqf al Ahli* – family *waqf*. This kind is created for the benefit of the founder and his relatives to provide for their needs during their lifetime, and after their death, to be used for charitable purposes.

- *Waqf al-Khayri*. This kind of *waqf* is created for religious and/or charitable purposes from the outset. It may be for the welfare of poor people or for the establishment and/or upkeep of a mosque, hospital, cemetery, or other public facility.

The person who is appointed to administer the *waqf* is called the *mutawali*, and is often, in the first place, the founder. The founder may appoint another *mutawali* to succeed him, or in his stead, and if the founder does not do so, a *mutawali* can be appointed by a judge. Such an appointment would often, but not necessarily, be of a relative of the founder. A woman or a non-Muslim may be a *mutawali*. The *mutawali* can receive a salary for his services.

Conditions for the establishment of a *waqf*

1. The property dedicated to the *waqf* must be in existence and owned by the founder (*waqif*) at the time the *waqf* is created.

2. The founder must be an adult person of sound mind.

3. The *waqf* must be perpetual and must commence before the founder's death.

4. A *waqf* must be absolute and (according to the Shias) unconditional.

---

8   'Abdur Rahman i Doi, *Women in Shari'ah,* 1990, pp 336-337.
9   Jamal Nasir, *The Islamic Law of Personal Status*, 1986, p 247.

5. An undivided share of property cannot be declared a *waqf* for the purpose of a mosque or cemetery, but it may be a valid *waqf* for other purposes.

6. The object of the *waqf* must be capable of being identified with reasonable certainty.

7. The purpose of the *waqf* must be acceptable to *Shariah*.

8. A *waqf* made on the founder's death bed (*mard al-mawt*) may not exceed one third of the estate without the consent of the heirs.

A *waqf* can be created orally or by writing.

Comparison between a *waqf* and a trust[10]

1. A *waqf* should be created for a religious and/or charitable purpose recognised by *Shariah*. A trust may be created for any lawful purpose.

2. The founder of a *waqf* cannot take any benefit for himself (except to some extent according to the Hanafi school). The founder of a trust may be a beneficiary.

3. Property in a *waqf* vests in God. Property of a trust vests in the trustee.

4. The *mutawali* acts essentially as a supervisor and has fewer powers than a trustee.

5. A *waqf* must be perpetual, irrevocable and unalienable. It is not essential for a trust to have these characteristics.

6. A *waqf*, unlike a trust, does not result for the benefit of its founder, when its objects are exhausted. It is applied for some purpose which is similar to its original objects.

Advantages and disadvantages of *waqf*

S Khalid Rashid[11] says that the institution of *waqf* has been criticised in India, because the number of *waqf* there are now innumerable, and much *waqf* property has fallen into disrepair because of lack of funds or indifference of *mutawalis*. Also where *waqfs* have been created for the benefit of a family, the numbers of people in a family have in many cases multiplied to the extent that very little benefit can be

---

10   Ibid p 252; S Khalid Rashid, *Muslim Law*, 1990, pp 159 – 160.
11   Ibid p 161.

received by any individual sharer. Another criticism is that some *waqf* property could now be put to better use if it were able to be alienated from the *waqf*.

On the other hand, those who defend the idea of the *waqf*, point out that it prevents family property being squandered by spendthrift heirs and preserves the property for the benefit of future generations.

9

CONTRACEPTION, ABORTION AND NEW MEDICAL TECHNOLOGY[1]

Neither contraception nor abortion is new. From the time of recorded history, women have been trying to prevent conception, or after it has occurred, to abort an unwanted foetus, while others have been seeking means to conceive after they have failed to do so naturally.

From the *Quran*

In the *Quran*, there is no specific mention of contraception. There are two verses condemning infanticide:

> Kill not your children for fear of want: We shall provide sustenance for them as well as for you: Verily the killing of them is a great sin.[2]
> Kill not your children on a plea of want;[3]

There is general agreement that these verses were revealed to prohibit the custom of infanticide which was practised among the Arab tribes of the time, especially in relation to female children. Some scholars, such as Maulana Maududi, in India, have drawn an analogy between the prohibition of killing children for fear of want mentioned in these verses, and limiting the birth of children through contraception for economic reasons. There does not seem to be as sound basis for this

---

1   Material in this chapter is largely drawn from Abul Fadl Mohsin Ebrahim, *Abortion, Birth Control and Surrogate Parenting*, American Trust Publications, 1991.
2   17:31.
3   6:151.

reasoning since contraception does not involve any killing, and at the time contraception is used, no child has yet come into existence.[4]

In *Sura Al-Baqarah*, verse 233 encourages breastfeeding: "The mothers shall give suck to their offspring for two whole years. . ."

There was much controversy in the early Muslim community about whether it was permissible for a husband to have intercourse with his wife while she was breastfeeding an infant, apparently for fear that a new pregnancy might cause harm to the existing child. The Prophet decided that such intercourse was to be permitted since he had observed that there was no prohibition against doing so among other communities with whom the Muslims were in touch, and their children suffered no harm. However, as breastfeeding generally operates to reduce the likelihood of conception, this encouragement from religion to continue breastfeeding for two years, if possible, would have resulted in spacing in the number of children a woman might produce, as well as benefiting the baby she was already caring for.

In the *Sunnah*

There are several *ahadith* which deal with contraception. *'Azl*, or *coitus interruptus* was practised by the Arabs at the time of the Prophet. Several *ahadith*[5] mention the practice:

> Jabir narrates, we used to practice *'azl* in the Prophet's (*pbuh*) lifetime and he was informed about this and he did not forbid it.

> 'Umar ibn al Khattab (may Allah be pleased with him) narrates, the Prophet (pbuh) forbade the practice of *'azl* with a free woman except with her permission.

> Abu Sa'id (may Allah be pleased with him) narrates, the Jews say that *'azl* is minor infanticide, so the Prophet (pbuh) said, "The Jews are wrong: for if Allah wanted to create something, no one can divert Him".

These *ahadith* indicate that the Prophet was aware of the practice of *'azl*, and did not condemn it. However, if a man intended to practise it with a free woman (remembering that slavery was still practised at the time) she must agree because she was entitled to have children if she wished and also to experience sexual satisfaction.

---

4   Abul Fadl Mohsin Ebrahim, *Abortion, Birth Control and Surrogate Parenting,* American Trust Publications, 1991, p 21.

5   Ibid pp 22-23.

There is also a *hadith* in which the Prophet is reported to have himself likened *'azl* to minor infanticide. This is considered by some scholars to be a weak *hadith*, but Imam al Ghazali explained the apparent contradiction as being that the "minor" infanticide lies in the intention not to produce a child and as such it may be likened to the Prophet's remarks about "minor disbelief" as being something undesirable but not forbidden. It may be noted that in Islam, while procreation of children is one of the purposes of the marriage relationship, it is not the sole or dominant purpose, mutual love and support between the parties and prevention of illicit sex also being of importance.

The opinions of the scholars

There is general agreement among the scholars of all the major schools of Islamic jurisprudence that contraception is acceptable, providing that the wife consents. Some consider it within the category of actions classed as *makruh* (undesirable) since it deprives women of sexual fulfilment and the benefit of having children. However, if there is some genuine need, as may result from a threat to the life or health of the mother or genuine financial difficulties, there is no objection to it.

A modern scholar, Shaykh Ahmad al Sharabassi from Egypt, has approved the use of contraception to prevent the transmission of genetic defects which can now be established by genetic screening.[6]

Abul Fadl argues that of the reasons advanced by the scholars in favour of contraception, only a threat to the mother's life or health is an unquestionably sound reason.[7] In theory the state treasury, the *bait ul-mal*, should be able to provide funds to alleviate poverty and the extended family, normal in Muslim countries, should be available to help take care of children where a family becomes very large, in other circumstances. However, whether or not these arguments are sound in theory, these benefits are not always available in practice, and they do not take into consideration the pressing need in many Muslim countries, such as Egypt and Bangladesh to limit population numbers because of national poverty and the need for protection of the environment.

---

6   Ibid p 26.
7   Ibid p 27.

Another modern scholar, Dr 'Abdur Rahman i Doi would allow contraception only in the following cases:[8]

- if childbearing or delivery would endanger the life of the mother;

- if there is any fear of special financial, educational or other problems in respect of children which would stop a man from fulfilling his religious duties;

- if it forces a man to accept unlawful things or unlawful food just for the sake of his children;

- if there is a problem of ruining the health of the children. If the father or mother is suffering from a contagious disease which can be transmitted to the children, but this does not apply to hereditary diseases like diabetes and other such diseases;

- if there is a danger that the parents would not be in a position to give proper training (*tarbiyyah*) to the children as required by Islam.

Dr 'Abdur Rahman i Doi argues that except in these cases contraception is not allowed since it "amounts to losing one's trust in Allah". He dismisses fears of overpopulation as unfounded, and does not apparently consider the effect on the mother's health of too frequent childbearing or of having too large a family to care for.

Contraception in the Muslim world

Nawal El Saadawi mentions that contraception was practised in the Muslim world in the Middle Ages.[9] A famous physician, Abou Bakr al Razi, in the 9th century, described various methods of contraception, other than *coitus interruptus*. Some of these were the placing of medicaments at the opening of the uterus before sexual intercourse. These were intended either to close up the opening or expel the semen. Some substances used were tablets of cabbage, wax secreted by animal's ears, the droppings of elephants and calcium water. It is not stated how effective these methods were or whether there were any side effects!

Another famous Muslim physician was Ibn Sina, known in Europe as Avicenna, who died in AD 1037. He wrote *Al Kanoun fil Tib* (the Laws of Medicine) in which he described 20 different

---

8 *Women in Shari'ah*, 1992, pp 129-130.
9 *The Hidden Face of Eve*, 1980, p 67.

methods of contraception in a way which Nawal El Saadawi describes as "remarkably accurate and detailed considering the relatively early stage of scientific development at which he was writing".[10] Imam al Ghazali, writing in the 11th century, mentioned the use of a condom made out of gut as a means of contraception.

In modern times, the governments of many Muslim countries have recognised the necessity for promoting family planning, and have sought religious sanction for doing so. In 1937, the Mufti of Egypt delivered a ruling which approved of contraception for medical or social reasons and even accepted abortion provided that it was carried out before 16 weeks.[11]

In Southeast Asia, Professor Hooker has found a variety of responses to the question of contraception in *fatawa* issued by religious authorities in various States in Malaysia.[12] A 1965 *fatwa* from Kelantan stated that the family planning program was "an attempt to restrict the freedom of Islamic family life and it is also contrary to the law of nature". Having said that, it went on to allow contraception in three circumstances:

- Where the health of the wife would be endangered.
- Where either or both of the parents have an infectious disease.
- In cases of severe poverty.

Fatawa from Trengganu in 1976 and Selangor in 1979 allowed contraception for health reasons but prohibited sterilisation and abortion, in the case of the Trengganu *fatwa*, absolutely after four months. A similar ruling was made by the National Council for Religious Affairs in Malaysia in 1981.

Since then, numerous previously unthought-of methods of contraception have been invented.

Some of these are reversible and some irreversible. It is generally agreed that the reversible methods are permissible, though some consider them undesirable, but there is a difference of opinion about the irreversible methods.

Methods such as tubal ligation, vasectomy and hysterectomy for contraceptive purposes are opposed by some scholars on the basis that

---

10   Ibid p 68.
11   Ibid p 69.
12   See MB Hooker, "Fatawa in Malaysia 1960-1985", *Arab Law Quarterly*, Vol 8 June 1993, p 93.

the Prophet prohibited castration in a well known *hadith*,[13] and because it amounts to mutilation of the human body which is prohibited in Islam.[14] However, others disagree saying that vasectomy and tubal ligation are not like castration and can be reversible.

Today most Muslim countries permit contraception, although most of them prohibit abortion. Among the first countries to introduce family planning programs were Egypt, Tunisia, Pakistan and Turkey. In Southeast Asia, both Malaysia and Indonesia have well established, government sponsored, family planning programs. The fact that in some areas of the Muslim world conservative *mullahs* preach against the use of contraception is more indicative of the fact that this issue has not been publicly discussed in all countries and some religious leaders are themselves not well informed on the topic.

However, Muslim scholars have pointed out that contraception should be practised only within marriage, and they strongly disapprove of making contraceptive devices freely available, especially to minors and unmarried persons as is the practice in Western countries. Contraception when practised for the purpose of enjoying illicit sex without risk is clearly *haram* (prohibited).

Abortion

The prohibition of abortion is based on the verses of the *Quran* quoted above. However, Nawal El Saadawi mentions that illegal abortion has been rife in Egypt and other Arab countries with its attendant risk of death, medical complications and sterility for the women who undergo it.[15] In fact she says, at the time she was writing (1980), that as many as one quarter of all pregnancies in Egypt ended in illegal abortion, and about 80 per cent of cases involved married women who had previously had two or more children.[16] A doctor herself, who has seen at first hand the tragic results of botched back yard abortions, she advocates the legalisation of abortion to allow poor women as well as the rich to obtain abortions under proper medical care and conditions of cleanliness.

---

13   Abul Fadl Mohsin Ebrahim, *Abortion, Birth Control and Surrogate Parenting*, American Trust Publications, 1991, p 34.
14   'Abdur Rahman i Doi, *Women in Shari'ah,* 1990, p 131.
15   Nawal El Saadawi, op cit p 72.
16   Ibid.

However, Nawal El Saadawi's opinion is not in line with that of the traditional Muslim jurists. Some, like Imam al Ghazali and the Maliki scholar, Ibn Gazey would not allow abortion in any circumstances. Generally the scholars of the Maliki, Hanbali and Shafii schools oppose abortion absolutely, while the Hanafi school would permit it, in the first 120 days of pregnancy, if there is some valid reason such as danger to the mother's life or health or the life of an existing infant dependent on its mother's milk for survival. Those who consider that abortion is not prohibited within the first 120 days of pregnancy base their opinion on a *hadith* in which the Prophet is reported to have said that human life does not exist in the embryo before that time.

In the *Quran* there are many references to the development of the foetus, and in one of them it is described as follows:[17]

> Man We did create from a quintessence (of clay);
> Then We placed him as (a drop of) sperm in a place of rest, firmly fixed;
> Then We made the sperm into a clot of congealed blood;
> Then of that clot We made a (foetus) lump;
> Then We made out of that lump bones and clothed the bones with flesh;
> Then We developed out of it another creature: so blessed be Allah, the best to create!

The Prophet said that the first three periods mentioned in the verse each lasted 40 days and at the end of that time (120 days) the soul is breathed into the foetus by an angel.[18] This is the reason for the opinion that abortion may be permissible up to 120 days. However, an alternative opinion is that the time of ensoulment, when the human individual first begins to exist, should be put at between 40 and 45 days after conception.[19] If this view were to be generally accepted, abortion would be permissible only within the first six weeks or so of pregnancy. The opinion of other scholars is that abortion is not permissible at any stage.

From the writings of Muslim physicians of the classical period, such as Al Razi (d AD 923), Ibn Sina (d AD 1037) and Ibn Hubal (d AD 1213), it can be seen that abortions were considered justified in

---

17   23:12-14, see also 22:5.
18   *Sahih Muslim, Kitab al-Qadr*, 5:496, quoted in Abul Fadl Mohsin Ebrahim, *Abortion, Birth Control and Surrogate Parenting*, American Trust Publications, 1991, p 77.
19   S Aksoy, "What makes a person?", *The Fountain*, Vol 2 No 14 Apr-June 1996, p 30.

their times if the life of the mother was in danger.[20] Al Razi mentioned, justifying his opinion by reference to the writings of the great Greek doctor, Hippocrates, that abortion should be allowable in circumstances where a very young female had become pregnant, and for those women with small reproductive organs for fear that they might die if the foetus reached full growth. Ibn Sina allowed abortion in similar circumstances, or when the woman suffers from a disease of the uterus. Ibn Hubal thought that knowledge of contraceptive and abortive medicines should not be disseminated among the common people, but should only be available to physicians to use in cases they thought appropriate.

Among modern writers, Dr 'Abdur Rahman i Doi and others would permit abortion when the mother's life is in danger,[21] but there is disagreement on whether abortion may ever be legitimate in other circumstances, such as rape or the existence of deformity in the foetus.

In Saudi Arabia a *fatwa* has been issued stating that the abortion of deformed foetuses cannot be permitted.[22] Such a predicament should be considered a trial from the Almighty. It is also noted that the life span of grossly deformed foetuses is naturally short, and if abortion is allowed it might lead in time to acceptance of other measures such as euthanasia for the handicapped.[23] Unfortunately, this view does not take into account the mental and physical suffering of a woman who knows that her child will still inevitably die, but only after she has endured the full term of a futile pregnancy and the labour and dangers of childbirth.

If a woman is raped, Abul Fadl Mohsin Ebrahim argues that there is no objection to her seeking medications against pregnancy[24] (the morning after pill?) on the basis that it is allowable to get rid of the semen before it settles in the womb. The author is uncertain of the morality of permitting abortion once that initial time has passed querying whether the right of the foetus to life should take precedence over the right of the woman not to be compelled to bear a rapist's

---

20   Abul Fadl Mohsin Ebrahim, *Abortion, Birth Control and Surrogate Parenting*, American Trust Publications, 1991, pp 90-93.
21   'Abdur Rahman i Doi, *Women in Shari'ah*, 1990, p 133.
22   Abul Fadl Mohsin Ebrahim, *Abortion, Birth Control and Surrogate Parenting*, American Trust Publications, 1991, p 86.
23   Ibid p 88.
24   Ibid p 84.

child. He takes refuge in the theory, frequently expounded by conservative Muslims, that rape would not occur if there could be:

> an end to all forms of indecent exposure of the body in public; ban pornographic motion pictures, literature and songs; curtail the free intermingling of sexes; and stop the use of women as an enticement in advertisements to sell goods or products of any sort.

However, he does admit that such measures cannot guarantee the non-occurrence of rape, and certainly it would seem that even in the strictest of Muslim countries where women are hardly allowed to leave their homes, rape has not been eliminated. Also many rapes are unfortunately perpetrated by close family members, even by fathers and grandfathers, and the abovementioned measures would have no effect on this form of social evil. The particular problem which exists in many Muslim countries is that women who admit to having been raped are ostracised, and are fearful to complain lest their reputation be ruined for life. In such cases the early measures advocated by the author cannot be used and the dilemma remains.

It seems that this is a question which demands a great deal more consideration from Muslim scholars, who must decide the question which has also plagued their contemporaries in the West, of when and in what circumstances legal abortion can be permitted. This is particularly important in view of the unforgiving attitudes which exist in Muslim societies towards illegitimate pregnancies and the numbers of unsanitary illegal abortions being performed.

Another complication to the question is the increasing expertise of medical science in neonatalology. According to a Muslim doctor in the United States, Dr Shahid Athar,[25] there is at least one instance of an infant being saved after birth at three-and-a-half months, within the 120-day period within which abortion is permitted by some jurists.

Punishment for illegal abortion is provided for in Islamic law. The scholars are agreed that *diyat* (blood money) may be payable if the foetus is aborted, or alternatively, *kaffarah* (expiation) or *ghurrah* (compensation) may be required. *Diyat* is required to be paid to the heirs of a deceased person by the person who brought about the death, but the jurists of the four major schools differ as to the exact circumstances in which *diyat* rather than *ghurrah* should be paid in the case of abortion. *Kaffarah* means to atone for a sin usually

---

25   "The Islamic Perspective in Medical Ethics", *Internet, http://www.safaar. com/im1.html*

through fasting, but in the past also through freeing a slave. A result could therefore be that a doctor who performs a non-therapeutic abortion after the fourth month of pregnancy would be liable to pay a share of the *diyat*, and expected to atone for his sin by fasting for two consecutive months as *kaffarah*. If before the fourth month, he should pay the *ghurrah* in compensation. The woman who seeks an abortion can also be liable in the same way.[26]

Modern reproductive technology: the Islamic view

Islam frowns on celibacy and encourages every Muslim to marry and have children. However, the *Quran* mentions that children will not be granted to everyone who wishes for them:[27]

> To Allah belongs the dominion of the heavens and the earth.
> He creates what He wills (and plans).
> He bestows (children) male or female according to His Will (and Plan),
> Or He bestows both males and females, and He leaves barren whom He will:
> For He is full of Knowledge and Power.

In the past, Muslims have attempted to overcome the problem of infertility through polygamy (in the case of men where the wife has been barren), and by fostering the children of others, since adoption is not recognised in Islamic law.

In contemporary times, new advances in medical science have provided new methods of overcoming infertility, which of course may be due to medical problems in either the husband or the wife. Such methods are principally artificial insemination, in vitro fertilisation or surrogate parenting. Consideration of these methods presents new challenges to Muslim scholars, as also to those concerned with medical ethics in Western societies.

Some writers have argued that a person afflicted with infertility should simply accept his or her lot, but the general view is that it is quite acceptable to seek a cure through medical science, relying on the Prophet's saying that "for every disease there is a cure".[28] However, any medical intervention sought should be strictly within the bounds of Islamic law and morality.

---

26   Ibid p 102.
27   42:49-50.
28   Abul Fadl Mohsin Ebrahim, *Abortion, Birth Control and Surrogate Parenting*, American Trust Publications, 1991, p 55.

Artificial insemination by the husband

Some scholars have expressed doubts about artificial insemination where the husband's sperm is used because the usual method of collecting the sperm is through masturbation. Most of the scholars consider masturbation to be a sin, if not definitely forbidden. An argument in favour of it is found in the legal principle that "necessity makes what is forbidden allowable". Thus masturbation should not be prohibited if its purpose is to provide a means to enable an otherwise barren couple to have children. There is no objection to this kind of artificial insemination otherwise.

Artificial insemination by donor

All the scholars agree that artificial insemination by a donor is prohibited in Islamic law. In Egypt, Shakyh Mahmud Shaltut, formerly the head of *Al Azhar* university, issued a *fatwa* as follows:[29]

> Artificial insemination with the sperm of a foreign person, is, under the *Shari'ah*, a grievous crime and a great sin and is tantamount to adultery, for their essence is the same and their result is also the same.

Abul Fadl Mohsin Ebrahim believes that it would also be forbidden for a man to store his sperm in a sperm bank and for his widow to be impregnated with it after his death. This is because death brings the marriage relationship to an end, at least after the period of *iddah* (four months and ten days) has expired. Pregnancy should only occur within the marriage relationship.

In vitro fertilisation

In vitro fertilisation involves the fertilisation of a woman's ovum with sperm outside the body under laboratory conditions, after which one or more fertilised ova are implanted within the woman's uterus. It can be resorted to for the purpose of overcoming infertility where the woman's fallopian tubes are absent or damaged. One result of this process is that many more fertilised ova may be produced than are required, and those not wanted will eventually be destroyed. Those, who, following Imam Al Ghazali, believe that human life begins at conception, oppose in vitro fertilisation for this reason, unless only as many ova are fertilised as are intended to be implanted. In practice this is not likely since the difficulty of obtaining ova and sperm and

---

29   Ibid p 59.

127

the likelihood of some attempts at fertilisation failing, leads medical experts to recommend that more than one or two ova be fertilised, and possibly some can be frozen for future use. On the other hand it can be argued that under natural conditions, excess numbers of fertilised ova are expelled from the uterus, and so there is little difference.[30]

If more embryos are produced than are needed, and some are frozen for future use, there is the possibility of complicated questions of inheritance, if an embryo is implanted in the mother after the death of the father. This question has already arisen to perplex the Tasmanian Supreme Court in the case of *Re Estate of K; Ex parte Public Trustee*.[31] The answer in Islamic law is most likely that as the marriage has come to an end on death, the implantation is outside the marriage relationship and the child is illegitimate and does not inherit.

Where in vitro fertilisation involves the implantation of another woman's ovum, whether fertilised or not, the same objections would arise under Islamic law as arise with artificial insemination by donor. This practice would not be allowable as being like adultery. The resulting child would not truly be a child of the marriage relationship.

Surrogate parenting

In recent years there have been numerous instances of surrogate parenting brought about through medical technology in various countries, and the ethics and legal complications arising from it have posed many problems for people in the West as well as Muslims.

A surrogate mother is one who is implanted with a fertilised ovum belonging to another woman and brings it to term in her uterus, or alternatively is fertilised by another woman's husband and agrees to hand over the child to that couple when it is born.

In the latter case, the procedure would clearly be termed adultery under Islamic law and is undoubtedly illegal.

If the fertilised ovum is the product of husband and wife who for some reason cannot support the pregnancy herself, the situation is less clear cut. The concept of the wet nurse who feeds a child in place of its mother is well known in Islam, and in fact it is considered that there is so close a relationship between the wet nurse and child that

---

30   Ibid p 62.
31   See Nicola Watts, "When a Father Dies – Has a Frozen Embryo Rights to an Inheritance?", *ALMD Advance*, 3 June 1996.

they become as family, so that the usual rules of affinity apply to marriages between the child and the wet nurse's own children.

Abul Fadl believes that drawing an analogy between employing a wet nurse and surrogate parenting is going much too far, and any contract for surrogacy would be illegal under Islamic law,[32] since it involves a "sale" of a child where the surrogacy agreement is made for money. Also, again, there is an element of adultery in involving a third person in an essential part of the marriage relationship.

The *Quran* says: "None can be their mother except those who gave them birth". According to *hadith*, the Prophet said "The child is of the bed" meaning that a child is the child of the woman who gives birth to it. This answer to the question of who is the "true mother" of the child renders surrogacy agreements null and void. Moreover, acceptance of surrogate motherhood would give rise to many evils, which Abul Fadl lists as follows:[33]

- It is tampering with the ways of God in the normal process of procreation.

- It would encourage unmarried women to "lease" their wombs which would undermine the institution of marriage and family life.

- It might tempt married women to employ a surrogate to relieve themselves of the inconvenience of pregnancy and childbirth.

- It could encourage bitter legal disputes over children as has already happened in the United States.

- It could create confusion in blood ties, for example, in a case where a grandmother gave birth to her daughter's child.

Abul Fadl Mohsin Ebrahim therefore concludes that of all the possibilities in new reproductive technology, the only ones which would be legal under Islamic law would be artificial insemination by the husband, and possibly in vitro fertilisation where the fertilised ovum was derived from the married couple. Otherwise, polygamy (for men only) or fostering are the only remaining alternatives.

---

32   Ibid p 64.
33   Ibid.

Other advances in modern medicine: organ transplantation

According to Islamic teachings, the human body should be treated with respect whether it is living or dead. According to a *hadith* recorded by Abu Daud, the Prophet told a man who had broken the bone of a dead person which he had found in the cemetery, that it was equally sinful to break the bone of a dead person as of a living person. Islamic funeral rituals require that the body be washed, wrapped in white, and buried (not cremated) as soon as possible. Anything which might lead to mutilation of the deceased's body such as a post mortem, unless it is absolutely necessary, is not approved.

From this it might seem that organ transplantation might not be in accordance with Islamic principles. However, that this is not the case can be demonstrated from a study of the sayings of the Prophet, the writings of Muslim jurists and physicians, and the practices of the past among Muslim peoples.

Guidance can be sought from the *Sunnah* of the Prophet. The Prophet's attitude to medical treatment was that it should be sought by those in need of it, since God has created a cure for every disease. The Prophet encouraged his cousin, Sa'd ibn Abi Waqqas to consult Al-Harith, a well known physician of the time, and himself recommended the use of honey as a medicine and other remedies known then. The well known *hadith* in which the Prophet said "search for knowledge even as far as China" can equally be applied to new medical knowledge, and thus, new methods of treatment should be sought and applied wherever they are beneficial.

Dr MA Albar[34] says that Arab surgeons, following those of other ancient civilisations, were expert at tooth transplantation a thousand years ago, and the subject of tooth and bone transplantation was fully discussed in Imam Nawawi's (d AD 1271) books of jurisprudence *al-Majmu* and *Minhaj al-Talibin*. Another early Muslim surgeon, Zakaria al-Qazwini (d AD 1283), even advocated the use of porcine bone grafts as they took better than other materials, and despite the fact that the pig is regarded as unclean by Muslims. This was on the basis of the jurisprudential rule that otherwise forbidden food and products become permissible when there is no reasonable alternative available and the object is to save or benefit human life. Of course,

---

34 "Organ Transplantation", *The Fountain*, Vol 2 No 12, Oct-Dec 1995, p 34 at p 35.

early Muslim surgeons were not aware of the possibilities of transplantation of other organs of the body such as the liver, heart, as are carried out today, but their practices indicate that in principle, transplantation was not considered forbidden.

In the 20th century, the question of organ donation and transplantation has been considered by Muslim scholars. There have been numerous *fatawa* dealing with these issues, and as a result approval has been given for blood transfusions, corneal transplants, skin transplants and the transplantation of other organs, whether from the dead or the living.[35] In the case of deceased persons, *fatawa* have sanctioned organs being removed from those who have given their consent before death, or with the consent of the relatives. In some cases, it would be permissible to harvest organs from unidentified bodies with the sanction of an order from a Magistrate. Such *fatawa* have been issued in Egypt, Kuwait and Saudi Arabia.[36] A *fatwa* issued at Jeddah in 1988 by the Fourth International Conference of Islamic Jurists approved all previous *fatawa* on organ transplantation and stressed that trading in organs should be forbidden and donations made only on the principle of giving a benefit to those in need.

There are still some areas where the scholars have been unable to agree or have as yet, made no decision. There has been no agreement about whether brain death is accepted as the point of departure of the soul from the body, and no decision on whether it is ethical or otherwise to use tissues from anencephalics or aborted embryos, or embryos produced but not used for in vitro fertilisation. However, these matters remain controversial and as yet undecided in the West also.

Cosmetic surgery

While there is no doubt that surgical intervention can and should be sought by a person suffering from an illness, the stricter Islamic scholars would not allow anything in the nature of cosmetic surgery, which is designed just to improve a person's appearance and make him/her more attractive to others.

According to *ahadith*, the Prophet forbade some practices which were resorted to by the Arabs of his time in the belief that they would make the person more physically attractive. These were tattooing,

---

35   Ibid pp 35-36.
36   Ibid.

cutting and shortening the teeth, or widening the gaps between them, or even plucking excess hairs from the eyebrows. The use of wigs and hairpieces was also disapproved by the Prophet, even, in a *hadith* recorded by Al-Bukhari and Muslim, in a case where a girl had lost her hair due to disease. The basis of the prohibition is that it is a type of deception and an encouragement of personal vanity which is not acceptable in Islam. People should be more concerned with their religious duties and with helping other people than with their own beautification, which, for women particularly, may be "a way to adultery" if it attracts the attention of men outside the family.

There is some authority that cosmetic surgery may be permissible where its purpose is to correct some gross defect, which causes undue embarrassment and suffering to the person who is afflicted with it.[37] Some scholars allow the removal of excess facial hair (excepting the eyebrows) under this category. If this seems to conflict with the Prophet's ruling not to allow the wearing of a wig to conceal hair loss, it must be remembered that the girl concerned would not have attracted public attention and subsequent embarrass-ment, as she would not have been seen in public without a head covering in those days.

Circumcision

There is nothing in either the *Quran* or the *hadith* that would lead to the conclusion that circumcision is compulsory for either males or females. Nevertheless there is a long standing tradition that Muslim boys be circumcised usually at or before the age of 12. In some Muslim countries circumcision is an important "rite of passage" for boys and is celebrated by family and community parties.

Although widely believed to be an Islamic practice, female circumcision in any form is not required by Islam. There are some *hadith* in which the Prophet sought to limit it. As the intention of female circumcision is to lessen female desire, it would be in contra-diction to the Islamic principle that both men and women are entitled to sexual fulfilment in marriage. Female circumcision is practised by Muslims in some countries, especially in Africa, but it is also practised in those regions by Christians, Falash Jews and animists.

---

37   Yusuf al-Qaradawi, *The Lawful and the Prohibited in Islam*, 1989, p 89.

Euthanasia

There is no doubt that euthanasia is totally forbidden in Islamic law. Suicide is specifically forbidden: "Do not kill yourselves; indeed, Allah is merciful to you".[38]

The Prophet warned his followers that to commit suicide is to commit a grievous sin, which will result in severe punishment in the Hereafter. There is one *hadith* which relates that a certain man was in such severe pain from his wounds that he cut his own wrist and bled to death. The Prophet commented that because of this, he would be deprived of the Garden (of Paradise).

It is equally forbidden to kill someone else even with the object of alleviating suffering: "Take not life which God has made sacred except by way of justice and law".[39]

A person may make a "living will" requesting that his or her life should not be prolonged by artificial means once their death is inevitable. Doctors and nurses should use their best efforts to alleviate pain and make a terminally ill person comfortable, but the final decision of the term of a person's life is in God's hands.

On the question of AIDS patients, Dr Shahid Athar says:[40]

> The Islamic perspective, though not clearly defined, would be the prevention of the disease, and after its occurrence treating it like any other disease, ie tuberculosis, syphilis or small pox. We never question the lifestyle of patients with other common diseases ie diabetes, hypertension, coronary heart disease in order to discriminate (against) them or restrict their care. AIDS may be a "wrath of God" because of certain lifestyles, but many "innocent" people are affected by it. Therefore, they should not be penalised. In each community every attempt should be made to prevent the spread of the disease but once it has affected an individual full attention must be given to lessen his or her suffering and maintain the dignity and quality of life.

Therefore, it can be seen that Islamic law follows a middle course, but upholds strong moral standards in this area. It allows contraception by most means and in most circumstances, but it condemns abortion, except in extreme circumstances. It allows Muslims to take advantage of the benefits of modern reproductive technologies, where they are used within the marriage relationship. It allows organ transplantation to save people's lives and health, but it condemns surgery which is undertaken for reasons of vanity. Suicide and euthanasia are both condemned as being contrary to the law of God.

---

38   *Quran*, 4:29.
39   Ibid 6:151.
40   "The Islamic Perspective in Medical Ethics", *http://www.safaar.com/im1.html*

القانون الجنائيى ❂

10

ISLAMIC CRIMINAL LAW

The classification of crimes

In Islamic law, crimes are classified in three ways:

- *Hudud*
- *Qisas*
- *Ta'azir*

The word *hudud* (singular *hadd*), means limits, and *hudud* crimes are those specifically mentioned in the Qur'an as transgressing the limits which God Himself has placed on people's behaviour. The *Hudud* crimes are:

- Theft (*Al-sariqa*)
- Highway robbery (*Al-hirabah*)
- Drinking alcohol (*Khamr*)
- Unlawful sexual intercourse (*Zina*)
- False accusation of unchastity (*Al-qazf*)

Some jurists also include murder and apostasy (*Al-riddah*) among the categories of *hudud* crimes.

Let us look at these crimes one by one:

Theft (*Al-sariqa*)

The prescribed punishment is cutting off the hand. This is subject to the following strict conditions:

1. The thief must be an adult.
2. He must be sane.
3. He must have a criminal intent.
4. He must not have been forced to commit the theft by hunger or emergency.
5. He must not have been under duress.
6. The property stolen must be more than a prescribed amount in value.
7. He must know that it is owned by someone, not a commodity which is common or government property.
8. It must have been taken from a place where it was kept in custody.
9. It must be of value – commodities such as wine and pork which are forbidden by Islam are considered to have no value in this context.

Additionally, the theft must be proved by the evidence of two reliable male witnesses, or by a voluntary confession made twice before the court. The penalty will not be imposed when the property stolen is of trivial value or belongs to a close relative of the thief.

Also, if the thief repents before the sentence is executed, the *hadd* penalty is averted.

Highway robbery (*Al-hirabah*)

This refers to robbery with violence. There are differences among the jurists as to whether the offence can only relate to robbery on the highway or whether armed holdups in urban areas are also included. The penalty varies according to whether the robber has killed or injured the victim or simply robbed or threatened to rob him or her. The prescribed penalties are:

- death – if the robber has killed but has not got away with the stolen property;
- crucifixion – where the robber has killed and got away with stolen property;
- cutting off the hand and foot on opposite sides – robbery with violence where the robber does not kill the victim;
- exile – where the robber frightens the victim but does not kill or get away with the stolen property.

The conditions and evidential requirements are similar to those for theft.

Drinking alcohol (*Khamr*)

The consumption of alcohol in moderation was at first allowed in Islam. Later, it was forbidden completely. The jurists consider that the prohibition applies with equal force to drugs and other intoxicants of whatever kind.

The penalty for drinking alcohol is either 40 or 80 lashes, depending on which school of law is followed. The evidence of two just witnesses is required to prove the offence, and the offender must be an adult, sane and not forced to drink by duress.

Unlawful sexual intercourse (*Zina*)

Zina includes rape, adultery and fornication between unmarried persons, though the Maliki jurist Al-Dasuqi classified rape under the heading of *Al-hirabah*. The jurists differ as to whether homosexuality attracts the *hadd* penalty for *zina*.

The concept of *zina* causes much difficulty for Westerners, since nowadays, adultery is scarcely even considered a matrimonial offence in our society. However, we might remember that it was viewed more seriously in the past. The Romans used to parade an unfaithful wife naked on a donkey, allowing the crowds to insult her and spit upon her. The Babylonians drowned an adulterous wife and the Hebrews stoned her to death.[1] Up until about the 16th century in England, adultery was an offence punishable by the ecclesiastical courts. The punishments varied from a fine to mutilation – one penalty was cutting off the nose. Until the middle of the present century, adultery and indeed, all sex outside of marriage was regarded as reprehensible. Adultery was a matrimonial offence leading to divorce, and women, found guilty of adultery usually lost custody of their children and were deprived of their property. Women were treated more severely than men.

In Islamic law, men and women should be treated equally with regard to *zina*. There is some difference of opinion among the jurists as to the penalty. The Qur'an prescribes 100 lashes, but the majority of the jurists agree that, on the authority of *hadith*, that the proper

---

1   AJ Schmidt, *Veiled and Silenced: How Culture Shaped Sexist Theology*, 1989, p 47-48.

punishment for married adulterers is stoning to death, and the unmarried should be awarded 100 lashes.

However, the evidence required to convict a person of *zina* liable to *hadd* is particularly strict. The offence must be proved by the *shahadah* evidence of four *adil* (trustworthy) male Muslims, each present at the same time, who must each have seen the act of penetration with their own eyes. *Shahadah* evidence is the strongest kind of evidence; there cannot be even the slightest shadow of doubt. To be *adil*, a witness must be proven to be of impeccable character; otherwise his evidence will be rejected. Using these standards, it is almost impossible to obtain a conviction for *zina*.

The other way *zina* may be proved is by confession, but confession also is subject to rigorous standards. The confession must be voluntarily made on four separate occasions before the court, when the person confessing is aware of the nature of the offence and the prescribed punishment. The Saudis, who are no slouches at enforcement of the criminal law, say that a conviction for *zina* is obtained only about once every hundred years in their country.

There is controversy concerning whether the pregnancy of an unmarried woman should be taken as confession of *zina*. The majority of the jurists believe that it should not, as there may be other explanations for the pregnancy, for example, the woman may have been raped, or have genuinely believed that she was married to the man concerned. However, Imam Malik believed that an unexplained pregnancy should be treated as a confession of *zina*, unless the woman demonstrated her lack of consent at the time by raising the alarm or laying a complaint soon after. The unquestioning adoption of this view has led to absurd and unjust results as the *Safia Bibi*[2] case in Pakistan shows.

In the *Safia Bibi* case, a young housemaid, who was almost blind, claimed that she had been raped by her employer, as a result of which she gave birth to an illegitimate child. Her father laid a complaint of rape against the employer, which complaint was dismissed for want of evidence. However, the trial court took the girl's pregnancy as evidence of her culpability and convicted her of *zina*, sentencing her to imprisonment, whipping and a fine. The case received a great deal of adverse publicity and the conviction was set aside by the Federal Shariat Court.

---

2   PLD 1985 FSC 120.

The case illustrates the dilemma confronting those who wish to cling to a strict traditional view of Islamic law. The definition of *zina* includes rape, and, where the same evidential standards are imposed, it becomes virtually impossible for a woman to prove that she was raped since few rapists choose to commit the crime in the presence of four upright Muslim men. On the other hand, the unfortunate victim, who has admitted sexual intercourse by laying the complaint, may be prosecuted while the rapist goes free. The Modern thinking is that the evidential standard mentioned in the *Quran* for *zina* should not be applied to rape, since there are *hadith* in which the Prophet convicted men of rape on the evidence of the victim alone. There is no doubt that the traditional approach can lead to injustice – an analysis of decisions of the courts in Pakistan has shown a bias against female testimony and a tendency to arrest and imprison women for *zina* on the basis of unsubstantiated allegations.[3]

False accusation of unchastity (*Al-Qazf*)

If a person accuses another of unlawful sexual intercourse and cannot prove it by producing the necessary four witnesses, the accuser will be punished with 80 lashes. Furthermore, his or her evidence will be considered worthless on all future occasions.

Apostasy (*Al-Riddah*)

Apostasy is rejection of Islam in favour of another religion or atheism. The jurists differ about whether apostasy should be considered a crime liable to *Hadd* punishment, and whether it should be punished by death in any case. This matter was no doubt of considerable interest to Salman Rushdie when the Ayatollah Khomeini issued a *fatwa* (religious order) condemning him to death for his book, *The Satanic Verses*.

The traditionalist jurists rely on *hadith* which indicated that the Prophet put to death people who resiled from Islam during his lifetime. The alternative view is that these were instances when the young Muslim community was in grave danger from its many enemies and changing religion then was a betrayal of the community. This is no longer the situation in the modern world. Holders of the latter view rely also on the *Quran*ic verse: "Let there be no compulsion in

---

3   Rose Ismail (ed), *Hudud in Malaysia: The Issues at Stake*, 1995, p 25-26.

religion",[4] but the traditionalists say this means only that it is not permissible to convert non-Muslims by force.

In relation to the Salman Rushdie case, most Muslims agree that the Ayatollah, an Iranian, had no jurisdiction over Rushdie, an Indian with British citizenship living in Britain, and in any event he should have been given a fair trial, as is required by Islamic law. Furthermore, the best response would have been to boycott Rushdie's works and otherwise ignore him, since the making of the *fatwa* gave him and his publishers enormous publicity and no doubt, much greater sales than he otherwise would have had.

Cruel and unusual punishments?

These are the crimes and punishments which people in the West think of when they describe Islamic law as cruel and barbaric. It is easy to forget that even in Western countries, until comparatively recently, the law condoned punishments at least as severe and sometimes even more horrible than the *Hudud* punishments. In Medieval England, blinding and castration were common punishments, under Henry II loss of hand and foot became very fashionable,[5] and up until 1790 the penalty for treason was disembowelling, beheading and quartering in the case of a male and being burnt alive in the case of a female.[6] Whipping was a frequent punishment and the effect of the cat o' nine tails is graphically described in many books about convict life in Australia. At the beginning of the 19th century, more than 200 crimes attracted the death penalty in England, and children as young as nine were hanged, sometimes for trivial offences.[7] As recently as 1952, two men were hanged for murder in Darwin.

These things are mentioned so that we can remind ourselves that humane treatment of criminals is a comparatively recent idea, and that the Islamic system has never had a monopoly over harsh punishments. The society in which the Qur'an was revealed was a tribal society. Physical punishments were the norm at that time throughout the world, and by comparison with others, the *Hudud* punishments were not unusual or unduly harsh. Today, our standards have changed, but periodic calls for the re-introduction of capital punishment and

---

4   2:256.
5   Pollock and Maitland, *The History of English Law*, Vol 2, 1985, p 461.
6   J Hostettler, *The Politics of Criminal Law*, 1992, p 134.
7   Ibid p 65.

requests by some aboriginal people for the law to recognise traditional tribal punishments such as spearing or clubbing of offenders show that the question is not settled for all time.

Secondly, Western commentators who condemn Islamic criminal law rarely have more than a passing acquaintance with it, and even more rarely, do they have any knowledge of the Islamic law of evidence. For the *hadd* punishment to be inflicted in each of the above cases, strict proof is necessary, and in some cases, for example the punishment for *zina*, the proof required is so strict that it might be difficult to imagine an instance where such proof could be obtained.

Thirdly, there is an overriding principle expressed in a *hadith* of the Prophet, that whenever there is any doubt at all, the *hadd* penalty should not be applied.

Another modern, minority, view is that the *hudud* penalties should not apply except in a just Islamic society. Since no such society exists in the world today, there is at present no requirement for application of the penalties.

Qisas

Qisas can be described as "equality in retaliation" similar to the Old Testament concept of "an eye for an eye and a tooth for a tooth". The authority for *qisas* is found in verses of the Qur'an such as the following:

> We ordained therein for them: Life for life; eye for eye; nose for nose; ear for ear; tooth for tooth, and wounds equal for equal. But if anyone remits the retaliation by way of charity it is an act of atonement for himself. And if any fail to judge by what God has revealed, they are wrong-doers.[8]

'Abdur Rahman i Doi explains that *qisas* was intended to limit the vicious blood feuds which the Arabs of the time pursued with great fervour, sometimes from generation to generation. *Qisas* gave the strict legal right to inflict the same hurt on the wrongdoer as the wrongdoer had perpetrated on the victim, but no more. However, it was recommended that the victim, or his heirs in case of death, remit the penalty, whether it be death or mutilation in return, and accept instead, compensation or *diyat* from the wrongdoer. A table of maims set out the appropriate compensation for various types of injury. If the

---

8   Qur'an 5:48.

wrongdoer did not have the funds to pay it, his relatives were expected to contribute.

Diyat can be thought of as victim's compensation. Under our system of law, until recently, when an offender was sentenced, the victim went home forgotten and without compensation for his/her injuries or loss. Victims and their families are often upset with the sentences handed down to offenders, and there has been some suggestion recently that it might be desirable to give victims some say in the punishment given to the perpetrator. In Islamic law, *qisas* performs both these functions. It allows the victim or his or her family to say whether the offender should be executed or receive the same injury he has inflicted on the victim; alternatively they can take compensation from him instead. Traditionally, *diyat* was set at 100 camels for the death of a person, and proportionally for lesser injuries, but today, monetary equivalents are calculated by the courts.[9]

A recent example of the application of *qisas* in Saudi Arabia occurred in the Gilford case which was widely reported in the Western press. Two British nurses were accused of murdering an Australian nurse, Yvonne Gilford, at the hospital where they all worked, and tried in Saudi Arabia. The victim's brother, Frank Gilford from South Australia, was given the responsibility under Saudi law for deciding whether to demand the death penalty or to accept financial compensation and allow the British nurses to go free. Ultimately, he accepted *diyat*, most of which was to be donated to an Adelaide hospital for a children's ward in memory of his sister, and the British nurses returned to Britain without further penalty.

Ta'azir

Ta'azir crimes are all those which are not included in the above categories. Their nature and the punishment for them may be determined by the ruler, or the state and awarded at the discretion of the judge.

Exceptions to criminal responsibility

The following people are held not to be legally responsible for their crimes:

---

9   For example, *The Criminal Act* (Sudan) s 42(1).

- children, up to the age of puberty;
- insane people;
- people who commit a crime while sleeping.

The criminal is solely responsible for his crime. His relatives must not be made to suffer, except in the case of payment of *diyat*, when the criminal's relatives on his father's side are responsible for payment.

The application of Islamic criminal law in the modern world

Saudi Arabia

Islamic law remains uncodified, as is still interpreted according to the traditional rules.

Iran

Islamic criminal law has been enacted in statutory form – *The Hudood and Qisas Act* 1982

Pakistan

The relevant statutes are the *Offences against Property (Enforcement of Hudud)* Ordinance 1979, *Offence of Zina (Enforcement of Hudood)* Ordinance 1979 and Ordinance on *Qisas* and *Diyah* 1990.

Sudan

The relevant Sudanese statute is the *Criminal Act* 1991. It however, does not apply the *hudud* punishments to the southern States where most of the population are non-Muslims.

Malaysia

Islamic criminal law used to apply in most States before the coming of the British.[10] More recently, the government of the Malaysian State of Kelantan passed the *Syariah Criminal Code (II) Act* in 1993 which sought to impose traditional Islamic criminal law in Kelantan. However, bringing it into operation would have required an amendment to the Malaysian Constitution, and this the Malaysian Government was not prepared to support. The proposal now appears to have been abandoned.

---

10   Ahmad Mohamad Ibrahim, "Suitability of the Islamic Punishments in Malaysia", *IIUM Law Journal*, Vol 3 No 1, January 1993, p 14.

The criminal jurisdiction of the *Syariah* courts in Malaysia is limited to offences punishable by imprisonment of up to three years or a fine up to RM5000 or whipping up to six strokes. Only Muslims can be dealt with by the *Syariah* courts and they can be punished for offences against the religion of Islam such as *khalwat* (close proximity of a sexual nature), and drinking alcohol.

Note that whipping, as carried out under Islamic law, is not so severe as that inflicted by the *rotan* in Malaysia and Singapore under the ordinary Penal Code.

Arguments for and against Islamic criminal law in the modern world

Against

- The punishments are cruel and unacceptable in the modern world. Civilised societies have long ago abandoned mutilation, whipping and crucifixion as punishments. Most advanced societies have abolished the death penalty.

- They do not assist in the rehabilitation of the offender.

- Islamic criminal law leads to injustice. There is no doubt that in Pakistan – where case studies are more readily available than from Iran or Saudi Arabia – there have been cases where the unthinking application of the traditional version of Islamic criminal law has resulted in great cruelty and injustice. The *Safia Bibi* case mentioned above is one such instance. However, the most outrageous cases have been ones where Islamic law was not properly applied, since sometimes even lower court judges do not seem to have a proper knowledge of the law they are supposed to apply. These cases were invariably overturned on appeal to the Federal *Shariat* Court.

- Women are unjustly treated by the law as it has been interpreted in most countries where Islamic criminal law is in force. It is extremely difficult for women to prove rape, and a woman making an accusation of rape runs the risk that she herself will be punished for *qazf*, if not *zina*. In Pakistan, there have been many cases where women have suffered because of the conservative interpretation put on the law by the authorities.

- The law is out of date in the modern world and does not take account of changing social attitudes.

- *Qisas* allows a victim to take revenge on the criminal. Individuals, even if wronged, should not be allowed to punish offenders themselves or to determine their punishment. That is for the state to decide.

For

- The severity of the *hudud* punishments is a deterrent to crime. According to the Saudis, the existence of Islamic criminal law in their country has resulted in it being remarkably free of crime. The deterrent effect of harsh penalties such as cutting off the hand for theft, has reduced the incidence of theft to a very low level. Thus there is also little need for armoured cars and security measures which are used in other countries to prevent theft. Furthermore the existence of the deterrent and low incidence of crime means that the *hadd* penalty is, in practice, rarely applied. The same applies to the other categories of *hudud* crimes.[11] However, cynics might believe that the comparative absence of crime in Saudi Arabia has more to do with the extremely repressive political system in that country, than the righteous application of Islamic criminal law.

- The imposition of *hadd* punishment is strictly controlled by the law of evidence and the principle that when there is any doubt the *hadd* penalty must not be imposed. According to a *hadith* of the Prophet; "Ward off punishment from the Muslims as far as it lies in your power, if there is any other way out (for the offender) to be let off, then let him off, for if the Imam commits error in forgiving, that is better than his error in inflicting punishment".[12]

- Repentance sets aside the penalty for *al-sariqa, hirabah* and possibly *zina* and drinking alcohol.[13] It does not set aside the punishment for *qazf* as the person's reputation has already been injured by the false accusation.

---

11   See comments by Saudi representatives, quoted in 'Abdur Rahman i Doi, *Women in Shari'ah,* 1990, pp 246, 260-261.

12   Al-Tirmidhi, *Jami'al-Sahih*, Vol IV p 33, quoted in Hashim Mehat, *Sentencing in Malaysian Law,* 199?, p 48.

13   Ibid p 323.

- In practice the *hudud* penalties are rarely applied. Where Islamic criminal law is interpreted in accordance with the spirit of the Qur'an, and applied in accordance with the strict rules of evidence, the *hadd* penalties would be rare. On the information which is available about the imposition of criminal punishments in the past, there is evidence that imprisonment was imposed more frequently than whippings or amputations.[14]

- *Qisas* empowers a victim to punish or accept compensation from the criminal. The victim will be more likely to feel that justice has been done. Under the common law system the victim feels overlooked by the legal process and often receives no compensation.

- *Qisas*, if chosen by the victim, is strictly limited to inflicting no greater hurt than has been inflicted on the victim. The Iranian Act goes into great detail about this and requires equality in the location, soundness and amount of injury (ss 60-62). It forbids imposition of *qisas* in conditions where the injury may become infected (s 67) and requires the weapon used to be sharp, unpoisoned and "suitable for the execution of the *Qisas*, because it is not lawful to give pain to the offender in excess of the quantum of his offence" (s 68). The acceptance of compensation (*diyat*) is encouraged instead.

---

14   Irene Schneider, "Imprisonment in Pre-Classical and Classical Islamic Law", *Islamic Law and Society,* Vol 2 No 2, 1995.

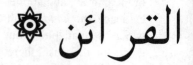

11

EVIDENCE IN ISLAMIC LAW

The importance of evidence

In Islamic law, as it is in the common law, the law of evidence is of great importance in any trial or legal adjudication. As we have seen, when looking at the criminal law of Islam, evidence plays an important part in mitigating the effect of the *Hudud* laws on society because a conviction can only be obtained if the most stringent evidential requirements are met. Thus, in the absence of four morally upright male Muslim witnesses who are prepared to testify that they have personally witnessed the sexual act, a conviction for *zina* cannot be obtained, and if a penalty be imposed, it must be the lesser penalty of *ta'azir*.

Evidence in the *Quran*

There are many verses in the *Quran* which attest to the importance of justice in legal (and other) matters. Let us look at a few examples:

In legal proceedings justice is all important:

> O you who believe! Stand out firmly for God, as witnesses to fair dealing, and let not the hatred of others to make you swerve to wrong and depart from justice. Be just: that is next to piety: and fear God. For God is well acquainted with all that you do.[1]

---

1   5:9.

Evidence must be given without bias, even if it is against the interests of the person testifying or against the interests of his family or friends:

> O you who believe! Stand out firmly for justice, as witnesses to God, even as against yourselves, or your parents, or your kin, and whether it be (against) rich or poor: for God can best protect both. Follow not the lusts (of your hearts), lest you swerve, and if you distort (justice) or decline to do justice, verily God is well acquainted with all that you do.[2]

Those who have information concerning a matter before the judge should not fail to co-operate in giving testimony:

> The witnesses should not refuse when they are called upon (to give evidence).[3]

Evidence should not be concealed:

> Conceal not evidence; for whoever conceals it, – his heart is tainted with sin. And God knows all that you do.[4]

Evidence in the *Sunnah*

There are a number of *ahadith* also which emphasise the importance of evidence in judicial proceedings. One of the best known is as follows:

> 'Ali said: The Messenger of Allah (may peace be upon him) sent me to Yemen as a judge, and I asked: O Messenger of Allah, are you sending me when I am young and have no knowledge of the duties of a judge? The Prophet replied: Allah will guide your heart and keep your tongue true. When two litigants sit in front of you, do not decide till you hear what the other has to say as you heard what they first had to say; for it is best that you should have a clear idea of the best decision. Ali said: I had been a judge (for long), or he said (the narrator is doubtful) : I have no doubts about a decision afterwards.[5]

In another *hadith*, two men were reported as arguing over their inheritance. They came to the Prophet to decide the issue. Neither had any evidence except his own assertion that he was entitled to the property. The Prophet said:

> I am only a human being, and you bring your disputes to me, some perhaps being more eloquent in their plea than others, so that I give judgment on their behalf according to what I hear from them. Therefore,

---

2   4:135.
3   2:282.
4   2:283.
5   Sunan Abu Daud, Vol 3, *Kitab al-Aqdiyya*, quoted in Mahmud Saedon Awang Othman, "The Importance of Evidence", 1992 IIUM notes, pp 11-12.

whenever I decide for anyone which by right belongs to his brother, he must not take anything, for I am granting him only a portion of Hell.

According to the *hadith*, on hearing this reminder of the consequence of a decision made in error without supporting evidence, the two men wept and agreed to divide the property up in an amicable way.[6]

On another occasion, two men referred their dispute about ownership of a farm animal to the Prophet. Since neither had any evidence to support their claim, the Prophet ordered the animal to be divided into two and shared between them.[7]

The onus of proof

As in the common law, the onus of proof normally lies on the plaintiff. Where the plaintiff's claim is accepted by the court, the defendant then has the obligation of answering the claim. It is also well established that a person accused of a crime is to be presumed innocent until proven guilty.

Proof may be of different standards:

- *Yaqin* (certainty). This is the highest standard of proof. It can be disproved only by another certainty. This standard is required in *hudud* cases, since the Prophet said; "set aside the penalty of *hudud* in cases of doubt".

- *Zann* (conjecture) This exists where there is a strong probability of the correctness of evidence but it does not attain the standard of certainty. It is more like the common law standard of "the balance of probabilities". It can be accepted to prove less serious offences.

- *Shakk* (suspicion) This is suspicion or doubt which falls between certainty and uncertainty but where neither is dominant. It would not normally be accepted by the court.

- *Wahm* (fancy) This is supposition or mere probability and is not given any weight as evidence before the court.

---

6   Ibid pp 13-14.
7   Ibid p 15.

Types of evidence

Bayyinah

Bayyinah is broadly defined as whatever clarifies, explains and shows the existence of any right in a suit before the court. It includes the evidence of witnesses and the special knowledge of the judge. According to one of the jurists, Ibn Qayyim, *bayyinah* is a wide and embraces all types of evidence, and includes *shahadah*. It includes the evidence of people who are not eligible to give *shahadah*, including women and non-Muslims. It may also include an oath when the defendant refuses to take an oath, circumstantial evidence, and the clear likeness between two people in cases regarding proof of parentage, in summary, any type of evidence which is likely to lead to the truth being established.

Shahadah

According to most of the jurists, *shahadah* is a special type of *bayyinah*, though some assert that they are one and the same thing. Ibn Rifa'h, a Maliki jurist, defined *shahadah* as a statement which makes it obligatory for a judge to give judgment based on this statement when it is made before him if the person who makes the statement is *adil* (just) and the statement is supported by the required number of witnesses or the oath of the claimant.

Shahadah is oral evidence, given before a judge in court, which must commence with the word "*asshadu*" ("I bear witness"). Such a statement must be based on certainty and not on speculation or deduction.[8] *Shahadah* must be given in relation to the interest of another person over another person and not in relation to the interest of the person giving the evidence. *Shahadah* therefore represents a type of proof which is strict and narrow and is not easily acceptable. However, if it meets the strict requirements it must be accepted by the judge. He has no discretion to reject it.[9]

Only certain persons are deemed to be entitled to give *shahadah*. They are people who are:

- Adult – that is having attained the age of puberty, but some jurists are of the opinion that the *shahadah* evidence of a child who has

---

8   Mahmud Saedon Awang Othman, "The Concept of Bayyinah in Islamic Law", 1992, p 11.

9   Ibid p 13.

reached the age of discretion (*mumayyiz*) may be valid in some cases, for example, murder.

- Sane (*'aqil*) – all the jurists agree on this point.

- Muslim – but if the person against whom the evidence is given is a non-Muslim, some jurists would accept the *shahadah* evidence of a non-Muslim.

- Sighted – some jurists do not accept the *shahadah* evidence of a blind witness, but the Malikis, Shafiis and Hanbalis accept such a person's evidence except in *hudud* cases.

- Able to speak – some jurists would accept evidence of a dumb person given through understandable sign language if it is necessary due to lack of other witnesses.

- *Adil* – this means that the witness must have a good reputation and blameless behaviour. If a Muslim, the witness should be one who is known to adhere to the requirements of Islam, to abstain from major sins and not to persist in minor sins. If a non-Muslim, the witness should be believable according to his religion. *Shahadah* evidence is not accepted from a witness who is known to have a bad character.

- Male – in cases of *hudud*. In such cases the requisite number of witnesses, either two or four, must give *shahadah* evidence.

- Also, the witness must not be biased against the defendant. Bias may arise out of family relationships, known enmity or conflict of interest.

Where a witness is not competent to give *shahadah*, normally his or her evidence can be accepted as *bayyinah*, the difference being that the judge is bound to accept *shahadah*, but has the discretion to accept or reject *bayyinah*.

Iqrar (confession)

Iqrar is an admission or confession made by a person that he or she is bound by a right or interest of another person or has a liability towards that other person. *Iqrar* can be made in or out of court. In the latter case it must be made before two *adil* witnesses to be binding. In the case of *zina*, the jurists differ. Some say the confession must be made before four *adil* witnesses, others before the court only and repeated four times in different sessions of the court, and others that it can be accepted even if made before only two witnesses.

For *iqrar* to be valid the following conditions apply:[10]

- The person making the confession must be sane and an adult.

- It cannot be made through a *wali* (guardian).

- It may be accepted from a child who has reached the age of discretion (*mumayyiz*).

- The person who benefits from the confession need not be an adult or sane.

- The confession should be made voluntarily without conditions.

- A confession made under the influence of intoxicants cannot be accepted in *hudud* cases.

- A confession made at the time of death-illness can be accepted.

Qarinah (circumstantial evidence)

The concept of *qarinah* in Islamic law is very like that of circumstantial evidence in common law systems. Its meaning is something which indicates the existence or non-existence of a fact or can be made a proof of it. An example of *qarinah* from the *Quran* is in the story of Prophet Yusuf (Joseph).[11] His master's wife was attracted by his good looks and tried to seduce him. As he was a virtuous youth, he ran away from her. She grabbed him from behind and tore his garment. Confronted by her husband, she accused Yusuf of trying to seduce her. A witness pointed out that the fact that his garment was torn from the back indicating he had been fleeing from her, whereas if he had been attacking her, the tear would have been at the front. Thus his innocence was proved from evidence of the location of the tear.

Qarinah has been accepted by most of the Muslim jurists, though some say that it is only a weak method of proof. Others would accept it even in *hudud* cases, for example Imam Malik held that an unexplained pregnancy by an unmarried woman could be taken as proof of *zina* on her part, but the other schools do not accept this ruling since it is possible that her pregnancy may have been caused without fault on her part. Caliph Omar is said to have imposed the *hadd* penalty for drinking alcohol on a man because alcohol could be smelled on his breath. However, some *ulema* do not agree with this, because the accused person may have been forced to drink alcohol or drunk it by mistake. In theft cases, some jurists consider that

---

10   Mahmud Saedon Awang Othman, Evidence Notes, IIUM 1992.
11   12:23-29.

possession of stolen property can be taken to be sufficient proof of theft in the absence of satisfactory explanation to the contrary.

There is a difference of opinion among the scholars as to whether *qarinah* can be a way of proof in a murder case. Some say that being in possession of the murder weapon indicates guilt especially if this circumstantial evidence is strengthened by the relatives of the victim taking the requisite number of oaths (50), that the accused was the killer.

The judge should evaluate *qarinah* evidence according to whether it is weak or strong, and reject any that is weak. To be acceptable, *qarinah* should attain the standard of *yaqin* which means that it should be reliable and free from any reasonable doubt.

Documentary and forensic evidence

In the early period of Islam, reliance was placed primarily on the oral evidence of witnesses who appeared in person before the judge. This was because at that time, few people were literate, and most had to rely on scribes to write any document for them. Thus oral evidence was more reliable. However, the *Quran* itself requires that in certain types of commercial transactions, writing is at least recommended, if not obligatory.[12] In the *Sunnah* also, it is recorded that the Prophet accepted documentary evidence. One *hadith* records that the wife of Ashim al-Thahabi was permitted to inherit from the blood money of her husband because of a letter written to the Prophet.[13] The Prophet himself sent letters to rulers of neighbouring countries and his deputies in other parts of Arabia. There was no religious objection to reliance on writing, so long as it could be authenticated. Authentication might be by a seal, or recognition of the person's handwriting by a reliable witness.

As the Muslim empire expanded, and the volume of commercial transactions grew, more reliance had to be placed on written documents. At different times, Islamic empires stretched from Al-Andalus (modern Spain) in the west to India in the east. Complex business ventures required documentation, and the difficulty of travelling such vast distances meant that personal attendance was not always possible. In the *Mejelle*, the 19th century civil code of the

---

12   2:282.
13   Mogamad Faaik Gamieldien, *Documentary Evidence,* unpublished paper 1993.

Ottoman empire, the acceptance of documentary evidence was expressed through the maxim:

Correspondence by writing is like talking to one another.[14]

Other clauses in the *Mejelle* allow written admissions to be accepted in the case of a confession written at the request of the person making it, and signed and sealed by the maker (Article 1607); a merchant's entries in his books may be accepted as an admission of debt (Article 1608); vouchers and receipts are acceptable as admissions (Article 1609); and a written acknowledgment of debt, which is signed and sealed, may prevail over oral evidence to the contrary (Article 1610).

There is some difference of opinion among the jurists as to the value of a document which is not properly attested. Some jurists would accept such a document if the handwriting of the writer was known and confirmed. Ibn Hanbal established three conditions for the acceptance of such writing:

- that the written document had been kept in safe-keeping;
- that its source was known, so that the source could be referred to if necessary;
- that there should be no doubt concerning the authenticity of the writing.

Furthermore, it was concluded that a judge is entitled to act on authenticated correspondence received from another judge in matters relating to property rights, but not in relation to *hudud* or *qisas* matters. Official documents and books kept by the court are also acceptable documentary evidence.

Today, properly attested legal documents and new technologies for sending and recording evidence such as faxes and computer records are reliable and have come to be accepted in Islamic law as elsewhere.

Who may give evidence?

As we have seen above, only certain types of persons are qualified to give *shahadah* evidence, which is required for a conviction in *hudud* cases. The conditions are not so strict when the evidence to be given comes under the broader classification of *bayyinah*.

---

14   Article 69.

It is clear that an adult Muslim man who is sane and recognised as *adil* can give evidence whether *shahadah* or *bayyinah*.

The evidence of a person who is *fasiq* (not *adil*) or an unbeliever can be heard, and accepted if the judge finds that it can be verified. This also applies to the evidence of a person who is known not to have a good memory.

The evidence of a child can be accepted if the child has reached the age of discretion (*mumayyiz*), which is considered to be ten years of age.

The evidence of a person who is biased because of family relationship or enmity towards the other party can be placed before the judge, who can then decide whether to accept or reject it according to the circumstances.

Likewise the evidence of a dumb person given through signs or writing or a blind person may be accepted as *bayyinah*.

The evidence of an expert witness may be received even if he is a non-Muslim and he is giving evidence against a Muslim. Otherwise the evidence of a non-Muslim will not be received against a Muslim.

The evidence of women

This is a subject about which there has been considerable controversy. Tradition dictates that women cannot be witnesses in *hudud* crimes, though the Zahiri school allowed the testimony of eight women in the place of four men in cases of *zina*.[15] There is no prohibition against women as witnesses in the *Quran* or the *Hadith* (except for the qualification in 2:282 which we shall consider below) and the reasons usually advanced for the traditional view is that women are too inexperienced in the ways of the world, too tender hearted and too emotional to be involved in unsavoury court proceedings. This, however, is the opinion of the jurists, who have apparently chosen to ignore the Prophet's example, recounted in at least two *hadith*, where he imposed the *hadd* punishment on a rapist on the evidence of the victim alone.[16]

Verse 282 of *Sura Al-Baqarah*, the second *sura* of the *Quran*, is as follows:

---

15   S Mahmassani, *Falsafat al-Tashri fi Al-Islam*, 1987, p 177-178.
16   The two *hadith* are recorded in the *Sunan* of Tirmidhi and are quoted by Kaukab Siddique in *Liberation of Women thru Islam*, 1990, pp 91-92.

O you who believe!
When you deal with each other,
In transactions involving
Future obligations
In a fixed period of time,
Reduce them to writing.
Let a scribe write down faithfully as between
The parties: let not the scribe
Refuse to write: As Allah has taught him,
So let him write. . .
And get two witnesses
Out of your own men,
And if there are not two men,
Then a man and two women,
Such as you choose,
For witnesses,
So that if one of them errs,
The other can remind her. . .

From this verse the jurists have assumed a general rule that the evidence of one man is equal to that of two women. Mahmassani says:[17]

> In addition to her lack of practical experience, the Arab woman was customarily secluded from men. The *shari'ah* took cognizance of this fact and accepted the testimony of women only in matters where women could be expected to have knowledge of necessary information. In economic transactions, where women are usually less informed than men, a woman's testimony was considered as half that of a man.

In matters where women could be expected to have information, or even be the only source of information, such as childbirth and lactation, the evidence of women, even one woman alone, is to be accepted. The Hanbali and Hanafi schools accept the evidence of one woman witness in such matters, but the Malikis require two by analogy to the usual number of male witnesses in other matters, and Imam Shafii required four female witnesses.

In other matters such as property disputes, Imam Malik would accept the evidence of two women with the oath of the plaintiff as the necessary proof, as would some of the Hanbali jurists, and the Zahiri school would always accept the evidence of twice as many women witnesses as were required for men in a particular case. According to tradition, the Caliphs Omar and 'Ali accepted the testimony of four women in cases of divorce, dowry and similar matters.[18]

---

17   Ibid p 180.
18   Ibid p 181.

Some modern Muslim scholars consider the rules limiting or excluding women as witnesses to be obsolete, at least in societies where women are as well educated as men. Furthermore, 2:282 refers to a particular type of financial transaction, and there is nothing in the *Quran* to indicate that it should be applied as a general rule.[19] Where witnesses are referred to elsewhere in the *Quran*, no gender is specified so that in other matters both men or women should be equally competent to be witnesses.

Attempts to apply the traditional *Shariah* rules concerning women as witnesses in the modern world have caused injustice and are opposed by women's groups. We have already noted the practical impossibility for women in proving *zina* liable to *hudud*. Women can give *bayyinah* evidence in such cases, and the *ta'azir* penalty can be applied, but it is anomalous that, for example in Pakistan, the penalty for rape under the statute is a maximum of 25 years while the penalty for *zina* liable to *hadd*, which includes consensual sexual intercourse, is death by stoning if the parties are married, and 100 lashes if they are not.

In 1984 in Pakistan, the Law of Evidence introduced by General Zia's Government reduced women's testimony in financial matters to half that of a man. This is clearly not just, or even sensible as a general rule, and is contrary to the spirit of the *Quran*.

The importance of the oath (*Al-Yamin*)

The oath plays a more important part in the Islamic law of evidence than it does in the common law. The reason is that Islamic law is a religious system of law and it is understood that those who come before the court will mostly be Muslims who will have a belief in God and a belief that they risk severe punishment in the hereafter if they lie on oath. Thus an oath can sometimes be accepted as proof or to strengthen the evidence of other witnesses. There is no strictly prescribed form of oath, but it should commence with the Arabic words "*Wallahi, Wabillahi, Watallah*" ("By God"). It is not necessary to place the hand on a copy of the *Quran* while making the oath, though many people do so.

The oath may be taken by the defendant at the request of the plaintiff where the plaintiff has a clear claim but insufficient evidence

---

19   Amina Wudud-Muhsin, *Qur'an and Woman*, 1992, p 86.

to prove it. If the defendant refuses to take the oath, judgment can be given for the plaintiff. The plaintiff may also take an oath to clarify doubts concerning his claim, or when the defendant refuses to take an oath, it is "returned" to the plaintiff.

In cases concerning property, where there is only one witness available, an oath may be taken to prove the claim.

An oath may also be taken for the purpose of strengthening evidence. This oath may be requested by the judge, especially in cases where the defendant is missing, or has died or is insane or a minor. In extreme cases the judge may request the witness to take the oath in the mosque after *Asr* prayer on Friday to emphasise the religious importance of taking an oath. If the witness is a non-Muslim, he or she may take an oath according to their religion, but the oath is not accepted from a person who is an atheist. Oaths are not acceptable in *hudud* cases at all.

One very unusual use of the oath is in case of divorce by *li'an*, where a husband accuses his wife of adultery and she denies the charge. Normally, an accusation of adultery, which cannot be proved through the evidence of the four *adil* witnesses required by the *Quran*, leaves the accuser open to the punishment of 80 lashes for *qazf*. In this case, however, if the husband swears four oaths that the wife has committed adultery, and then a fifth oath. calling down the wrath of God upon himself if he is lying, and the wife, in turn, swears four times that she has not committed adultery, and a fifth oath in the same terms as that of the husband, the result is that they are irrevocably divorced.

A recent report from Malaysia[20] tells of a case in which an oath was taken by a man accused of rape under the Malaysian Penal Code, which is a civil law statute. The accused took a solemn oath, denying the charge, in the form prescribed by Islamic law in a mosque in Kelantan after *Asr* prayer, in the presence of the Imam of the mosque, the Senior Sessions judge, the prosecutor, his solicitor and the mother of the victim. He was later acquitted by the Sessions Court on the basis that the defence had raised a reasonable doubt as to his guilt. It was noted that this was the first recorded instance of an accused taking an oath in relation to criminal proceedings in the civil courts in Malaysia.

---

20   *Malaysian Law News*, March 1996, p 5.

القانون التجاري ✦

12

ISLAMIC COMMERCIAL LAW

Guidance from *Quran* and *Sunnah*

There are many verses in the *Quran* which encourage trade and
commerce. At the time of the Prophet, trade routes crisscrossed the
Arabian peninsula and the people of Mecca were in the forefront of
trading activity. The Prophet himself had been a successful businessman, as agent for his first wife, Khadijah. The traditions[1] relate that
she first employed him to take charge of a trading expedition to Syria
on her behalf. Later, she was so impressed by his honesty and trust-
worthiness that she offered to marry him and he accepted the offer.
After the marriage he undertook further trading ventures to differing
places in Arabia, including Yemen and Bahrain.

Not surprisingly, the attitude of Islam is that there is no
impediment to honest and legitimate trade and business, so that people
may earn a living, support their families and give charity to those less
fortunate. Islam does not expect believers to give away all their
possessions and live the life of ascetics.

However, just as Islam regulates and influences all other spheres
of life, it also governs the conduct of business and commerce.
Muslims should conduct their business activities in accordance with
the requirements of their religion to be fair, honest and just towards
others. Also, they should not allow their business activities to
dominate so that making money becomes a first priority and they

---

1   Majid Ali Khan, *Muhammad the Final Messenger*, 1983, pp 62-64.

158

neglect religious duties. In particular, all trading must cease during the time of the Friday congregational prayer.[2]

In the *Quran* there are many exhortations to honesty and reliability in commercial transactions. For example:

> O you who believe, fulfill all obligations,[3] also
> Give full measure when you measure; and weigh with a balance that is straight; that is most advantageous and the best of policy.[4]

There are also some specific verses in the *Quran* dealing with trade and commerce, for example verse 282 of Sura al Baqarah which advises that contracts concerning future obligations should be written down and witnessed:

> O you who believe!
> When you deal with each other in transactions involving future obligations
> In a fixed period of time, reduce them to writing.
> Let a scribe write down faithfully as between the parties:
> Let not the scribe refuse to write:
> As Allah has taught him, so let him write.
> Let him who incurs the liability dictate,
> But let him fear his Lord Allah and not diminish anything of what he owes.
> If the party liable is mentally deficient, or weak, or unable himself to dictate,
> Let his guardian dictate faithfully.
> And get two witnesses, out of your own men. . .

An "on-the-spot" transaction need not be reduced to writing, but people are cautioned: "take witnesses whenever you make a commercial contract".[5]

In the following verse there is further advice:

> If you are on a journey, and cannot find a scribe,
> A pledge with possession (may serve the purpose)
> And if one of you deposits a thing on trust with another,
> Let the trustee (faithfully) discharge his trust,
> And let him fear his Lord.
> Conceal not evidence; for whoever conceals it –
> His heart is tainted with sin.
> And Allah knows all that you do.

In the *hadith* there are many statements of the Prophet concerning the necessity for honesty and fair dealing in trade. One such *hadith* says:

---

2   *Quran* 62:9.
3   Ibid 5:1.
4   Ibid 17:35.
5   Ibid 2:282.

"A trustworthy and an honest and truthful businessman will rise up with martyrs on the day of Resurrection".[6]

The aim of the Islamic economic system is to allow people to earn their living in a fair and profitable way without exploitation of others, so that the whole society may benefit. Islam also emphasises the welfare of the community over individual rights. This is in line with recent Western thinking which criticises open market approaches to economic management because they emphasise monetary growth at all cost without regard for quality of life and the widening gap between rich and poor in society.[7] Islamic religious precepts are clearly opposed to the doctrines of capitalism which is seen by Islamic countries to threaten their societies[8] by undermining *Shariah* values.

Principles of the Islamic economic system

Property rights

In principle God is the absolute and eternal owner of everything on earth and in the heavens. However, God has appointed man His vice-regent on earth and entrusted him with God's possessions. Man's ownership of earthly property is therefore a trust (*amanah*) to be enjoyed conditionally so long as man follows the *Shariah* and remains worthy of the trust.[9] People have the right to use natural resources for the benefit of mankind. However, the whole earth is a trust from God and should be looked after by the people who have charge of it and who will ultimately be accountable to God for their actions. The Prophet is reported as saying:

> Never a Muslim plants a tree, but he has the reward of charity for him, for what is eaten out of that is charity; what is stolen out of that, what the beasts eat out of that, what the birds eat out of that is charity for him.[10]

Normani and Rahnema[11] mention that property rights in Islamic law may be divided into three categories – public property, state property and private property. Public property includes forests, pastures, rivers and mines and everything which is found in the sea. Land which is

---

6   Ibn Majah quoted in 'Abdur Rahman i doi, *Women in Shari'ah,* 1990, p 350.

7   N Baydoun and P Blunt, "Notes on Islam, Culture and Organisational Behaviour", 1997, unpublished paper, Northern Territory University, p 2.

8   Ibid.

9   Farhad Normani and Ali Rahnema, *Islamic Economic Systems*, 1995, p 66.

10   Sahih Muslim, *Kitab al-Buyu*, (3764).

11   Farhad Normani and Ali Rahnema, *Islamic Economic Systems*, 1995.

uncultivated (*mawat*) also generally falls into the category of public property. This *mawat* land can be converted into private property by anyone who is willing to take it up and cultivate it and things taken from public property, for example fish caught from the sea, trees felled for timber, also become appropriated to private ownership. The state exercises supervision over all public property and should ensure that there is no exploitation of it contrary to public benefit. For example, the Prophet prohibited the withholding of water where it is to be used to grow herbage or for the use of animals.[12]

There are differences of opinion among the jurists on the status of mines. One line of traditions indicates that the Prophet considered mines a public utility which should always remain common property under state control. Another line of authority suggests that mines can be private property based on a tradition that the Prophet himself gave ownership of a gold mine to one of his companions, subject only to a requirement to pay *zakat*. Some scholars hold that open and accessible mines belong in public ownership, whilst inaccessible mines can be owned privately. However, there is no consensus, and much the same differences apply also to such things as water rights.[13]

Some property is explicitly mentioned in the *Quran* as belonging to God and the Prophet. This includes a proportion of the spoils of war (*anfal*), property surrendered to the Muslims, and various other types of property both movable and immovable such as uncultivated (*mawat*) land, the estates of people who die without an heir and other unclaimed property. Such property can be granted to private individuals by the state, but can equally be taken back by the state if the individual holding it does not put it to productive use. The often quoted example is the land given by the Prophet to Bilal, which was taken back by Caliph Omar because Bilal had not cultivated it and was allowing it to go to waste.

The right to private ownership of property is allowed. Property may be acquired through inheritance, gift, purchase or by taking up common property and/or things on it, as mentioned before. Wealth may be accumulated provided that it is gained fairly. Honest and conscientious work can even be considered a type of worship (*ibadah*). There are differences among the jurists concerning whether

---

12   Sahih Muslim, *Kitab al-Buyu* (3800), (3801).
13   Ibid p 68.

any limits should be placed on the extent of private ownership.[14] However, too much emphasis on materialism can lead to spiritual poverty. Simplicity and moderation are to be preferred to luxury and ostentation in private life. In fact, men are prohibited from wearing gold ornaments and silk clothing except if suffering from a skin disease which obliges them to wear softer fabric. Both men and women are forbidden to use gold and silver utensils or silk furnishings in the home.[15]

Business methods

The paramount principle in business is honesty and fair dealing. The Muslim business person should therefore be a person of high moral values[16] who would not set out to exploit others. Monopolies and price fixing are prohibited. Generally the market should be free and not subject to manipulation. This is so that people will not be exploited by the more powerful in business transactions. The Prophet forbade the practice of townspeople going out to meet desert tribesmen on their way to market so that they could buy their goods cheaply, relying on the tribesmen's ignorance of the market price, and so obtain an unfair profit and reduce competition in the marketplace. Hoarding is forbidden when the intention is to force up the price in times of scarcity and so profit at the expense of others.

People engaging in trade and commerce should behave equitably. Vendors of goods should not hide any defects in them, nor lie about the quality of the goods. There is no doctrine of *caveat emptor* in Islamic law. A *hadith* describes an incident which occurred one day when the Prophet was visiting a market. He thrust his hand into a heap of grain and found it wet underneath. He scolded the merchant for attempting to deceive buyers by hiding the bad wheat under the good.[17] Likewise the merchant should be accurate in weighing and measuring goods.

---

14   For a full discussion of this point, see Farhad Normani and Ali Rahnema, *Islamic Economic Systems*, 1995, pp 70-77.

15   Yusuf al-Qaradawi, *The Lawful and the Prohibited in Islam*, 1989, p 98.

16   N Baydoun and P Blunt, "Notes on Islam, Culture and Organisational Behaviour", 1997, unpublished paper, Northern Territory University, p 5.

17   Quoted in Yusuf al-Qaradawi, *The Lawful and the Prohibited in Islam*, 1989, p 261.

Dealing in stolen goods is prohibited. The Prophet said: "He who buys stolen property, with the knowledge that it was stolen, shares in the sin and shame of stealing".[18]

It is prohibited to sell *haram* goods. Thus Muslims may not deal in alcohol, pigs or pork products, idols and statues and other commodities forbidden by Islam. Muslims therefore may not own liquor shops, or shares in companies owning breweries, piggeries and similar businesses. Similarly Muslims should not earn money from *haram* activities such as prostitution or fortune telling.

In a just Islamic society there should be an equitable distribution of wealth. This does not mean that some people would not be richer than others since people are not equal in their abilities or in their opportunities to acquire wealth, but there should not be extremes of wealth and poverty because the rich have an obligation to help the poor. It is charity for a creditor to remit some of the debt for a debtor who is unable to repay it because of misfortune.

Likewise, people of means have a legal obligation under *Shariah* to pay *zakat* to assist those who are less fortunate. Both *zakat* and the Islamic system of inheritance, which ensures that the property of a deceased person is distributed among all the heirs in stated proportions, have an important role to play in preventing the accumulation of wealth in the hands of a few and in making money available to circulate for the good of society.

The prohibition of *riba*

Unlawful gain (*riba*) is prohibited.[19] The word *riba* is often translated as "interest", but its meaning is wider than this. Nabil Saleh defines *riba* in its *Shariah* context as:

> an unlawful gain derived from the quantitative inequality of the counter-values in any transaction purporting to effect of the exchange of two or more species (*anwa'*) which belong to the same genus (*jins*) and are governed by the same efficient cause (*'illa*).[20]

Riba is not confined to paying interest in the form of additional money on monetary transactions but it also means that commodities such as cereals, dried fruits and legumes should not be exchanged

---

18   Ibid p 264.
19   Dr Ala'eddin Kharofa has pointed out that the early Christian church also condemned usury. A canon of the Third Lateran Council in 1179 stated that "Manifest usurers shall not be admitted to communion, nor if they die in their sin, receive Christian burial". *Usury, "Interest" or Riba*, 1993, p 17.
20   Nabil Saleh, *Unlawful Gain and Legitimate Profit in Islamic Law*, 1986, p 13.

except in equal quantities and with immediate effect.[21] The rules are complex, varying with the type of commodity, and there has been much disputation among the scholars concerning exactly which types of transactions amount to *riba* and in what situations.

In practice much of the modern discussion of *riba* centres on the unlawfulness of charging interest on loans. A few scholars say that only excessive interest (usury) if forbidden but the great majority forbid the giving or taking of interest of any kind. The rationale behind the prohibition is that allowing interest permits the strong to prosper at the expense of the weak, so that the rich become richer and the poor poorer. Yusuf al-Qaradawi gives four reasons for the prohibition of interest:[22]

- Taking interest implies taking another person's property without giving him anything in exchange. The lender receives something for nothing.

- Dependence on interest discourages people from working to earn money. Money lent at interest will not be used in industry, trade or commerce all of which need capital, thus depriving society of benefits.

- Permitting the taking of interest discourages people from doing good. If interest is prohibited people will lend to each other with good will expecting nothing more back than they have loaned.

- The lender is likely to be wealthy and the borrower poor. The poor will be exploited by the wealthy through the charging of interest on loans.

The prohibition of interest has posed problems for sincerely religious Muslims, since the prohibition extends to borrowing at interest as well as lending. This makes it difficult for practising Muslims to find a legitimate way to acquire major items such as a house or car. As a way of avoiding interest in commercial enterprises, Islamic banks and co-operatives have now been set up in most Muslim countries. However, these are still few and far between, and where such facilities do not exist, Yusuf al-Qaradawi says that "if a person is driven to borrowing money on interest due to some pressing need, the sin will be on the lender alone". Nevertheless, such need is limited to the necessities of life, the exact amount needed and no more, and the

---

21 'Abdur Rahman i Doi, *Shari'ah: The Islamic Law*, 1989, p 380.
22 Yusuf al-Qaradawi, *The Lawful and the Prohibited in Islam*, 1989, p 265-266.

borrower must continue to search for ways to escape from the predicament of paying interest.[23]

Gharar (uncertainty)

Uncertainty (*gharar*) is forbidden. In legal and business terms *gharar* means to undertake a venture blindly without sufficient knowledge or to undertake an excessively risky transaction.[24] *Gharar* applies in a number of circumstances:

- When the seller is not in a position to hand over the goods to the buyer.
- The subject matter of the sale is incapable of acquisition, for example the sale of fruit which is not yet ripened or fish or birds not yet caught.
- Speculative investments such as trading in futures on the stock market.
- Where the purchaser is not given the opportunity of inspecting goods before purchasing them.

However, minor uncertainties can be permitted where there is some necessity.

To avoid *gharar* it is necessary that:

- the subject matter of the transaction be in existence;
- the characteristics of the subject matter be known;
- the parties to the contract should have such control over the subject as to be able to ensure that exchange will take place;
- if performance is to take place in the future, the date of performance should be certain.

The concept of *gharar* has led to the condemnation of some or all types of insurance by Muslim scholars, since insurance involves an unknown risk. This has lead to the development of *takaful* (co-operative) insurance in some Muslim countries. This is discussed in Chapter 13.

---

23   Ibid p 267.
24   Mahmood M Sanusi, "Gharar", *IIUM Law Journal,* Vol 3 No 2, 1993, p 87.

Islamic forms of business organisation

Islamic business enterprises can be placed into two major categories:[25]

Ijarah or wage-rent enterprises

Wage-rent enterprises, based on *ijarah* (hire), in which the person with capital hires labour for a specific job or time and at a fixed wage. The financier receives all profit and is responsible for all losses. Such an enterprise may be arranged by a sole proprietor, or as a partnership (*shirakah*).

Profit-sharing enterprises

These can be concluded in agriculture (share-cropping), horticulture or trade according to the traditional scholars. The majority of modern jurists agree that this principle can be extended to industrial production.

Many enterprises are carried on through partnerships. There are a number of different forms of partnership recognised by Islamic law:[26]

Shirkah al-'Inan (limited partnership) – in this kind of partnership, partners contribute capital, property and/or labour. Profits and losses are shared in an agreed manner. The difference between this and other forms of partnership is that each partner is only the agent and not a surety for his co-partners and so a partner is not liable for a debt contracted by his co-partners and is only able to sue someone with whom he himself has contracted.[27]

An exception to this is the *inan sharikat a'mal (abdan)* partnership where partners contribute labour. One partner can bind the others in undertaking to perform work for an employer and each is entitled to claim the total salary due from the employer.[28]

Mudaraba or *Qirad:* (dormant partnership) – a *qirad* is a contract whereby one person (the dormant partner) gives funds or property to another on the basis that the lender will share in the active partner's profits in a proportion agreed in advance. They may not agree on a fixed return since this would amount to *riba*. If there is a

---

25   See Farhad Normani and Ali Rahnema, *Islamic Economic Systems*, 1995, pp 95-98 for greater detail on this.

26   These are discussed more fully in Abdur Rahman i Doi, *Shari'ah: The Islamic Law,* pp 365-367.

27   Nabil Saleh, *Unlawful Gain and Legitimate Profit in Islamic Law*, 1986, p 93.

28   Ibid.

loss they share the loss proportionally also, but the liability of the person who has provided the capital is limited to the amount of that capital. The dormant partner remains the owner of the capital, but takes no active part in the enterprise. The trader is responsible only for negligence or breach of contract. Legitimate expenses of the venture such as employees' wages and travelling expenses are deductible from the capital. The contract can be determined by either party on notice to the other.

This kind of partnership is called *muzar'a* when it is applied to share-cropping of agricultural land. The scholars disagree, however, about whether share-cropping is always permissible.

Musharakah – when two or more people combine their resources to invest in an enterprise, a *musharakah* partnership is formed according to Islamic law. All parties have the right to share in decision making and profit making. Losses are borne in proportion to capital subscribed. There are various categories of *musharakah:*[29]

- *Shirkat al-mulk* – joint ownership of property without joint exploitation of capital, as when people merely share ownership of an asset.

- *Shirkat al-Aqd* – two or more persons combine to carry on a business in partnership with profits to be shared. All partners may contribute some capital and labour or services.

- *Shirkat al-Wujuh* – this is a credit partnership which purchases commodities on credit and resells immediately. Profit is distributed in an agreed ratio.

Norhashimah Mohd Yasin has summarised the rules governing *musharakah* as follows:

- *Musharakah* can be for a general or specific transaction for a specified period of time, which may be extended if the partners agree.

- All partners should receive regular information concerning the operation of the business and its finances.

- Partners must agree in advance before entering a new *musharakah* contract with others.

---

29   See Norhashimah Mohd Yasin. "Shariah Contracts Used by Islamic Banks", *Al-Nahdah*, Vol 17 1997, pp 5-6 for an extensive discussion of this topic.

- The proportion of profit to be shared must be agreed at the time of making the contract. There are different opinions among the scholars as to whether the ratio of profit must conform to the proportion of capital invested by each partner.

- The ratio of sharing the loss must be in accordance with the proportion of investment.

- Ideally the capital should be in money, rather than commodities. If the latter, the monetary value must be estimated.

- The *musharakah* contract is terminated on death or the giving of notice.

The *musharakah* contract is extensively used in Islamic banking.

The modern company

Most of the scholars agree that the modern corporation is acceptable in an Islamic economy, and that investments can be made in the stock market providing that the companies involved trade only in *halal* commodities. This is similar to the modern concept of ethical investment. An intending purchaser of shares should give careful consideration to the activities of the company to ensure that none of them is contrary to Islam.

Under Islamic law it is lawful to own ordinary shares in companies, but it has been pointed out that it would not be lawful to hold preference shares since these offer a pre-determined rate of return which amounts to *riba*.[30] Similarly it is not lawful to invest in debentures or futures.

Employment and industrial relations

Islam encourages people to go out and earn their living through honest work. Yusuf al-Qaradawi says:

> It is not permitted to the Muslim to avoid working for a living on the pretext of devoting his life to worship or trust in Allah, as gold and silver certainly do not fall from the sky. It is also not permissible for him to depend on charity while he is able to earn what is sufficient for his own and his family's needs through his own efforts.[31]

Any sort of work should be regarded as acceptable so long as it does not involve anything prohibited by Islam. Thus making and selling

---

30   Nublan Zaky Yusoff, *An Islamic Perspective of Stock Market,* 1992, p 71.
31   Yusuf al-Qaradawi, *The Lawful and the Prohibited in Islam,* 1989, pp 125-6.

wine, beer and spirits, or prostitution or exotic dancing are considered *haram* occupations which must be avoided by Muslims.

Islam emphasises the dignity of labour, and the employee or labourer is entitled to a fair wage and decent treatment by his employer. The *Mejelle*, the commercial code of the Ottoman empire, contained various provisions as to the hire of labour, for example "the right of the common employee to pay arises on the work being done" (art 424). Also "if someone employs a workman without naming a wage, if there is a known daily wage, he gives the known wage, if not, he gives a wage, equivalent to the work" (art 565); "Bakshish (tips) given by outsiders to servants, cannot be counted towards their wages" (art 567).

Zakat and taxation

The obligation to pay *zakat* is one of the five pillars of Islam and is incumbent on every Muslim who possesses assets of a value above the *nisab* (legal threshold). The purposes of *zakat* are set out in the *Quran*:

> The alms are only for the poor and needy, and those who are employed to administer the funds, for those whose hearts have (recently) been reconciled (to Islam), for those in bondage and in debt, for the cause of Allah, and the wayfarers.[32]

Some writers have described *zakat* as a form of taxation. Others have translated it as "alms" suggesting that it is purely a charity. It has also been called "an act of worship expressing a Muslim's gratitude for God's *financial* gifts".[33] It is similar in concept to a tithe, its purpose being to discourage the concentration of wealth and to "purify" the surplus wealth of the relatively well-to-do by redistribution to the poor.[34] It discourages hoarding and encourages the return of idle wealth into economic activity for the benefit of society generally.

Zakat is assessed as 2.5 per cent of the total of the payer's genuinely owned assets held for one full year after deducting his or her liabilities. *Zakat* must be paid annually and is usually paid before the end of the month of *Ramadan*. *Zakat* is payable not only by individuals but by corporate entities such as Islamic banks. *Zakat* should be paid into the public treasury, called the *Bait ul-Mal*, from

---

32   *Quran*, 9:60.
33   Nabil Baydoun, notes on Islamic Financial System, NTU, 1997.
34   Ibid.

where it is paid out by the authorities to assist those in need. Thus *zakat* funds form the basis of a social security system.

In non-Muslim countries such as Australia, and some Muslim countries, *zakat,* is a voluntary payment, although a religious obligation. In other Muslim countries it is a compulsory and is collected by the state authorities. In Malaysia, payment of *zakat* is compulsory and is collected by the state[35] but Muslim taxpayers are allowed to off-set their *zakat* against the amount of their income tax.

As well as *zakat*, most scholars allow that the Islamic state may have recourse to other forms of taxation to raise revenue for administration, defence and public purposes, since *zakat* may be used only for the purposes set out in the *Quran*. However, taxation has proved to be a contentious issue for modern states like Sudan and Pakistan which have sought to "Islamise" their economies. Not only has there been a lack of agreement among the scholars on individual aspects of taxation – for example, whether indexing or proportional taxation are allowed – but the world has become much more complex, so that the traditional solutions of the past are not always still appropriate.

Not surprisingly, there remains a wide gap between the theory of Islamic taxation and its practice in modern Muslim states.

Other forms of Islamic taxation – *Ushr, Kharaj, Khums* and *Jizyah*

Ushr is a traditional levy on agricultural produce, while *kharaj* is a tax on agricultural land. *Ushr* is imposed at the rate of one-tenth or one-twentieth of the produce at the time of production depending on whether the land is irrigated or non-irrigated. *Kharaj* is paid annually on land on the basis of actual production. In some countries the *ushr* on agricultural produce is termed *zakat*. *Khums* is an obligatory tax, recognised in the Shia schools rather than the Sunni, of one fifth on mineral deposits such as gold, silver and oil, and also, traditionally, on the booty received in war. This should be paid to the *bait ul-mal* to be used for the welfare of the poor. These taxes are not imposed in all Muslim countries.

Jizyah was an annual tax imposed on non-Muslims living in an Islamic state. Non-Muslims were not required to pay *zakat*, nor were

---

35   N Baydoun and P Blunt, "Notes on Islam, Culture and Organisational Behaviour" 1997, unpublished paper, Northern Territory University, p 6.

they obliged to render military service. Their financial contribution to the public treasury was by way of *jizyah*.

Contract law

The general principle of the Islamic law of contract is contained in the *Qura*nic verse: "O you who believe, fulfill all obligations".[36] The definition of contract (*al-'aqd*) is similar to that in the common law, but is wider in that it includes dispositions which are gratuitous as well as endowments and trusts. A contract consists of an agreement made between two or more people. The elements of contract are quite similar to those of the common law:

- Offer and acceptance – a contract requires an offer (*ijab*) and acceptance (*qabul*). The contract can be oral or in writing, made by signs or gestures or by conduct, or through an agent. If the offer is sent by writing it remains in force until received by the other party who must then reply promptly.

- Consideration – is essential. As in the common law, consideration may consist of money, goods or services. It must be something which is capable of being given, or if an action, performed. It must not consist of a substance which is illegal according to Islamic law.

- Capacity – the parties entering into a contract must be legally competent. A minor, an person of unsound mind, an insolvent person, a person legally declared a prodigal, an intoxicated person or a person suffering from an illness which leads to his or her death (*mard al-mawt*) cannot enter into a binding contract.

- Legality – the purpose of the contract must be legal. A contract to grow grapes for winemaking would be illegal as would a contract to sell firearms to criminals, or one to make a loan at interest.

- Absence of duress – the parties must enter into the contract of their own free will. A contract concluded under duress is null and void.

---

36   5:1.

The doctrine of option (*khiyar*) in contracts

Under the common law, once a contract is made it is binding on the parties to it. Islamic contract law allows the parties the option (*khiyar*) of withdrawing from a concluded contract in certain circumstances.

The doctrine of *khiyar al-majlis* gives each of the parties to a contract of sale the option of withdrawing from the contract so long as they have not physically separated. There is no time limit to the *majlis* (meeting) which only ends when one party leaves the meeting place. This principle only applies to contracts made in a face to face meeting and its purpose is to ensure that the parties are as sure as they can be about the transaction.[37]

Other types of option exist, such as *khiyar al-shart*, an agreed period of time in which either party may rescind; *khiyar al 'aib*, an option to rescind for fault existing in the goods or services at the time of the contract. This may arise out of the failure of the seller to make a full and frank disclosure of any defects existing in the goods as he is bound to do under Islamic law; *khiyar al ru'ya* – where goods are sold sight unseen but the buyer has the right to reject them upon sight; *khiyar al wasf* may be exercised where the goods do not meet the precise description in the contract.

The above options cannot be excluded and must be exercised within a reasonable time. These options are for the benefit of the buyer and preclude the common law idea of *caveat emptor*.[38]

Termination of contract

A contract may be terminated by mutual agreement. A contract may be set aside unilaterally by the innocent party in cases of duress, undue influence, misrepresentation or fraud. A contract can also be ended through frustration, or where a substantial and material change in circumstances makes it unduly burdensome for one party to perform the contract.

Assignment of contract

As in the common law, some contracts can be assigned to third parties. A transfer of a debt is called *halawah*. According to Coulson

---

37   See NG Coulson, *Commercial Law in the Gulf States,* 1984 for a full discussion of Islamic contract law.
38   Ibid.

halawah has a much narrower scope than assignment under the common law, since it is restricted to a simple triangular situation where A the creditor assigns the debt owed to him by B to his own creditor C. The debts owed by A and B must be equal otherwise the assignment is technically void, but the law will see the transaction as being in the nature of an irrevocable power of attorney to collect the debt.[39]

Remedies for breach of contract

Certain remedies are available to the injured party without judicial sanction.[40] These include termination of the contract, withdrawal under the option of *khiyar*, withholding payment or performance or set-off. The court's assistance must be sought to obtain the remedies of damages, specific performance, rescission or civil imprisonment.[41]

Major types of contract

- *Bay'* (sale) – this is the unconditional and immediate transfer of the ownership of an existing and determined object of legal value, capable of delivery for a fixed price.[42] The subject matter of the sale must be lawful. A contract for the sale of something at a future time, or for an unspecified price is void. A contract for barter is permitted, but there must be immediate delivery of the goods.

- *Bay 'al Wafa* – is a sale in which the vendor retains a right of redemption of the property and may repay the purchase price by instalments over a fixed period. This is really a type of mortgage transaction, designed to avoid the prohibition on *riba*. Some scholars believe that this should properly be classified as a pledge or *rahn*.

- *Istisna* – this is a contract for the sale of goods to be manufactured and can be revoked by either party before the goods are manufactured.

- *Ijara* (hire) – no distinction is made between the hire of real property and chattels. This term is also used for employment

---

39   Ibid.
40   SH Amin, *Islamic Law in the Contemporary World*, 1985, p 68.
41   Ibid.
42   NG Coulson, *Commercial Law in the Gulf States*, 1984.

contracts. The nature of the hire must be precisely defined, the amount of rental or wages must be fixed and the period of time must also be precisely determined.

- *Hiba* (gift) – the transfer of ownership must be absolute and unconditional. The scholars differ on the question of when a gift becomes binding and effective.

- *Ariyya* (loan) – this refers to the loan of a particular and identifiable piece of property with or without conditions attached.

Islamic arbitration (*Tahkim*)

The arbitration of disputes is highly recommended in Islamic law. In marital disputes, the *Quran* specifically recommends the appointment of arbitrators (*hakam*) one each from the family of the husband and the wife.[43] In non-family disputes also, arbitration is recommended in *Sura Al-Hujarat*:[44]

> If two parties among the Believers fall into a quarrel, make peace between them. . .
> Make peace between them with justice; and be fair
> For Allah loves those who are fair (and just).

Vincent Powell-Smith has noted that the earliest record of an arbitration agreement in the Islamic world was one between Ali bin Abi Talib and Muawiyat bin Abi over the succession to the Caliphate in the very early days of Islam, and was very similar in content to modern arbitration documents.[45] All the Sunni schools agree that people in dispute are entitled to refer their differences to an arbitrator; however, the Shia Ithna-Ashari school does not approve of arbitration.[46]

One difference between Islamic arbitration and arbitration under common law rules is that only an existing dispute can be referred to arbitration under Islamic law, since any agreement concerning a dispute which might arise in the future would constitute *gharar*. Another difference noted by Professor Powell-Smith is that in Islamic law an agreement to arbitrate an existing dispute is revocable by either party up to the time the award is made.

---

43   *Sura An-Nisaa* 4:35.
44   49:9.
45   *Aspects of Arbitration: Common law and Shari'a compared*, 1995, p 7.
46   Ibid p 9.

174

Under *Shariah*, the scope of arbitration is limited to private disputes, usually concerning commercial transactions and property rights. There are differences between the schools concerning the precise matters which can be arbitrated. The law applied is, of course, *Shariah*, and again there will be variations according to the opinions of the prevailing school in the locality where the arbitration takes place.

Shariah law is more strict than the common law with regard to the qualifications of the arbitrator, and the evidence and procedure to be applied in the arbitration.[47] The arbitrator must have similar qualifications to those which are required of a *qadi* (Islamic judge). He must be an adult Muslim man (not a woman according to all but the Hanafi school), *'adl* (just), free from physical defects, for example deafness, which might impede the arbitration and learned in *Shariah*. However, the Hanafis say that being learned is not necessarily a prerequisite for an arbitrator since he can avail himself of professional advice.

Once the arbitration award is made, it becomes binding in the same way as if made by a court, according to the majority of scholars, and is enforceable by the court. It may be challenged in the same way as a court judgment and set aside if found to be contrary to *Shariah* principles.[48]

---

47   Ibid pp 39, 53.
48   Ibid p 61.

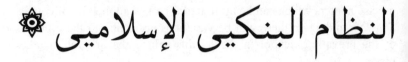

النظام البنكيى الإسلاميى ❋

13

ISLAMIC BANKING

The beginnings of Islamic banking

As mentioned above, one of the great difficulties sincere Muslims face in modern life is being able to obtain finance for major purchases and capital for carrying on business without infringing the prohibition against *riba*. No solution for this problem was immediately apparent in traditional jurisprudence, since, in the days of the Prophet, society was much simpler, and financial and business transactions much less complex. The practical effect of the prohibition of *riba* was that money could be lent only out of charity, interest free, or as participant in trade or a commercial transaction.

During the period of European colonisation, most Muslim countries were induced by their colonial masters to adopt banking and financial systems based on European models. Little serious thought was given to the establishment of Islamic banks and economic systems based on the *Shariah* until well into the 20th century, when the resurgence of Islamic thought and identity led to the questioning of interest based banking systems as being inappropriate and undesirable in Muslim countries.

Since Islam prohibited interest but permitted trade, Islamic economists exercised their ingenuity to formulate a system of banking through trade, with the bank as participant in ventures undertaken by its customers, and sharing in their profit or loss. Since there was no precedent for the modern commercial bank in Islamic history, the structures of ordinary banks were able to be adapted for use in Islamic banking. Thus, where normal banking practices do not conflict with Islamic principles, Islamic banks have been able to adopt normal banking procedures and practices. In some countries such as Iran and Pakistan, Islamic banks operate under the laws generally applicable to all banks, while in others, such as Turkey and Malaysia, special legislation has been passed to enable Islamic banks to operate.[1] Other vehicles for Islamic financing take the form of investment companies and investment funds.

Principles of Islamic banking

- The giving and taking of interest is prohibited in all transactions. The point has been made that Islamic banking is broader than mere interest free banking since banks should be actively concerned with promoting the social benefits of an Islamic economy.[2]

- Business and trade activities are undertaken on the basis of *halal* profit. Not only should interest based transactions be avoided, but banks should offer finance and/or participation only to businesses which are engaged in activities legal under Islamic law, for example an Islamic bank could not finance a brewery, piggery, casino or similar *haram* enterprise.

- Transactions should be free from *gharar* (unreasonable uncertainty or speculation).

- Making money from money is not acceptable to Islam. Money has no value in itself. It is not acceptable that money should be hoarded or left in a bank without productive investment.

- Financial transactions should be in line with Islamic principles, of discouraging hoarding and encouraging social justice. Islamic banks have religious committees to advise them on the propriety of their activities under *Shariah*.

- *Zakat* is to be paid by the bank. Like any Muslim individual, the bank also has an obligation to contribute to the assistance of the poor and disadvantaged in society.

---

1   Said Zafar and Shameela Chinoy, "Submission on Islamic Financial Institutions, Canada", 1997, p 2.
2   Al-Omar and Abdel-Haq, *Islamic Banking*, 1996, p 21.

Financing structures used by Islamic banks

- *Mudarabah*: a contract whereby one party (*rabb al-mal*) contributes capital while the other (*mudarib*) provides work and management skills. The bank lends money to a customer for a business venture and in return receives a specified percentage of the venture's profits for a pre-determined period of time. The share of the profit covers repayment of the principal of the loan plus a profit for the bank. If the venture incurs a loss, the loss is shared by the bank. The bank is not liable for losses beyond the amount of money loaned, and the *mudarib* can lose only his time and effort.

- *Musharakah*: a partnership, usually for a short period of time, to carry out a specific project. It is similar in nature to a joint venture. *Musharakah*, in relation to Islamic banking, can be either permanent – without a specified period – the bank participating in the equity and receiving an annual share of the profit, or diminishing/ decreasing partnership in which additional payments can be made over and above the bank's share of the profits so that the bank's equity gradually reduces to nothing at which point it ceases to be a partner.[3]

- *Murabahah* – in this case, commodities are purchased by the bank and sold to the customer at cost plus an agreed profit. Normally the customer may pay by instalments. The use of *murabahah* by Islamic banks has been criticised since the bank is able to finance the buyer without taking any risk itself. It is simply a cost plus profit sale which has the appearance of just being a device to circumvent the prohibition of interest.[4]

- *Bay Bithaman Ajil* (BBA) – this is similar to *murabahah*. In modern practice BBA is used for longer term financing of assets such as buildings and machinery while *murabahah* is for short-term finance for example working capital. BBA is a deferred payment by instalments, while *murabahah* is a deferred payment by lump sum.[5]

---

3   Norhashimah Mohd Yasin, "Shariah Contracts Used by Islamic Banks", *Al-Nahdah*, Jan-June 1997, p 5.
4   Ibid p 7.
5   The two are not distinguished in all jurisdictions. Ibid, p 5.

- *Bay' Al-Salam* – this is a contract of sale of a specified commodity in which the price is paid in full in advance for goods to be delivered at a future time at an agreed price.[6] It can be used to buy goods where the seller needs working capital before he can deliver.[7]

- *Ijara* – direct lease financing – the bank purchases an asset and leases it to the customer for a term, the bank receiving an agreed charge or rent.

- *Bai'Al-Takjiri* – lease ending with ownership (hire purchase finance) – this is the same as *ijara* except that the bank and the customer agree that the customer will eventually purchase the asset at an agreed price with all lease rentals previously paid forming part of the price.

- *Istisna* – this is the giving of an order to a workman to make something, with agreement to pay a definite price on completion. This method of financing can be used for a house under construction. The bank can contract with a customer who wishes to purchase a house (or other item) and a parallel contract with a builder or hire a builder to construct it. Payment of instalments can begin before the house is completed or on completion.

- *Qard ul-Hasan* – benevolent loan – the borrower is obliged to repay only the amount of the loan, but *Shariah* encourages the borrower to pay something beyond the principal amount without demand from the bank. In practice, Islamic banks use this method only for charitable purposes or for buying Government Investment Certificates.[8]

- *Al-Wadiah* – is a contract of trust or safe keeping. The bank accepts deposits from customers and guarantees the safety and return of the funds. The bank is entitled to use the depositor's money and keep the profits.

- *Rahn* (pledge) – Islamic banks are able to take security for loans by this method.

---

6   Ibid p 8.

7   "Islamic Funding Structures and Financing Vehicles", *Nida'ul Islam*, Nov – Dec 1995.

8   Norhashimah Mohd Yasin, "Shariah Contracts Used by Islamic Banks", *Al-Nahdah*, Jan-June 1997, p 10.

The first Islamic banks

The first Islamic bank was set up as an experiment at Mit Ghamr, a rural area outside Cairo, Egypt, in 1963. The aim of its founders was to encourage local people to save, invest in local enterprises, undertake small development projects and so raise the standard of living in the community. Emphasis was placed on understanding local conditions, providing simple facilities which could be easily understood and used by customers and developing a relationship of trust between the bank and the villagers.

The Bank introduced three types of accounts:

- Savings and Loan fund – minimum deposit 5 piasters (5c), with freedom of deposit and withdrawal. Regular savers in this type of account were entitled to short-term loans for productive ventures with free technical advice provided by the bank.

- Investment fund – people who wished to invest in profitable enterprises could use this fund to invest either directly or indirectly through entrepreneurs. Withdrawal could be restricted in accordance with the nature of the investment and its liquidity requirements.

- Social Service fund – money for this fund was provided from *zakat* and other donations. Its purpose was to assist savers who fell into financial difficulties as a result of misfortune.

The bank participated in the losses suffered by its customers' ventures as well as their profits and provided technical assistance free of charge where needed.

Following the success of this first experiment in Islamic banking, eight other Islamic banks had been set up in Egypt by 1967, including one in Cairo with 250,000 depositors. However, apparently for political reasons,[9] the experiment was brought to an end in 1967. Evaluations of the performance of the bank demonstrated that the bank had been influential in promoting social change in the areas in which it operated, by mobilising the savings of small depositors, changing attitudes of villagers from passive acceptance of their lot towards active concern for the community and checking the trend for villagers to migrate to the city by encouraging local industry.[10]

---

9   Al-Omar and Abdel-Haq, *Islamic Banking*, 1996.
10   Ahmed A El Naggar, "Islamic Banking in Egypt, a model and a challenge" in Ataul Hoque (ed), *Readings in Islamic Banking*, 1987, p 265.

In 1973, the Amanah Bank was set up in the Philippines to cater for that country's Muslim minority. It did not last long and its failure has been blamed on the possibility that it was really only a propaganda gimmick for the Marcos regime, rather than a genuine attempt at Islamic banking.[11] Another Islamic bank, the Amanah Islamic Investment Bank, was set up in 1990.

Islamic banks or Finance Houses (some Muslims wish to avoid the connotations of the word "bank") were set up in Dubai in 1975, Kuwait in 1977, Bahrain in 1979 and Qatar in 1981. In Sudan and Egypt, the Faisal Islamic banks (named after Prince Muhammad Ibn Faisal of Saudi Arabia, a leading proponent of Islamic banking) opened their doors in 1977. Islamic banks have also been set up in Jordan, Turkey, Malaysia, Indonesia, Tunisia, Sudan, Sri Lanka, Nigeria and more recently in the former Russian republic of Kazakhstan.

In Europe and America, Islamic banks or Finance Houses, or where registration as a bank is not possible under local law, Islamic investment companies, have appeared in Luxembourg, Switzerland, Canada, Denmark, Britain and the United States. Islamic banks are now operating in 45 countries. There are now over 130 Islamic banks around the world managing more than US$120 billion in funds.[12] As well, many conventional banks have opened Islamic desks. Obstacles to setting up Islamic banks in the West include the fact that most states have banking statutes requiring banks to keep a prescribed proportion of their deposits with the central bank in deposits which are interest bearing, and require payment of interest on savings accounts.

In Saudi Arabia, where all aspects of life are supposed to conform to *Shariah* anyway, there was reluctance for a time to authorise an Islamic bank since this suggested that existing financial institutions might not be Islamic.[13] After some decades, a licence was granted to the Al-Rajhi Banking and Investment Corporation which eventually became the most profitable in the region, and one of the largest.

---

11   *Asiaweek*, 30.10.1992, p 62.
12   Said Zafar and Shameela Chinoy, "Submission on Islamic Financial Institutions, Canada", 1997, p 5.
13   Andrew Cunningham, "The growth of Islamic financing", *Project and Trade Finance,* February 1994, p 35.

Some countries decided to go further than merely setting up, or allowing Islamic banks to operate, by decisions to Islamise their entire economic systems. Following the revolution of 1979 in Iran, a new Law of Usury-Free Banking was passed in 1984, which provided that all Iranian financial institutions were to be Islamised by 22 March 1985.

In Pakistan, the Constitution provides that the laws of the country should be brought into conformity with *Shariah*. Under the regime of Zia ul-Haq, in 1979, the government commenced an attempt to Islamise the financial system by eliminating interest among other measures. Advisory committees were set up and plans devised, but progress was slow. Interest free counters were opened in all the five nationalised banks in 1981 and necessary changes made to the banking and other laws to accommodate Islamic banking. Indications are, however, that the process of Islamisation of the financial system has a long way to go in Pakistan and it is still opposed by some powerful interests.

Overall, it seems that Islamic banking has expanded greatly from its small beginnings in Egypt in 1963. There are now Islamic banks and/or finance institutions in nearly all countries with a Muslim majority and many in Muslim minority countries also. While some Muslim countries have tried to operate their whole economies under Islamic principles, in most areas Islamic finance remains a niche market,[14] albeit one of growing importance. When Islamic banking first began, Western observers believed it was doomed to failure. Clearly, this prediction was incorrect.

A look at one Islamic bank in practice

The following section will provide detail about the structure and operation of one specific Islamic bank, Bank Islam in Malaysia.

Bank Islam was supported by the Malaysian Government and established under the *Islamic Banking Act* 1983. The passage of the Act was preceded by 11 months of research by a government sponsored committee which studied the operation of the Faisal Islamic Bank in Egypt and Sudan. It concluded that the principle of sharing profits and losses was acceptable and could be promoted in four ways – through *Mudarabah, Murabahah, Musharakah* and *Wadiah*.

---

14   Rodney Wilson, "Going Global", *The Banker*, March 1995, p 45.

A difficulty existed with regard to short-term investments by the bank, as it would be unable to buy treasury bills and short-term government securities because of the prohibition against interest. A new *Investment Act* 1983 was passed, allowing the government to issue short dated investment certificates which would carry dividends rather than interest.

The *Islamic Banking Act* 1983 is modelled on the conventional Malaysian *Banking Act* 1973, with modifications to bring it into line with Islamic principles. Like other Malaysian banks, the Islamic bank is under the control of the Central Bank, *Bank Negara*.

The structure of Bank Islam is similar to that of commercial banks, with a Board of Directors heading departments dealing with investments, funding and administration. There is also a religious supervisory council which consists of between three and seven Islamic scholars whose role is to ensure that the bank complies with Islamic law.

Bank Islam's initial paid up capital was RM80 million, of which 30 per cent was taken up by the Federal Government, 10 per cent by PMFB (Pilgrims Management and Fund Board), 5 per cent by Perkim, 25 per cent by religious departments of the States and 30 per cent by various other government agencies. In 1990/91 the Bank took steps to expand its equity and shares were listed on the Kuala Lumpur stock exchange. The paid up capital of the bank is now RM133.4 million.[15]

Types of accounts

Savings

The bank guarantees savings deposited on an *Al-Wadiah* basis, but is not obliged to pay any rewards to the savers. The bank may, at its discretion, pay cash rewards from their profits at the end of the financial year.

Investment

Depositors authorise the bank to invest their money in any of its projects on the basis that after the expiry of the specified period, the account holder will get an agreed share of the profits. There are two kinds of investment account, both operated on the *mudarabah* principle.

---

15   BIMB, *Islamic Banking Practice*, 1994, p 155.

- The special investment account accepts deposits from the government and corporate customers. Modes of investment and ratios of profit distribution may be individually negotiated.
- The general investment account, accepts deposits on a term basis (from one month to 48 months). The bank manages the investment funds. The profit sharing ratio is 70:30 of gross profits, of which the customer receives 70 per cent. The minimum investment is RM500.

Current account

This is operated in the same way as in conventional banking systems but on the principle of *Al-Wadiah* and no interest is paid. The bank uses these funds to generate a profit and provides the customer with services such as cheque books and other current account facilities. The minimum deposit is RM500.

Trade finance

Methods of trade finance are:

- Letter of credit under the principle of *Al-Wakala* – The bank may require the customer to deposit the full amount of the value of goods to be acquired under the principle of *Al-Wadiah*. The bank charges fees and commissions for its services.
- Letter of credit under the principle of *Al-Musharakah* – The customer places with the bank a deposit for his share of the goods under *Al-Wadiah* principles. The bank issues the letter of credit and uses customer's deposit and its own share of the finance. The customer receives and uses goods as per agreement. Profit is divided between bank and customer as per agreement.
- Letter of credit under the principles of *Al-Murabahah* – The customer requests bank to acquire the goods using its own financing. The bank sells the goods to the customer at cost plus profit margin for settlement by cash or on a deferred payment (*bai bi-thamin ajil*) basis.
- Letter of guarantee – The bank may require the customer to place a certain amount of deposit with the bank under *Al-Wadiah* principle. The bank charges a fee for its service.
- Working capital under the principle of *Al-Murabahah* – The bank purchases or appoints the customer as its agent to purchase the goods required and the bank pays from its own

funds. The bank sells the goods to the customer on price plus cost basis. The customer may settle the sale price on a deferred basis, usually 30, 60 or 90 days.

Islamic banks may also provide services such as safe deposit, bank drafts, travellers cheques, clearance trustee and nominee services and other usual banking services for a fee.

Liquidity requirements

The bank is required to maintain statutory reserves with Bank Negara, the central bank.

Subsidiaries

At the end of 1994 Bank Islam had five subsidiaries:

- *Al-Wakalah* Nominees Sdn Bhd – this is a wholly owned nominee company.

- *Syarikat Takaful Malaysia* Sdn Bhd – the purpose of this subsidiary is to conduct Islamic insurance operations.

- *Syarikat Al-Ijarah* – this company was formed for the acquisition of immovable and movable fixed assets and is a wholly owned subsidiary.

- BIMB Securities and BIMB[16] Unit Trust Management.

An evaluation of the success of Bank Islam Malaysia

At the end of 1994 Bank Islam had 35 branches throughout Malaysia, plus 25 "mini branches". Branches were equipped with ATMs. BIMB's staff increased to 1061 in 1994. While its market share is still very small, it is growing steadily.

While the majority of the Bank's customers are Muslims, surveys have shown that the bank is also popular with non-Muslims as the profit paid to investors is comparable with or slightly higher than that of commercial banks.[17]

BIMB has avoided the practice of Muslim banks overseas which have collected small amounts from a large group of depositors and channelled the money to a small group of entrepreneurs. 74.2 per cent

---

16   BIMB stands for *Bank Islam Malaysia Berhad* (Limited).
17   In 1994 the rate of return was 1 per cent higher than that of commercial banks according to the *Far Eastern Economic Review*, April 1995.

of its accounts for financing and investment involve sums of less than RM1000 to RM100,000. Also much financing has gone to business institutions such as PMFB which represent Muslim interests.

BIMB's success has led other Malaysian banks to introduce "Islamic counters" or to Islamicise their own banking business completely. Bank Raykat began converting to Islamic banking in 1993. Bank Raykat was set up to help farmers gain access to cheap credit, but its chairman, Affifudin Omar, was quoted in *Asiaweek*[18] as saying that the bank had found that many rural people were reluctant to use the banking system because of the interest taken and paid. Some refused interest which made it difficult to reconcile accounts.

However, some people have queried whether Islamic banks like Bank Islam represent a proper approach to Islamisation. It has been argued that a proper approach would be first to adopt an Islamic constitution for the country so that all development would proceed in an Islamic framework. However, Islamic banks have been successful in various countries where there is no overall policy of Islamisation, for example, in Turkey. But, in Islamic terms, the financial viability of the bank is not itself sufficient; and the bank should be an instrument for establishing a just and efficient economic order.

The banks have an over-dependence on "second line techniques", that is *murabaha, bai bi-thamin ajil* and *ijara*. These are considered by some to be just interest under another guise. Mark-ups are about the same as the interest charged by commercial banks. The banks should actively promote the first line techniques, such as *mudaraba* and *musharaka*, to help achieve the ultimate objective of Islamic banking that is alleviation of economic injustice as manifested by inequitable distribution of income and excessive concentration of wealth.

The banks have been accused of being concerned only with profits and neglecting welfare. However, the counter-argument is that the banks are commercial organisations and have a duty to protect the interests of depositors and shareholders.

The banks need to find new ways to mobilise deposits given that an Islamic bank cannot promise its depositors any specified return on their funds. In the long term, encouragement of the Islamic value system of moderation in spending and prohibition of hoarding should be encouraged.

---

18   17.3.1993, p 61.

Other Islamic financial institutions in Malaysia

Tabung Haji (Pilgrims Management and Fund Board)

Traditionally the Malays were agricultural small holders and did not have a great deal of excess capital. Their principal aim in saving was to accumulate sufficient funds to make the *hajj* to Mecca, usually in their old age. Funds used for this purpose must be *halal*, and could not be tainted with *riba* (interest) which is forbidden. Therefore the Malays were reluctant to invest in banks or other savings institutions which paid interest, and tended to keep their money in cash under the bed, or buried in tins in their compound etc.[19]

Another common way of raising finance for the *hajj* was through *jual janji* where a loan could be obtained on security of the intending pilgrim's land without payment of interest.

In 1959, Ungku Aziz, then an economist at the University of Malaya, submitted a working paper to the government containing a proposal to establish a financial institution to solve the financial problems of pilgrims, allowing them to invest their savings without interest. Ungku Aziz estimated that about M$3 million was spent each year by pilgrims. Savings in cash under the mattress were clearly unproductive and at risk, and could clearly be put to better use.

The Pilgrims Savings Corporation was set up in 1963 following consultations with the Grand Mufti of Egypt who studied the plan and found it to be free of *riba*. In 1951 there was a merger with the Pilgrims Affairs Office which looked after the welfare of pilgrims. As a result of the merger the Pilgrims Management and Fund Board (*Tabung Haji*) was formed.

The purpose of the Board is to manage the savings of intending pilgrims and invest their money collectively in *halal* investments in industry, trade and commerce. According to Razali Hj Nawawi, by about 1988, *Tabung Haji* was one of the strongest Islamic financial institutions, totally owned and managed by Muslims. At its establishment in 1963, it had 1281 depositors with savings of M$46,600. By December 1985 it had 867,957 depositors with savings of M$1531 million.

---

19   Radiah Abd Kader, 1991 p 139.

Organisation of PMFB

PMFB is a semi-government body under the Prime Ministers Department. The Board of Directors formulates policies and implements programs.

Financial structure

Funds for operating are from two sources:

1. government grants;
2. PMFB funds generated from investments and fee for services .

- *Mobilisation of deposits* – deposits are accepted from depositors on the *Shariah* principle of *al-wadiah* whereby depositors allow PMFB to use their deposits for investment. Profits from investment are then distributed among investors after payment of *zakat* and other necessary expenses.

- *Membership* – limited to Malaysian Muslim individuals. Minimum deposit is RM2. No account book is issued, but each member is given an account number and receives bi-annual statements. A bonus is calculated at the end of the year. Deposits can be made at Post Offices or by salary deduction. Withdrawal of funds is subject to some restrictions.

- *Utilisation of funds* – only *halal* investments may be made in shares and through subsidiary companies and through short-term investments with Bank Islam.

Investment in shares is limited to selected Malaysian equities. Generally PMFB does not participate as a major shareholder but if it holds more than 5 per cent of shares, it is represented on the company's board. It acquires listed shares and those allocated for Malays, also through partnership and joint ventures with other companies

Subsidiary companies – there are five subsidiary companies engaged in such diverse industries as palm oil, rubber and cocoa plantations, palm oil processing, transport and trading especially providing flights and supplies for pilgrims, developing housing schemes for members and general public and other investment in land and building

Investment activities are carried out under *Shariah* principles of *mudaraba* (profit sharing), *musharaka* (equity participation) and *ijara* (leasing).

The growth of depositors has increased continuously, and these include members of the public and school children as well as intending pilgrims. Depositors are more concentrated in urban rather than rural areas. This may be because of low levels of rural income.

In summary, PMFB is primarily a service organisation not an investment institution. Its success has been in providing a vehicle for investment of the savings of the Malay community while at the same time providing services for pilgrims. About 13 per cent of Malays are members of PMFB and there is scope for further growth. PMFB also acts as an instrument in reducing the "capital deficiency gap" in Malay participation in business activities and spreads ownership over a large number of individuals through its ownership of investments.

New Islamic financial services in Malaysia

Stockbroking

BIMB Securities is a new subsidiary of Bank Islam (70 per cent owned through BIMB Securities (Holdings) Sdn. Bhd) It commenced operations on 19.8.94. It is a brokerage facility, which avoids short selling and does not deal in non-*halal* stocks – 270 of the 502 listings on Kuala Lumpur Stock Exchange are considered *halal*. It is expected to attract patronage from Islamic institutions such as PMFB, the Employees Provident Fund and overseas Islamic investment institutions.

Unit Trust Management Services

BIMB Unit Trust Management Bhd is a new wholly owned subsidiary of Bank Islam which commenced operations on 20 June 1994. It manages *Amanah Saham Bank Islam* (ASBI) *Tabung Pertama*, a unit trust fund established by the bank with a fund of RM150 million. Its 1994 profit before *zakat* and taxation was RM666,652, and after *zakat* and tax. RM452,043.

Pawnbroking (*Rahn*)

An Islamic pawnbroking service is now provided by 40 branches of Bank Raykat. A service fee is charged. Only gold can be pawned and loans are made up to 50 per cent of the pawned item. Six months is normally allowed to redeem the item, but if the customer cannot do so in that time he is granted a three-months extension, after which the item is sold, the bank's loan repaid and the balance returned to the customer. According to the *Far Eastern Economic Review*,[20] on a loan of RM2400, a customer would pay MR48 pm to a conventional pawnshop but only RM12 pm service fee to Bank Raykat.

Islamic Insurance (*Takaful*)

Objections by Muslims to conventional insurance arise from:

- *maisir* (the perceived element of gambling) – the insured may get back more than he has paid in premiums. This view is not accepted by all scholars as insurance merely compensates the insured for loss suffered and he does not make a profit.

- *riba* (interest) – investment of premiums in interest bearing deposits or un-Islamic businesses. Also interest is paid to the insured in some types of insurance.

- *gharar* (uncertainty) – both parties do not know their respective rights and liabilities until the occurrence of the insured event. However, the view of some jurists is that "the *Sunnah* does not forbid those transactions that fulfill genuine needs and are indispensable for certain desirable ends but which cannot always be altogether freed from indeterminacy or hazard".[21] The principle of necessity (*zarurat*) also renders insurance permissible according to some scholars but elements of uncertainty should be reduced as far as possible.

- Nomination clauses in life policies can enable Muslims to violate Islamic rules of succession – that is that a bequest cannot amount to more than one-third of the estate and cannot be made in favour of an heir. It has been held by courts in Pakistan (*Karim v Hanifa* PLD (1970) Karachi 683) that a nominee is an agent who receives the benefit on behalf of all the heirs. A *fatwa* to this effect was issued in Malaysia in September 1973.

---

20   13.4.1995, p 55.
21   Syed Khalid Rashid, "Insurance and Muslims", paper presented at IIU Malaysia on 13.10.1992, p 5, quoting Siddiqi *Insurance in an Islamic Economy*, 1985.

Principles of Islamic Insurance – (*Takaful* means "joint-guarantee")

1. *Riba* is avoided. Interest is neither taken nor given. Investments are not made in interest bearing bonds or other non-*halal* investments.

2. No business participation is made in anything prohibited by *Shariah*.

3. The *Takaful* contract attempts to determine the terms of the contract as clearly and definitely as possible to minimise ignorance and uncertainty.

4. Business is conducted on the basis of *mudarabah*.

5. There is no forfeiture of premiums if the policy lapses or is surrendered.

6. A nominee cannot retain the benefit of the policy for his own use but receives it as an agent on behalf of the heirs.

7. A *Shariah* advisory council oversees the operation of the scheme and advises on *shariah*.

8. The company pays *zakat* on its profits. *Syarikat Takaful* paid RM20,559 in 1991.

9. In Malaysia, *Takaful* insurance is not conducted through brokers or agents but directly by employees of *Syarikat Takaful Malaysia* through desks at Bank Islam branches and at 16 *Tabung Haji* offices (1992).

Types of insurance offered

General *Takaful* Insurance

Types of cover offered are fire, motor, accident, marine, personal accident, workers' compensation, employers' liability, business interruption etc. The participant determines the amount for which he wishes to insure, and pays the *takaful* contribution to the company. The amount of contribution is assessed on the value of the asset to be covered. The contract runs for one year and specifies that any profit will be shared in a given ratio if the participant does not make any claims. The company pools all contributions and invests them in *halal* investments. The participants agree that the company shall pay compensation from the general fund to any fellow participant who might suffer a loss, and also operational costs.

Family *Takaful*

This is an investment program to provide *halal* investment returns to the participant as well as mutual financial aid. Individuals participate to save regularly a sum of money to provide for dependants if they should die prematurely, or as contingency savings if they survive to maturity of the plan. The plan may be taken for terms of 10, 15 or 20 years. Participants must be between the ages of 18 and 50 years, and the plan must mature before the participant reaches 60 years.

The contract is also based on the *Mudarabah* principle. The participant decides the amount of insurance required and the amount he wishes to pay and the company determines the minimum amount of instalment (RM15 pm in 1988). The company maintains two accounts, the *Participant's account* into which as much as 95 per cent of the participant's contributions are paid as savings and investment and a *Participant's special account* where the balance of the contribution is credited as *tabarru'* (donation) for the payment out of compensation to claimants. The proportion credited to each account depends on the age group of the participant and the maturity period of the policy and is worked out by actuaries. The PA operates as a form of savings account while the PSA is a form of mutual fund.

Takaful as compared with conventional insurance[22]

Common features

- Both have specified maturity periods.
- The sum insured is paid to the policy holder if he survives.
- Benefits are paid to beneficiaries in case of premature death.
- Calculation of premium is done by actuaries taking the same factors into account.
- In the case of *Takaful*, the *tabarru'* portion is calculated by actuaries taking the same principles into account as with conventional insurance.

Distinguishing features of Family *Takaful*

- No element of forfeiture.
- No non-profit policies.

---

22   Ibid p 208ff.

- Same contribution/ instalment since there is no policy which does not share profits.
- Profit sharing ratio is clearly stated in *Mudarabah* contract and the method of determining profit is clearly known to both parties.
- Profit is calculated and credited monthly at annual rate of profit.
- The insured are participants.
- The company does not engage in practices or investments which are disallowed by *Shariah*.

Conventional insurance

- Forfeiture if premiums cease within three years (usually).
- There are both profit and non-profit forms.
- Premiums are high for part policies.
- Policy holders may not know how profits are determined and what proportion they may receive.
- Interval of determining the bonus is not known.
- Insured are clients not participants.

An Islamic financial institution in Australia – MCCA

The Muslim Community Co-operative (Australia) Ltd (MCCA) was founded in 1989 to offer *halal* investment and interest free finance to Muslims in Australia. MCCA began operations in Victoria with 10 members and $22,000 share capital, but has since (March 1997) opened a branch in New South Wales and grown to more than 2700 members with a share capital base of over $12 million.[23] MCCA was first registered as a co-operative, but consideration is presently (1998) being given to forming a credit union with a view to being able to offer improved services to members.

The main operating activities of MCCA involve *halal* forms of investment and borrowing such as *Mudarabah, Murabahah, Musharakah* and the Shared Equity Rental scheme under which MCCA participates in the purchase of a house for a member and becomes a co-owner of the property. The property is rented to the

---

23   MCCA News, Vol 1 No 2, April 1998, p 2.

member who pays rent while at the same time gradually purchasing MCCA's interest in it. MCCA also operates a *zakat* fund to help the needy and a *Qard Hassan* fund to assist members with unforeseen emergency expenses.

14

ISLAM AND MUSLIMS IN AUSTRALIA

The first Muslims

The first Muslims to visit Australia, before the time of European settlement, were almost certainly fishermen from the nearby islands of eastern Indonesia, who visited the northern shores of Australia to fish and to collect trepang. Evidence of their visits has been found in artifacts preserved around the shores of the Northern Territory, but it is clear that they made no permanent settlements, and their influence upon the Aboriginal people who came into contact with them was minimal.

The "Afghans"

It seems that the first permanent Muslim settlers in Australian were the men, mostly from northern India and Afghanistan, whose services were recruited during the 19th century to manage the camel caravans which played such a significant part in the opening up of the drier areas of Australia. From about the 1860s until modern methods of transportation made camel transportation redundant even in the outback in the 1920s, they carried goods and made a particularly significant contribution to the erection of the overland telegraph and railway lines in remoter areas.

Some became hawkers and were well known for their travels around the countryside supplying many of the everyday goods needed by settlers who were out of reach of a township. Most were peasants, illiterate even in their own language, who had set out across the seas from India in the hope of making themselves financially independent by working and sending money home to their families.[1]

Many of them were single men who returned or intended to return home when their work was finished, and few brought their wives out with them. That they tried to adhere to their religion is shown by the building of mosques – the first at Broken Hill in New South Wales, at Adelaide in 1890, Perth in 1904, and Brisbane in 1907. The Perth and Adelaide mosques are still in use but the one at Broken Hill is now a museum. Those early Indian settlers who inter-married with Aboriginal or white people mostly did not succeed in passing their religious faith on to their children, who were eventually assimilated into the wider community and are only recognisable now as descendants of the Afghans because of their Arabic sounding surnames.

The adoption of the "White Australia Policy" about the time of Federation meant that dark skinned people from India were no longer welcome in Australia, and in fact were declared to be prohibited immigrants. From then on until after the end of World War II, very few Muslims were able to come to Australia and the Muslim community virtually disappeared.

Post-war migration

After the Second World War, the White Australia Policy was still in force, but there was an urgent need for more migrants to come to Australia to work on developments such as the Snowy Mountains Scheme. Among the thousands of new settlers who were recruited from the war-torn lands of Europe were Albanians, Yugoslavs and Turkish Cypriots who happened to be Muslim, although white skinned. Turks from mainland Turkey were held to be Asian until 1968, after an agreement was signed between the Australian and Turkish governments.[2] From then on many Turkish migrants arrived to work in the factories of Melbourne and Sydney. Among the Lebanese, Christians were considered acceptable migrants earlier than Muslim Lebanese.

---

1   See Hanifa Deen, *Caravanserai*, 1995, for an interesting account of some of these early Muslims.

2   Ibid p 15.

With the easing and eventual abolition of the White Australia Policy in the 1960s, the way was made clear for more Muslims migrants to come to Australia. Many professional people arrived from Egypt, India and Pakistan, and refugees came from Lebanon and Palestine due to warfare and displacement of populations in those countries.

The Muslim population in Australia today

Today, the Muslim population is made up of settlers from at least 64 different nationalities. The largest communities are those of Lebanese and Turkish descent, but there are substantial numbers from the former Yugoslavia, the Indo-Pakistan sub-continent, South Africa (mostly people of Malay-Indonesian or Indian descent) and Egypt. There are also Muslims who have come to Australia from China, Vietnam, Indonesia, Somalia, Fiji and many other countries. It is probably more correct to speak of Muslim "communities" in Australia, rather than the Muslim "community", since they are so ethnically divided. Many ethnic communities have their own mosques where the language of their country of origin is mostly used, so that while Muslims of other ethnic backgrounds are not prevented from attending, they are discouraged by not being able to understand the parts of the service which are given in the vernacular (rather than Arabic, which is universally used for formal prayers).

There are no accurate figures for the number of Muslims in Australia, but the number of 300,000 has been estimated by Muslim organisations. The numbers recorded by the census are almost certainly an underestimate, since answering the question on religious affiliation is not compulsory, and many Muslims refrain from indicating their religion from fear of attracting prejudice. The majority of Muslims live in the urban areas of New South Wales (nearly one half) and Victoria (about one third),[3] though there are Muslim communities in all States and Territories.

A recent report commissioned by the Bureau of Immigration, Multicultural and Population Research found that Muslims have the highest rate of marriage in Australia, the lowest divorce rate and the lowest rate of out marriage of any religious group.[4] They have the

---

3   Bureau of Immigration, Multicultural and Population Research, "Muslims in Australia", BIMPR Bulletin, August 1995, p 49.
4   Ibid.

lowest proportion of couples living in de facto relationships and of births outside marriage.[5] These statistics indicate the adherence of Australian Muslims to the tradition of maintaining a strong stable family as the centre of society.

Muslims, multiculturalism and Australian society

Many of the newly arrived cling to the customs of their country of origin and, like the Greeks and Italians who migrated before them, tend to cluster together in low cost suburbs where they feel secure among their own kind. A few attempt to enforce even the most conservative habits of their homelands, such as the veiling of women in black and keeping their womenfolk secluded at home. Others go to the other extreme and become caught up in the materialism and secularism of mainstream society. Probably the majority follow a middle course, make some concessions to the society around them and take advantage of its benefits while trying to preserve their Islamic identity and ethnic language and culture.

While most Muslims place much importance on maintaining their ethnic and religious traditions, and passing them on to their children, the lifestyles of men are not usually radically different from that of mainstream Australians, except that they should not drink or gamble and many will endeavour to take time off to attend Friday prayers at the mosque. Most men are employed at ordinary occupations, wear Western dress at most times and only a few keep to wearing the ethnic clothes and untrimmed beards which the media depicts as typically "Muslim".

Women's dress and lifestyles are more varied. In practice, the lifestyles of Muslim women in Australia cover the whole spectrum, from liberal to extremely conservative. Many Muslim women in Australia are in the workforce, some in the professions, enjoying the same freedom of lifestyle as other Australian women. Some Muslim women wear *hejab* at work and at home; some do not. Probably a majority of Muslim women are at home, caring for their family as is traditional. The extent to which they participate in mainstream life varies, though it is likely that lack of English prevents many from taking part in activities outside the ethnic community.

---

5   "Greeks and Italians produce smaller families", BIMPR Bulletin, August 1996, p 34.

A minority of women, brought to Australia as brides from overseas, live confined to the home, unable to communicate in English and not permitted by their husbands to go out to meet outsiders. Some husbands insist that their wives even wear *niqab*, the face veil, when they leave the house, and some women wear it voluntarily. Even a few Australian converts have taken up the practice, believing apparently that it makes them more modest, and is required by Islam. This practice is being encouraged by some conservative elements among Muslims but others believe it creates a barrier between the *niqab* wearing woman and the rest of society. It might be noted that there should be no objection to asking a woman to remove her face veil when only women are present and there is no danger that she will be seen by a man.

Muslim youth, both male and female, are well represented in universities. Most Muslim parents encourage their children to study for a worthwhile career. However, a few still insist on removing girls from school as soon as they attain puberty for fear that they will compromise the family honour by becoming involved with boys. Many Muslim parents feel that allowing teenage boys and girls to mix freely in co-educational schools is contrary to Islamic teachings and may lead to sexual permissiveness and the degradation of morals, as well as a tendency for students not to concentrate fully on their studies.[6] Muslim parents would greatly prefer single sex schools, especially at secondary level. Generally, girls are closely chaperoned and most will not be allowed to attend parties and other social events with Australian friends.

Although the change in Australian Government policy from assimilation to multiculturalism has made it easier for Muslim migrants to adjust to life in Australia, Muslims still experience certain difficulties in reconciling their religion with an Australian lifestyle. Some of these difficulties are as follows:

1. Muslims frequently experience difficulty in obtaining time off from work to attend religious services. Attendance at the mosque for Friday prayers (usually held at 1 pm) is compulsory for men. The major feast days of *Eid ul-Fitr* and *Eid ul-Adha* are not recognised in Australia and, when they fall on a weekday, many Muslims face the option of losing a day's pay or foregoing proper

---

6   Aziza Abdel Halim, *Meeting Needs of Muslim Students in the Australian Education System,* 1989, p 13.

observance of the occasion. Of course not only Muslims, but Jews, Hindus and Buddhists suffer from this problem, and now that Australia is recognised as a multi-religious society, a case can be made out for some recognition of the major festivals of each faith, as happens in other multi-religious countries such as Malaysia.

2. Despite the public policy of multiculturalism, the Australian education system is still largely mono-cultural. Muslim children are sometimes encouraged by teachers to Anglicise their names and they are not encouraged to preserve their cultural or religious identities. Community languages are generally not taught in schools and almost nothing is taught of other peoples' cultures and religions. Muslim students experience difficulty in performing prayers at the appointed time, in observing the fast of *Ramadan*, while at school, and with school uniforms, especially in the case of girls. The wearing of shorts, short skirts and swimming costumes in public is not acceptable, and many Muslim girls also wish to wear *hejab* with their school uniform. Some teachers and students display a negative attitude to Islam which tends to alienate Muslim students from the education system.[7]

3. Some local councils and communities are still reluctant to allow Muslims to erect mosques or Islamic schools in their areas, citing reasons such as noise, traffic congestion and interfering with the amenity of the area to disguise prejudice. It appeared that a way had been discovered to overcome this problem when Muslim communities began to purchase disused churches, surplus to the needs of Christian communities, to convert them to mosques. It was widely believed that, council permission having been granted for these sites for use for public worship, no difficulty would be encountered either from councils or neighbours.

On this basis, the Bangladeshi community in Sydney purchased a church in Sefton from the Presbyterian church and converted it to a mosque. However, in October 1998, on the application of Bankstown Council, Justice Sheahan in the NSW Land and Environment Court, held that previous permission to use the

---

7   A full account of problems which Muslim students have experienced at school is given in Aziza Abdel Halim's work referred to above.

building as a church did not entitle the new owners to use it as a mosque. The decision was widely criticised and is being appealed. In the interim, the council imposed stringent restrictions on the use of the building, including a ban on entering after sunset, which effectively prevented performance of two of the five daily prayers. This judgment appeared to represent a serious setback for the Muslim community. However, the Premier of New South Wales, Mr Carr, has since announced plans to amend the *Environmental Planning and Assessment Act* 1979 (NSW) to broaden the definition of "places of worship" to include, as well as churches, places of worship of religions other than Christianity.[8]

4. Muslim women who dress in the traditional Islamic manner sometimes experience prejudice when out in public, because they are identifiably Muslims. This was particularly a problem during the Gulf War, which was a war supported by Western nations to liberate one feudal, undemocratic Arab state (Kuwait) from invasion by another undemocratic Arab dictatorship (Iraq). All Muslims became the enemy in the eyes of the media and less thoughtful Australians. Muslim women were abused and attacked on the streets because their dress showed them to be Muslims. Women who came from countries as remote from the hostilities as South Africa and India, and even Australian converts were subjected to abuse, not because they were thought to be Iraqis, or even Arabs, but simply because they were recognised as Muslims.

5. The prevalence of drinking alcohol and gambling as accepted and almost compulsory social customs in Australia makes life difficult for Muslims who wish to integrate into Australian society. Both are forbidden in Islam, but people who refrain from them are often treated as outcasts by mainstream Australians, and young Muslims may be considerably pressured by Australian work mates and friends to take up the habits.

6. In the past Muslims have not been able to obtain *halal* food in some places such as hospitals and similar institutions. Nowadays, most hospitals are aware of the need to cater for ethnic patients (not only Muslims), and even airlines can produce a (sometimes

---

8   Ardyn Bernoth, "Mosques win the battle to be places of worship", *Sydney Morning Herald*, 7.12.1998, p 1.

quite strange) version of Muslim food for travellers. Attempts by Muslims to educate food manufacturers have resulted in more labelling their food with the Arabic *halal* emblem (which should also help their export opportunities) but there is still widespread ignorance of the meaning of *halal* food or its importance to Muslims. Incidents such as the serving of ham sandwiches to a visiting delegation from a Muslim country by a caterer employed for the occasion, are still, unfortunately, not unknown.

7. The image of Islam as portrayed in the media is a constant source of distress to Muslims. Media reports concentrate on acts of terrorism which can be attributed to Muslims overseas, and the bizarre aspects of local happenings. No media report is complete, it seems, without a picture of veiled women standing in front of a mosque. Televised pictures of Muslims at daytime prayer (which is silent) are jazzed up by playing a background recording of *azan* (which is recited before but not during prayers), presumably to add to the exotic effect. These misrepresentations make Muslims feel defensive and tend to isolate them from the wider community.[9]

Muslim organisations in Australia

The organisation of Muslim communities is traditionally centred on the mosque. Unlike migrants of the Christian faith, the first Muslim migrants found no existing religious institutions in Australia to help them settle in. Islamic associations were formed and mosques built, and gradually wider associations formed, first on a State basis. The Islamic Society of New South Wales was formed in 1957, and the Islamic Society of Victoria in 1962. Similar societies were later formed in the other States and Territories. In 1964 the Australian Federation of Islamic Societies (AFIS) was formed as a representative body for all Australian Muslims. It was renamed the Australian Federation of Islamic Councils (AFIC) in 1976 and restructured in three tiers – local societies which each elect their own executive committee, State Councils which are made up of representatives of local societies and the national body at the top. Its head office is now in Zetland in Sydney. Annual elections are held for leadership

---

9   See Naomi Cass, "Our media portrayal", BIMPR Bulletin, November 1995, pp 28-31.

positions on AFIC, and an annual conference is held, usually at Easter.

AFIC is an umbrella organisation for Australian Muslims. Its functions include the following:

- liaising with Australian government and semi-government organisations concerning matters which affect Muslims;
- liaising with the various Muslim communities concerning religious matters such as the correct date for the commencement of *Ramadan* and the Eid feast days;
- certification of *halal* meat and other products for export to Muslim countries;
- founding and maintaining some Islamic schools;
- support for youth and women's groups in the Muslim community;
- welfare and community work.

Muslims and the Australian legal system

Most Muslim migrants have come to Australia from countries where the common law is not the legal system. They need therefore to adapt to unfamiliar legal concepts as well as different ways of administering the law. Even migrants from countries such as India, Pakistan and Malaysia, which have largely British based legal systems, are used to their personal law – marriage, divorce and succession at least – being governed by Islamic law.

Since Muslims are bound to obey Islamic religious law as well as that of the country they live in, it is possible that Muslims may sometimes be put in a position of conflict. Generally, however, there are very few areas where Islamic law directly conflicts with the secular law, although there are very considerable differences between them. There are, for example, areas where an activity is forbidden by Islamic law, but is legal under Australian law. Drinking alcohol, gambling and sexual relations outside marriage are not prohibited by Australian law although they are forbidden to Muslims under Islamic law. Muslims are not compelled to engage in these activities (although they may be under strong social pressure to do so) and so can obey Islamic law in these matters. Of course, if they choose to disobey Islamic law and take up drinking and gambling, or live in a de facto relationship, no sanctions can be imposed under the law.

There are also areas where Islamic law permits an activity which is forbidden by Australian law. Polygamy is an example of this. Under Islamic law a man may have up to four wives at one time, provided that he can maintain them and treat them all equally. Under Australian law having more than one wife is called bigamy and amounts to a crime, although there is no restriction on living in more than one de facto relationship at one time. Here, Muslims are able to obey both laws by refraining from marrying more than one wife. Polygamy is merely permissible under Islamic law and is by no means compulsory, or even recommended. Therefore Australian law imposes no hardship.

Family law

In Australia, the law governing Family Law is secular and universally applied, regardless of religion or ethnic background. There are a number of areas in which it differs from and conflicts with Islamic law.

Marriage

Although different rules apply, there should be no real difficulty concerning marriage. The *Marriage Act* 1961 (Cth) permits the solemnisation of marriage according to any rites a couple may choose, and in this respect, is much more generous than the law in England. Imams may become authorised marriage celebrants, and all the requirements of Islamic law – the consent of the bride's *wali* (if required), the payment of *mahr*, the offer and acceptance and the formal marriage contract – may all be complied with. As well, the requirements of Australian law regarding notice, consent, witnesses and registration can be met without difficulty. On the other hand there is no sanction if Islamic law is not complied with, for example, if the *mahr* is not paid or the bride's *wali* refuses his consent.

Islamic law permits a Muslim man to marry a Christian or Jewish woman but not a pagan or an atheist. It does not permit a Muslim woman to marry anyone other than a Muslim man. There is nothing in Australian law to prevent a Muslim complying with this law but no sanction applies to those who do not. This is not the situation in many Muslim countries where marriage to a non-Muslim is not permitted by law.

The age of marriage

Many Muslims have come from countries where it is the tradition that girls be married very soon after puberty. They find difficulty with the fact that Australian law does not permit marriage until both parties are 18. This problem is exacerbated by the felt need to ensure, especially where girls are exposed to the permissive environment of Australian society, that they do not form inappropriate and Islamically illegal sexual liaisons before marriage. This is despite the fact that most Muslim countries have now legislated to raise the minimum age of marriage to at least 15 or 16 for girls.

A real crisis develops when a young person, usually a girl, develops a romantic attachment or a sexual relationship with someone of the opposite sex while they are still below marriageable age according to Australian law. To make matters worse, in some Muslim cultures, the honour of the whole family depends on the purity of its womenfolk. All members of the family, parents, siblings and remoter relations, will be degraded in the eyes of society by loose or immoral behaviour on the part of any female. This is not Islamic law, but it nevertheless is a strongly held belief among those cultures.

On the other hand, Australian law does not forbid sexual activity on the part of anyone over the age of consent, and emphasises the right of the individual to choose his or her own sexual partner regardless of parental approval or consent. Furthermore marriage may not be permitted even where the girl is pregnant since magistrates do not necessarily view pregnancy as an exceptional circumstance warranting permission to marry under the age of 18 years.

Muslims cope with this kind of problem in different ways. Commonly, regardless of Australian law, if the proposed partner is acceptable to the family, a religious marriage will be celebrated. This ensures that the couple are married in the eyes of the community, and a formal ceremony which complies with Australian law may or may not be held when the legal age for marriage has been attained. There have been other cases where the father, or male relatives who have the responsibility for ensuring that family honour is upheld, have resorted to force, or even attempted murder, to prevent a sexual relationship between a young girl and a man regarded as unsuitable.[10] These cases

---

10   A trial of a Syrian man accused of conspiracy and incitement to murder his daughter for dating an Australian boyfriend disapproved of by the family is described in Michelle Gunn, "Daughter tells of dangerous liaison", *The Australian*, 1.6.1994, p 3.

often end in tragedy. In other instances, girls are hastily sent back to the home country for a suitable match to be arranged, when they are perceived to be in danger of indiscretion in Australia.

Arranged marriages are not uncommon among the Muslim communities in Australia, although it would be rare for parents to push their children into a marriage against their will. Young men and women are choosing their own partners more frequently, though opportunities to meet suitable Muslim partners are sometimes limited. Partners are sometimes sought overseas through relatives and friends in the home country.

Divorce

There are more areas of conflict between Australian law and Islamic law in relation to divorce. The *Family Law Act* 1975 requires anyone seeking a divorce in Australia to comply with its requirements. Religious divorce is not recognised at all, unlike religious marriage, which as mentioned above is quite acceptable to the state authorities. The reason for this is historical. The Christian church traditionally did not permit divorce at all, and so secular divorce was developed to meet the needs of those who could not live together in marital harmony. The rules relating to divorce under the *Family Law Act* are quite different to those under Islamic law. In particular, the *Family Law Act* recognises only one ground for dissolution of marriage, irretrievable breakdown, and requires a waiting period of at least 12 months before a party can file an application for divorce. No distinction is made between husband and wife as to the ability to make the application.

Some Muslims have expressed dissatisfaction with the provisions for divorce under the *Family Law Act*, in particular that the period of 12 months before dissolution can be applied for is too long, and no account is taken of whose fault it is that the marriage has broken down. There is no recognition of the concept of *nusyuz* (disobedience) on the part of a wife, or of faults recognised by Islamic law on the husband's side which would justify the wife in seeking divorce. In the division of property, agreements entered into in marriage contracts are not legally enforceable, and in custody, arrangements may be ordered which are quite contrary to Islamic law.

The result is that some Muslims have decided to disregard Australian laws entirely in family matters and have simply married and divorced under religious law. Neither marriage nor *talaq* divorce under the classical Islamic law requires the intervention of the court or any state official. Marriage under Australian law does not apparently confer any greater benefits than religious marriage, and divorce is costly and difficult. Therefore the anomalous situation sometimes arises where persons A and B have originally married under Australian and Islamic law at the same time; divorced under Islamic law; and then remarried different partners under religious law, so that according to Australian law, A and B will still be married, but according to the religious law, A is now married to C, and B to D. According to Australian law, the relationships between A and C, and B and D are de facto relationships, but in the eyes of the community, they are married. It is not unknown for polygamous marriages to take place in the same way, and being unrecognised by the law, they are not able to be regulated.

There does not seem to be any reason, in principle, why Australian law could not recognise religious divorce, as it recognises religious marriage, if parties choose that method of terminating their marriage. The argument that there must be equality between men and women in Australia is not applied to marriages, where, for example if Muslims belonging to the Shafii school want to marry according to Islamic rites, the consent of the bride's *wali* must be obtained. People could always have the alternative of choosing to marry and divorce under the civil law if they wished, as they do now.

Since mediation has become the desired method of settling disputes between divorcing parties concerning children and even property, and since mediation and arbitration are the recommended means of setting marital differences under Islamic law, there is a need for the Muslim community to set up their own family mediation service. At present, Muslim couples referred to mediation must attend upon non-Muslim mediators who cannot be expected to understand fully the cultural and religious issues involved. Normally, Muslims are reluctant to seek help from sources outside the community and will use Australian courts only as a last resort, and even then, the court's judgment will not necessarily resolve underlying problems which are caused by different family values.[11]

---

11   "Lebanese Families" in Des Storer (ed) *Ethnic Family Values in Australia*, 1985, p 196.

Wills and inheritance

In contrast to Australian law which allows freedom of testation (subject to Family Provision legislation), Islamic law lays down detailed and compulsory rules about inheritance. These rules are not recognised under Australian law.

Nevertheless, there is nothing to prevent a Muslim making a will which directs that his or her estate is to be distributed according to Islamic law, although the effect of doing this should be carefully considered in the context of current social conditions. A major difficulty might arise in ensuring that a surviving widow is properly provided for, since, under Islamic law, she is entitled to only one eighth of the estate if there are children, and one quarter if there are no children. Where the major or only asset is the family home in the name of the husband, and other heirs seek to realise their inheritance, this could place the widow in an unenviable situation. This situation can be overcome where steps are taken to ensure that the wife has sufficient property in her own name to ensure her financial independence if her husband predeceases her. There is no objection to a husband making a gift of property to the wife during his lifetime.

Another problem may be that in some circumstances, a portion of a deceased estate may be due to the *bait ul-mal*. Since there is no *bait ul-mal* in Australia, this provision of the inheritance law could not be put into effect.

Business and commercial law

The greatest religious difficulty for Muslims in a capitalist commercial system is the reliance upon interest in business transactions. It is extremely difficult for Muslims to conduct a business, or buy a home or car without being obliged to pay interest, which is forbidden in Islam. Even investing can be difficult as most investments are based on the receipt of interest on money invested. If the alternative of buying shares is chosen, Muslims should take care to invest only in companies carrying on *halal* enterprises that is they should not buy shares in a brewery, casino or other gambling enterprise, or in a business which sells goods which are *haram*.

An Islamic financing facility has now been set up in Victoria and New South Wales,[12] providing loans on a partnership basis (Shared Equity Rental) for home purchase as well as short-term loans. While this enterprise appears to be growing strongly, it is still a long way from being able to provide for all the financial needs of the Muslim community in Australia.

The future of the Muslim community in Australia

It is now more than 20 years since Muslims began to arrive in Australia in comparatively large numbers as migrants. The struggles of these early settlers have been well documented.[13] Since then a new generation has grown up of Muslim children born in Australia, or who arrived in Australia at a very young age. Only rough estimates can be made of the future growth of the Muslim community since it depends on so many variables such as immigration policies, conditions in overseas countries which encourage people to emigrate and so on. However, it seems likely that the numbers of Muslims will gradually increase,[14] and the number of Australian born Muslims will grow as a proportion of the total Muslim community. It remains to be seen to what extent these people will assimilate into the Australian community, or alternatively, preserve their identity as Australian Muslims.

---

12   Muslim Community Co-Operative Australia (MCCA,) 1342 Toorak Road, Burwood, Vic 3125.
13   See, for example, Margaret Pickles "Keynotes for Understanding, Differentiating and Managing Islamic Immigration Stresses: The Australian Experience", *Journal Institute of Muslim Minority Affairs*, Vol 11-2, July 1990 pp 263-272, and also Gulay Cevik, "Power or participation? Status of Turkish women", BIMPR Bulletin, August 1996 p 27.
14   Riaz Hassan, "The future of the Muslim Community in Australia", *The Australian Minaret*, December 1991, p 30.

GLOSSARY OF ARABIC TERMS

Letters in the Arabic alphabet do not correspond exactly to the Roman alphabet. Many words are transliterated in slightly different ways, according to the preference and tradition of the translator. In particular, "dh" and "z" are both used in words such as "*Ramadan*" which is also spelt "Ramadhan" or "Ramazan"; "u" and "oo" in words such as "hudud/hudood", and "q" and "k" in words like "*fiqh/fikh*". In South-East Asia "y" is frequently substituted for "h" in words like "*Shariah*". There are numerous other variations. Additionally, written Arabic contains marks which aid pronunciation. No attempt has been made to reproduce these in this text.

adat	custom (Malay/Indonesian)
adil	virtuous
adalah	justice
ahad	a solitary hadith, reported by only one person
ahadith	plural of hadith
alim	learned in the law
amana	trust
amin	trustworthy
amir	leader
amr	command
Ansar	the inhabitants of Medina who helped the early Muslim emigrants
aqd	contract
ayah	(pl *ayat*) sign, a verse from the *Quran*
azan	the call to prayer
bait ul-mal	public treasury
bai'	(also *bay*) a sale
batil	null and void
bayyinah	clear proof, evidence
bida'ah	innovation
da'if	weak

dhimmi	a non-Muslim subject under the protection of an Islamic state
diyah(t)	blood money, compensation for death or injury
faqih	(pl *fuquha*) a Muslim jurist
fard	obligatory
fasakh	annulment of marriage, divorce by the court on prescribed grounds
fasiq	transgressor against religious law
fatwa	(pl *fatawa*) a legal ruling
fiqh	Islamic jurisprudence
gharar	uncertainty, speculation
hadanah	(also *hizanat*) custody
hadd	(pl *hudud*) limit, prescribed penalty
hadith	(pl *ahadith*) narrative relating the deeds, sayings and tacit approvals of the Prophet
hajj	the pilgrimage to the Ka'aba, obligatory once in a lifetime
hakam	arbitrator
halal	legal, permitted
haq	right
haram	forbidden
hasan	good
hiba	gift
hijrah	the Prophet's migration from Mecca to Medina, which marks the starting point of the Islamic calendar
hukm	legal judgment, decision
ibadat	acts of devotion
iddah	the waiting period for a divorced wife or a widow before remarriage is possible
iftar	the meal which breaks the fast in *Ramadan*
ijab	proposal
ijara	hire
ijma	consensus of opinion
ijtihad	personal reasoning
il'a	a type of divorce
Imam	a person who leads prayers
iman	faith
iqrar	acknowledgment, confession
isnad	chain of authorities in a tradition
istihsan	juristic preference

istishab	presumption of continuity
istislah	consideration of public interest
jihad	struggle, religious war
jizya	tax on non-Muslims
jumhur	majority
khalwah	(Malay *khalwat*) close proximity raising suspicion of sexual misconduct
khamr	intoxicating drink, wine
khiyar	option
khula'	divorce by redemption
kitabiyyah	a Jewish or Christian woman
li'an	divorce by oath of adultery
madhab	school of Islamic thought
majlis	assembly, meeting
makruh	disapproved acts
mal	property
mufti	a religious scholar qualified to give *fatawa*
mahr	(*mas-kahwin* in South-East Asia) marriage gift from husband to wife, dower
mawat	waste land
mihrab	the niche in a mosque which shows the direction of Mecca
mimbar	the pulpit in the mosque from which the Imam delivers the Friday *khutba*
mu'amalat	a secular transaction
mubara'ah	mutual discharge
mudarabah	a type of partnership
mujtahid	a person who practises *ijtihad*
murabahah	sale at a specified profit margin
murtad	apostate
muta	temporary marriage approved by some of the Shia
muta'a	payment of compensation to a woman divorced without fault
nafaqah	maintenance
nass	text, an express injunction in the *Quran*
nikah	marriage contract
nisab	minimum limit
nushuz	(Malay *nusyuz*) disobedience (usually of a wife)
qazf	false accusation of unchastity
qadi	(Malay *kadi, kathi*) judge

qard	loan
qarinah	circumstantial evidence
qisas	permitted retaliation for death or injury
qatl	homicide
qiyas	analogical deduction
Quran	the Holy Book of Islam (spelt *Koran* in some texts)
rahn	pledge, pawn
rajm	stoning to death
Ramadan	the ninth month of the Islamic calendar, the fasting month
riba	interest, usury
rukn	pillar, essential part
Sahabah	the companions of the Prophet
sahih	valid, authentic
salah	(also *salat*) prayers
salam	a form of sale where the price is paid in advance
shahadah	the strongest kind of evidence
shakk	suspicion
Shariah	(also *Shari'ah;* Malay *Syariah*) the law of Islam
shiqaq	marital disharmony
shirkah	a type of partnership
shura	consultation
sultan	the ruler
sunnah	the accepted practices of the Prophet
sura	a chapter of the *Quran*
ta'azir	crimes for which the penalty may be determined by the judge
tafsir	science of interpretation of the *Quran*
talaq	divorce initiated by the husband
taqlid	imitation, being bound by the opinions of the traditional jurists
tayammum	ablution with clean sand, when no water is available
ulama	(sing *'alim*) religious scholars
ummah	the community of Muslims
'urf	custom
'ushr	an agricultural tax
wahm	supposition
wahy	divine revelation
wajib	obligatory
wali	guardian

waqf	(also *wakaf*) a trust
wasiyah(t)	will, bequest
wudu	ablution with clean water
yaqin	certain proof
zakah(t)	religious tax, alms
zann	doubt
zina	adultery, illegal sexual intercourse

BIBLIOGRAPHY

Primary sources

Quran, generally reference is made to the translation of Abdullah Yusuf Ali, Sh Muhammad Ashraf, Lahore, 1984

Sahih Muslim, translation of Abdul Hamid Siddiqi, Sh Muhammad Ashraf, Lahore, 1992

Secondary sources

Abdel Halim, Aziza, *Meeting Needs of Muslim Students in the Australian Education System*, Research Project, Sydney, 1989

Abdul Haseeb Ansari, "Fiscal Measures in Shari'a and the Modern Muslim State: Analysis and Proposals", *Religion and Law Review*, Vol IV, No 2, 1995, p 178

Abdul Majid, "An Aspect of Islamic Law in the Judgement of the Family Court of Australia in *In the Marriage of B and B* [Kidnapping]", *Asia Pacific Law Review*, Vol 4 No 1, 1995, p 91

Abdullah Muhammad Zin, *The 'Abbasid Caliphate*, Pustaka Antara, Kuala Lumpur, 1993

Abdullahi An-Na'im, "Towards an Islamic Reformation", in Norani Othman (ed), *Shari'a Law and the Modern Nation State*, SIS Forum Bhd, Kuala Lumpur, 1994

'Abdur Rahman i Doi, *Shari'ah: The Islamic Law*, AS Noordeen, Kuala Lumpur, 1989

— *Women in Shari'ah*, AS Noordeen, Kuala Lumpur, 4th ed, 1992

Abraham, Dulcie, "A Malaysian Christian Perspective", in Norani Othman and Cecilia Ng (eds), *Gender, Culture and Religion*, Persatuan Sains Sosial Malaysia, Kuala Lumpur, 1995

Abul Fadl Mohsin Ibrahim, *Abortion, Birth Control And Surrogate Parenting, An Islamic Perspective*, American Trust Publications, 1991

Ahmad Ibrahim, *Family Law in Malaysia and Singapore*, Malayan Law Journal Pte Ltd, Singapore, 1984

—   "The need to amend s 51 of the Law Reform (Marriage and Divorce) Act 1976", [1990] 2 *MLJ* lviii

—   "Fasakh for Failure to Maintain", *Journal of Malaysian and Comparative Law*, 1970, p 329

—   "Suitability of Islamic Punishments in Malaysia", *IIUM Law Journal*, Vol 3 No 1, January 1993, p 14

—   "The Administration of Islamic Financial Institutions", *Syariah Law Journal*, 1988, p 13

Ahmad, Qazi Ashfaq, "Islam and Muslims in Australia", in *Islam and Muslims in Muslim-Minority States*, p 317

Aksoy, S, "What makes a person?" *The Fountain*, Vol 2 No 14, April-June 1996, p 30

Ala'eddin Kharofa, *Usury, "Interest" or Riba*, AS Nordeen, Malaysia, 1993

Albar, MA, "Organ Transplantation", *The Fountain*, Vol 2 No 12, October-December 1995, p 34

Alkhateeb, Sharifa, "The Marriage Contract", *Sisters*, August/September 1996, p 15

Al-Omar, Fuad and Abdel-Haq, Mohammed, *Islamic Banking,* OUP, Karachi, 1996

Amin, SH, "Contemporary Legal Systems in the Muslim World", *Muslim Education Quarterly*, Vol 8 No 3, 1991, p 56

—   *Islamic Law in the Contemporary World*, Royston Ltd, Glasgow, 1985

Asghar Ali Engineer, *The Rights of Women in Islam*, IBS Buku Sdn Bhd, Selangor, 1992

Athar, Shahid, "The Islamic Perspective in Medical Ethics", *http//:www.safaar.com/im1.html*

Bank Islam Malaysia Berhad, Annual Report 1994.

Bank Islam Malaysia Berhad, *Islamic Banking Practice From the Practitioner's Perspective,* Kuala Lumpur, 1994

Bannerman, Patrick, *Islam in Perspective*, Routledge, 1988

Bates, Frank, "The Story of B: Australian Family Law and Policy in an Asian Context", *Asia Pacific Law Review*, Vol 3 No 2, 1994, p 33

Baydoun, Nabil and Blunt, Peter, "Notes on Islam, Culture and Organisational Behaviour", Working Paper, Northern Territory University, 1997

Brett M and Forman W, *The Moors*, Orbis Publishing Ltd, UK, 1984

Brown, Daniel, *Rethinking tradition in modern Islamic thought*, Cambridge University Press, Cambridge, 1996

Bureau of Immigration, Multicultural and Population Research, *BIMPR Bulletin*, Issue No 14, August 1995, August 1996

Buttar, PA, "Muslim Personal Law in Western Countries: The Case of Australia", *Journal Institute of Muslim Minority Affairs*, Vol 6 No 2, p 271

Butti Sultan Butti Ali Al-Muhairi, "Islamisation and Modernisation Within the UAE Penal Law", *Arab Law Quarterly*, 1995, p 34

Chandra Muzaffar, "Reformation of Shari'a" in Norani Othman (ed), *Shari'a Law and the Modern Nation State*, SIS Forum Berhad, Malaysia, 1994

Connors, Jane, "Towards a System of Islamic Finance in Malaysia" in Chibli Mallat (ed) *Islamic Law and Finance*, Graham and Trotman, London, 1988, p 57

Coulson, NJ, *Commercial Law in the Gulf States*, 1984

—   *A History of Islamic Law*, Edinburgh, 1971

Cunningham, Andrew, "The growth of Islamic financing", *Project and Trade Finance*, February 1994, p 35

Deen, Hanifa, *Caravanserai*, Allen and Unwin, Sydney, 1995

—   *Broken Bangles*, Anchor Books, Sydney, 1998

El Naggar, Ahmed A, "Islamic Banking in Egypt, a model and a challenge", in Ataul Hoque (ed) *Readings in Islamic Banking*, Islamic Foundation, Bangladesh, 1987

Esposito, John, *Islam, the Straight Path*, Oxford University Press, UK, 1984

Farhad Normani and Ali Rahnema, *Islamic Economic Systems*, S Abdul Majeed and Co, Malaysia, 1995

Golnar Mehran, "The Education of a New Woman in Postrevolutionary Iran", *Muslim Education Quarterly*, Vol 8 No 3, 1991, p 7

Hart, Michael J, *The 100: A Ranking of the Most Influential Persons in History*, Golden Books Centre Sdn Bhd, Kuala Lumpur, 1987

Hamidullah, M, *Introduction to Islam*, Sh Muhammad Ashraf, Lahore, 1974

Hammudah 'Abd al 'Ati, *The Family Structure in Islam*, American Trust Publications, 1977

Hashim Mehat, *Sentencing in Malaysian Law*, Kuala Lumpur.

Hassan, Riaz, "The future of the Muslim community in Australia", *The Australian Minaret*, December 1991, p 30

Holmewood, Aliah, "Misinterpretation of the Holy *Quran* – The Position of Women", paper presented at National Women's Conference, Auckland NZ, 1992

Hoodbhoy, Pervez, *Islam and Science*, S Abdul Majeed and Co, Kuala Lumpur, 1975

Hooker, MB, "Fatawa in Malaysia 1960-1985", *Arab Law Quarterly,* Vol 8 June 1993, p 93

Hostettler, J, *The Politics of Criminal Law*, 1992

Humphrey, Michael, "Religion, law and family disputes in a Lebanese Muslim community in Sydney" in Bottomley G and de Lepervanche M (eds), *Ethnicity, Class and Gender in Australia*, Allen and Unwin, Sydney, 1984, p 183

Hussin Mutalib, "Islamisation in Malaysia: between Ideals and Realities", in Hussin Mutalib and Taj ul-Islam Hashmi, *Islam, Muslims and the Modern State,* 1994

Ismail, Rose (ed), *Hudud in Malaysia*, SIS Forum (M) Bhd, Kuala Lumpur, 1995

Kabilsingh, Chatsumaru, "Women in Buddhism", in Norani Othman and Cecilia Ng (eds), *Gender, Culture and Religion*, Persatuan Sains Sosial Malaysia, Kuala Lumpur, 1995

Khawla Fadhil Mohammed Al-Zubaidy, "The experience of Muslim women: considerations of education and employment opportunities", *Muslim Education Quarterly,* Vol 8 No 3, 1991, p 48

Kaukab Siddique, *The Struggle of Muslim Women*, Thinkers Library, Singapore, 1987

— *Liberation of Women thru Islam*, Thinkers Library, Singapore, 1990

Lings, Martin, *Muhammad*, Foundation for Traditional Studies and AS Noordeen, Kuala Lumpur, 1983

M Abdur Rahman Khan, *Muslim Contribution to Science and Culture*, Sh Muhammad Ashraf, Lahore, 1946, reprinted 1973

Mahmassani, S, *Falsafat al-Tashri fi al-Islam* (trans Farhat J Ziadeh), Penebitan Hizbi, Malaysia, 1987

Mahmood M Sanusi, "Gharar", *IIUM Law Journal*, Vol 3 No 2, 1993, p 87

Mahmud Saedon Awang Othman, "The Concept of Bayyinah in Islamic Law", IIUM 1992

Majid Ali Khan, *Muhammad the Final Messenger*, Sh Muhammad Ashraf, Lahore, 1983

Mallat Chibli and Connors, Jane (eds), *Islamic Family Law*, Graham and Trotman, London, 1990

Mandelbaum, David G, *Women's Seclusion and Men's Honor*, University of Arizona Press, Tucson, 1988

Maudoodi, Maulana Abul A'ala, *The Laws of Marriage and Divorce in Islam*, Islamic Book Publishers, Kuwait, 1987

Maulana Ashraf Ali Thanwi, *Heavenly Ornaments*, (trans Mohammad Masroor Khan Saroha), Darul-Ishaat, Karachi, 1987

Mernissi, Fatima, *Women and Islam*, B Blackwell, Oxford, 1991

— *The Harem Within: Tales of a Moroccan Girlhood*, Doubleday, London, 1994

Mogamad Faaik Gamielden, "Documentary Evidence", unpublished paper, IIUM, 1993

Mohammad Hashim Kamali, *Principles of Islamic Jurisprudence*, Pelanduk Publications (M) Sdn Bhd, Selangor, 1989

Mohd Ariff (ed), *The Muslim Private Sector in Southeast Asia*, Institute of SE Asian Studies, Singapore, 1991

— *Islamic Banking in Southeast Asia*, Institute of SE Asian Studies, Singapore, 1988

— *The Islamic Voluntary Sector in SE Asia*, Institute of SE Asian Studies, Singapore, 1991

Mohd Fadzli Yusof, "Takaful Insurance Company Sdn. Bhd – Islamic Alternative to Insurance", *Syariah Law Journal*, 1988, p 87.

Nabil A Saleh, *Unlawful Gain and Legitimate Profit in Islamic Law*, Cambridge University Press, UK, 1986

Nasir, Jamal J, *The Islamic Law of Personal Status*, Graham and Trotman, UK, 1986

Nawal el-Saadawi, *The Hidden Face of Eve*, Beacon Press, Boston, 1982

Norani Othman (ed), *Shari'a Law and the Modern Nation-State*, SIS Forum (Malaysia) Berhad, Kuala Lumpur, 1994

— "Shari'a Law and the Rights of Modern Muslim Women: an overview of the implementation of CEDAW in Muslim societies", paper presented at CEDAW Conference, New York, 14 January 1995

Norani Othman and Cecilia Ng (eds), *Gender, Culture and Religion*, Persatuan Sains Sosial Malaysia, Kuala Lumpur, 1995

Norhashimah Mohd Yasin, "Shariah Contracts Used by Islamic Banks", *Al-Nahdah*, Vol 17, 1997, p 5

Nublan Zaky Yusoff, *An Islamic Perspective of Stock Market*, Dian Darulnaim Sdn Bhd, Malaysia, 1992

Oorjitham, KS Susan, "A Hindu Perspective", in Norani Othman and Cecilia Ng (eds), *Gender, Culture and Religion*, Persatuan Sains Sosial Malaysia, Kuala Lumpur, 1995

Pickles, Margaret, "Keynotes for Understanding, Differentiating and Managing Islamic Immigration Stresses: The Australian Experience", *Journal Institute of Muslim Minority Affairs*, Vol 11 No 2, July 1990, p 263

Pollock and Maitland, *The History of English Law*. Vol 2, 1985

Powell-Smith, Vincent, *Aspects of Arbitration: Common Law and Shari'a Compared*, Central Law Book Corporation Sdn Bhd, Malaysia, 1995

Radiah Abdul Kader, "The Malaysian Pilgrims Management and Fund Board and Resource Mobilization" in Mohd Ariff ed *The Islamic Voluntary Sector in Southeast Asia,* Institute of SE Asian Studies, Singapore, 1991, p 138.

Razali Hj Nawawi, "The Administration of Islamic Financial Institutions – Malaysia's Experience", *Syariah Law Journal,* 1988, p 1.

Said Ramadan, *Islamic Law, Its Scope and Equity*, Muslim Youth Movement of Malaysia, Kuala Lumpur , 2nd edn, 1992.

Said Zafar and Shameela Chinoy, "Submission on Islamic Financial Institutions Canada", unpublished submission to the Task Force on the Future of the Canadian Financial Services Sector, 1997

Schmidt, Alvin John, *Veiled and Silenced*, Mercer University Press, Macon Georgia, 1989

Schneider, Irene. "Imprisonment in Pre-Classical and Classical Islamic Law", *Islamic Law and Society*, Vol 2 No 2, 1995

Schulberg, Lucille, *Historic India*, Time-Life International NV, 1968

Shaista P Ali-Karamali and Dunne, Fiona, "The Ijtihad Controversy", *Arab Law Quarterly*, 1995, p 249

Shatzmiller, Maya, "Women and Property Rights in Al-Andalus and the Maghrib: Social Patterns and Legal Discourse", *Islamic Law and Society*, Vol 2 No 3, 1995

Sisters in Islam, *Are Muslim Men Allowed to Beat their Wives?*, Kuala Lumpur, 1991

Soraya Altorki, *Women in Saudi Arabia*, New York, Columbia University Press, 1986

Storer, Des (ed), *Ethnic Family Values in Australia*, Australia, Prentice-Hall Pty Ltd, 1985

Syed Khalid Rashid, *Muslim Law*, 1990

— "Insurance and Muslims", paper given in Public Lecture series at IIU Malaysia on 13 Oct 1992

Syed Othman Alhabshi and Nik Mustapha Nik Hassan (eds), *Islamic Civilization Present and Future Challenges*, IKIM, Kuala Lumpur, 1995

Syed Waseem Ahmad, "Islamic Insurance in Malaysia" in Mohd Ariff ed, *The Muslim Private Sector in Southeast Asia,* Institute of SE Asian Studies, Singapore, 1991, p 188

Tahir Mahmood, "Law and the Elderly in the Islamic Tradition – Classical precepts and modern legislation", *Islamic and Comparative Law Quarterly*, Vol IX, 1 March 1989, p 33

Tames, Richard, *The Muslim World*, London, Macdonald and Co, 1982

Tanzil ur-Rahman, *A Code of Muslim Personal Law*, Islamic Publishers, Karachi, 1978

Tyser, CR (translator), *The Mejelle*, Lahore, The Book House, reprinted

Watts, Nicola, "When a Father Dies – Has a Frozen Embryo Rights to an Inheritance", *ALMD Advance*, June 1996

Wilson, Rodney, "Going Global", *The Banker,* March 1995, p 45

Wudud-Muhsin, Amina, *Qur'an and Woman*, Penerbit Fajar Bakti Sdn Bhd, Malaysia, 1992

— "The Qur'an, Shari'a and the Citizenship Rights of Muslim Women in the Umma", in Norani Othman (ed) *Shari'a Law and the Modern Nation-State*, SIS Forum (Malaysia) Berhad, Kuala Lumpur, 1994

Yusuf al-Qaradawi, *The Lawful and the Prohibited in Islam*, Kuwait, International Islamic Federation of Student Organizations, 1989

Zainur bin Zakaria, "Religious freedom – right to wear the Purdah", [1993] 3 *MLJ* xxv

Zakariya Man, "Islamic Banking: the Malaysian Experience" in Mohd Ariff (ed) *Islamic Banking in Southeast Asia,* Institute of SE Asian Studies, Singapore 1988, p 67.

INDEX

223